By the Same Authors

Opera Scenes for Class and Stage

More Opera Scenes for Class and Stage

From One Hundred Selected Operas

MARY ELAINE WALLACE

ROBERT WALLACE

Southern Illinois University Press

Carbondale and Edwardsville

Printed in the United States of America

Edited by Teresa White

Designed by David Ford

Production supervised by Natalia Nadraga

Library of Congress Cataloging-in-Publication Data

Wallace, Mary Elaine.
More opera scenes for class and stage : from one hundred selected operas / Mary Elaine Wallace, Robert Wallace.
p. cm.
Includes index.
1. Opera—Production and direction. I. Wallace, Robert, 1945–
II. Title.
MT955.W22 1990
792.5—dc19
ISBN 0-8093-1429-0 89-10048
CIP
MN

The paper used in this publication meets the minimum requirements of American National Standard for Information Sciences—Permanence of Paper for Printed Library Materials, ANSI Z39.48-1984. ∞

Contents

Preface

As we cleared our desks after the completion of *Opera Scenes for Class and Stage,* we had no thought of ever developing a second volume. The scenes included in that first volume were, in general, from the most popular, full-length operas, those whose piano-vocal scores would be found in almost every music library. But soon after publication, requests began to arrive for scenes from contemporary opera and from the more rare and esoteric opera repertory. We were flattered, as well as curious, so eventually our work on *More Opera Scenes for Class and Stage* began. Using only published operas with scores available through music distributors and libraries, we chose another one hundred operas for inclusion in this book.

In the choice of excerpts, indexed by voices, we gave thought to those scenes suitable for university opera workshops, summer institutes, and training programs for singers with more mature voices. Musically, the choice varies from through-composed opera scores, which are difficult to excerpt because the music deliberately flows forward without pause, to scores clearly defined in short scenes—and from scores needing superb pianists, when an orchestra is not available, to scores with simple piano accompaniments occasionally enhanced by the use of one or two other instruments. We have used some excerpts requiring a chorus onstage, but more often, if a chorus is required, it is an offstage chorus and may consist of members of the workshop who have solo roles in other scenes on the program.

The feature most praised in the first book was the Table of Voice Categories, and this is again included. For example, if a scene is desired for two sopranos, a mezzo-soprano, and a baritone, one need only to consult that heading for a listing of all the scenes in the book using that particular combination of voices; one may then examine the description of each of those excerpts and select the one most suitable for the particular circumstances.

The libretti of these excerpts are not always as familiar as those in the first book; however, they are often fascinating plots with a variety of characters and action providing excellent training and program material. Again we recommend that those producing opera scenes for public performance should consider programs based on scenes with a theme. For example, it is possible to build a program commemorating a famous historical event or the anniversary of the birth or death of a composer. Also programs of American opera, bel canto opera, or commedia dell'arte style are possible. Operas with the same story but by different composers whose styles are contrasting could be used; for example, a director might choose scenes from *Romeo et Juliette* by Gounod (from our first book, *Opera Scenes*), *Romeo and Juliet* by Blacher, *I Capuleti ed i Montecchi* by Bellini, *A Village Romeo and Juliet* by Delius (all from *More Opera Scenes*), and *West Side Story*.

Singers wishing to extend their understanding of arias already learned in the voice studio find it helpful to sing the aria within the context of the operatic scene. We suggest you look in the Index of Arias and Ensembles in the back of each volume for an aria your singer may already know, and find out in which scene or scenes it appears. We believe that when the aria is performed in its true dramatic situation, it takes on a new perspective, a new vitality, and a new excitement.

Some have asked about staging directions, and we repeat that we feel this should be the creative product of the stage director in consultation with the singers. There are many factors that must be considered because of the stage area being used, and there are many adjustments to be made because of the physical attributes of each singer in the scene, the acting ability of each, and the working relationship established among them. These excerpts may be presented with sets, costumes, lighting, and all the other accoutrements of a staged work, or they may be done in the simplest way, relying on the singing and acting to portray the story. In all instances, no matter how simple or how complex, study and research by both the directors and the singers are important to the quality of the production.

Many of the operas included in this book are published only in their original language. Because operatic singers must study languages and learn to memorize entire operas in a foreign tongue, singing scenes without English translation is valuable training. Also, permission must be obtained from the publisher when using a contemporary work or a published translation; operas that are public domain and are sung in their original language do not require royalties.

It is our hope that this volume with over seven hundred scenes, used in conjunction with the first book containing approximately the same number of scenes, will make it possible for directors to find suitable material for any combination of voices they might have in their opera training program or for any opera scenes program they may be planning.

A Note on the Text

The Index of Operas and Index of Arias and Ensembles have been listed by the commonly recognized titles without consideration for articles, e.g., The Good Soldier Schweik, La Clemenza di Tito, "Ein grab? Nein, eine Leucht'!"

PUBLISHERS' ABBREVIATIONS

AF	Adolph Furstner, Berlin
AMP	Associated Music Publishers
Bel	Belwin Mills
B&H	Boosey & Hawkes, Inc.
Br	Broude Brothers, Ltd.
Brei	Breitkopf & Haertel c/o Associated Music Publishers
Car	Carish, S.A., Milano
Chap	Chappell & Co., Inc.
Chou	Choudens
Cur	J. Curwin & Sons, Ltd.
Dur	Durand
Esch	Editions Max Eschig
Fab	Faber Music, Ltd.
Gal	Galaxy Music Corp.
GS	G. Schirmer, Inc.
Heu	Heugel
HM	Hudební Matice, Praha
Int	International Music Co.
JW	Josef Weinberger, Ltd.
Kal	Edwin F. Kalmus c/o Belwin Mills
Ox	Oxford University Press
Pet	C.F. Peters Corp.
Pr	Praha
Ric	G. Ricordi
Sch	Schott und Söhne
SMP	State Music Publishers, Moscow
SZ	Casa Musicale Sonzogno
UE	Universal Edition
Wei	Weintraub Music Company

LANGUAGE ABBREVIATIONS

cz = Czech, e = English, f = French, g = German, i = Italian, r = Russian, sp = Spanish

PAGE REFERENCES

opt. = optional cut, trad. = traditional cut

pp. 21–36	The excerpt begins at the top of page 21 and concludes with the last bar of page 36.
pp. 114/2/1–131/1/3	The excerpt begins on page 114, second score, first bar, and concludes on page 131, first score, third bar.
pp. 98; 101/4/2–116; 120–31/1/3	The excerpt includes all of page 98; then cuts to page 101, fourth score, second bar, and continues through the last bar of page 116; then cuts again to the top of page 120 and continues through page 131, first score, third bar.
pp. 35–71 (trad. 45/1/3–48/1/1)	The excerpt begins on page 35, first score, first bar, and continues through page 45, to first score, third bar; then traditionally cuts to page 48, first score, first bar, and continues to the end of page 71.

VOCAL RANGES

S = soprano, M-S = mezzo-soprano, C = contralto, T = tenor, BAR = baritone, BS = bass.

The system used to notate vocal ranges is the one used by Quaintance Eaton in her reference works, *Opera Production* and *Opera Production II*, as diagramed below:

Soprano: B♭2–C5 Bass: F1–F3

Table of Voice Categories

Voice categories are grouped by range beginning with soprano (first), mezzo-soprano (second), tenor (third), baritone (fourth), bass (fifth), and then in combinations thereof.

In the chorus column, F = female, M = male, X = mixed, C = children, and O = offstage.

For the speaking roles, SpF = female, SpM = male, SpC = child. For the silent roles, SF = female, SM = male, SC = child, SX = extras. "Ad lib" following a letter abbreviation indicates any number of persons in that category.

OPERA	*EXCERPTS*	*LESSER ROLES*	*CHORUS*
	SOPRANO		
Capriccio	4	BS	
Hamlet	8		X
Les Mamelles de Tirésias	2a		
Porgy and Bess	1a		F opt.
Regina	2	SpF	
	5b		
Le Rossignol	3	M-S, T, BAR	F
A Tale of Two Cities	1a	M-S, T, BAR	
The Turn of the Screw	2a		
La Vida Breve	1c	T	M
	1d	T	
La Wally	1	BAR, BS	F
	MEZZO-SOPRANO		
Arlecchino	3a	SpM	
Carry Nation	3a		F
Miss Julie	1	S, 2SF	XO

OPERA	*EXCERPTS*	*LESSER ROLES*	*CHORUS*
Riders to the Sea	2a	2S	F
The Sojourner and Mollie Sinclair	2b	SM	
	TENOR		
Oberon	1	M-S or T, or 2SM	
	2	BAR or SM	
Porgy and Bess	5		X
Rusalka	2	BS, SF	F
The Turn of the Screw	1a		
	BARITONE		
Arlecchino	1	SpM, SF	
The Cunning Little Vixen	1	5C	
Les Mamelles de Tirésias	1		
The Pilgrim's Progress	3		
Porgy and Bess	3	2S, M-S, BAR	X
	3a	SM	X
	2 SOPRANOS		
Arabella	1b		
	3		
Cendrillon	2	3S, 3M-S, dancers	
La Clemenza di Tito	5	M-S	
The Cunning Little Vixen	7		
Elegy for Young Lovers	3a		
Jenůfa	3a		
	3b		
Regina	3		
Tiefland	2a		
The Turn of the Screw	2		
La Wally	6a		
	SOPRANO, MEZZO-SOPRANO		
Adriana Lecouvreur	5	3SM	
Anna Bolena	4		

OPERA	*EXCERPTS*	*LESSER ROLES*	*CHORUS*
Béatrice et Bénédict	3		
Black Widow	3a		
I Capuleti ed i Montecchi	4	BAR, BS	M
	4a		
Cendrillon	3		
La Clemenza di Tito	1a		
	2a		
Esclarmonde	1a		
	1c		FO
The Growing Castle	6	2BAR	
	7		
Hamlet	3	SM	
Hugh the Drover	1a		
Idomeneo	1		
	5a		
Linda di Chamounix	2a		F
	4		
I Lombardi alla Prima Crociata	1	T	
Maria Stuarda	2		
Oberon	3		X opt.
	3a		
Le Prophète	1		
	4	4SM	
	4a		
Il Ritorno d'Ulisse in Patria	4		
Roberto Devereux	1	T, 2BS	X
Rusalka	1b		
	5		
Semiramide	2	T	F
	2a	T	
	2b		
	4		
Signor Deluso	1a	BAR	
The Sweet Bye and Bye	1		
Troilus and Cressida	4a	MO opt.	
The Turn of the Screw	2		
La Vida Breve	1b		
The Wings of the Dove	2b		

OPERA	*EXCERPTS*	*LESSER ROLES*	*CHORUS*
	SOPRANO, TENOR		
Adriana Lecouvreur	1c		
Alceste	2		XO
	2a		
	3		MO
	3a		
L'Amore dei tre re	5	S or M-S, S or boy SO	
Anna Bolena	3a	BAR	
Arabella	6		
L'Arlesiana	2b	M-S	
	3a		
Attila	2		
The Boor	1		
Cendrillon	3		
The Cunning Little Vixen	7		
Double Trouble	1b	BAR or BS	XO
Edgar	1		
Elegy for Young Lovers	3b		
	4a		
	9		
Esclarmonde	2		FO
	3		
Fedora	1a		
	3	M-SO	
Giovanna d'Arco	2		
Gloriana	1b		
	3a	S, SF	
The Good Soldier Schweik	1		
Goyescas	1	SM	
	2		
Guillaume Tell	2		
	4		
Hamlet (Searle)	7	M-S, T	
He Who Gets Slapped	1		
	5		
Hugh the Drover	1b		
	2		
	3		

OPERA	*EXCERPTS*	*LESSER ROLES*	*CHORUS*
Idomeneo	1		
	3b		
	3c		
	5a		
Iolanta	3a		
Iris	3		
Jenůfa	4a		
La Jolie fille de Perth	1a		
	5		
Linda di Chamounix	2b		
	6a		
I Lombardi alla Prima Crociata	2		
	4		
Lucrezia Borgia	1	T, BAR, BS	
	5c		
Luisa Miller	5c		
Maria Stuarda	1b		
	3		
I Masnadieri	4		MO
Oberon	5		
L'Oca del Cairo	1d		
Of Mice and Men	2	BS	
	4		
L'Ormindo	4		
Il Ritorno d'Ulisse in Patria	2		
	3		
Roberto Devereux	2		
Romeo und Julia	3		
Romeo und Julia auf dem Dorfe	2		
	4		
Rusalka	3	SF	
	6	BS	
The Scarf	1		
Simon Boccanegra	2a		
	4b		
Sir John in Love	1	BARO	
The Sweet Bye and Bye	2		
	4		

OPERA	*EXCERPTS*	*LESSER ROLES*	*CHORUS*
Tiefland	5	BS	
	5a		
	6c		
Die tote Stadt	1b		
	2a		
	4		
Troilus and Cressida	1a	BAR	
	2c		
	3a	M-S, T	
I Vespri Siciliani	2a		
	4		
La Vida Breve	1e		
Le Villi	1		
La Wally	6b		MO
Wozzeck	5		

SOPRANO, BARITONE

OPERA	*EXCERPTS*	*LESSER ROLES*	*CHORUS*
Adriana Lecouvreur	1b		
	6a	SF	
Alceste	1		
L'Amore dei tre re	4		
Arabella	4a		
	7	SM	
Béatrice di Tenda	2	T	
	2a		
Black Widow	2		
	4		
The Boor	2	T	
	2a	SM	
	2b	SM	
	3a	T	
Il Campanello di notte	1		
Capriccio	1		
Cendrillon	4a		
Double Trouble	2		MO
Elegy for Young Lovers	5		
Ernani	1a	M-S	F
Giovanna d'Arco	3		
Gloriana	1a	SpM or SpF	

OPERA	*EXCERPTS*	*LESSER ROLES*	*CHORUS*
The Growing Castle	3	M-S, BAR	
Hamlet (Searle)	5		
Hamlet (Thomas)	1		
He Who Gets Slapped	4a		
Linda di Chamounix	5		
Luisa Miller	5b		
Les Mamelles de Tirésias	2		
Maria Golovin	1	MO	
	2	MO, C	
	4	M-S	
	5a		
I Masnadieri	3	T	XO
	3a	T	
Miss Julie	2		
	3		
Nabucco	2	SM	
L'Oca del Cairo	1b		
	2a		
Porgy and Bess	1b		X
	2	2T	X
	6		
Roberto Devereux	4a	T, BS	
The Scarf	2		
Simon Boccanegra	3		
Thaïs	2	TO	
	2a		
	3		
	4	M-S	F
	5a		
Tiefland	3		
L'Ultimo Selvaggio	3a		
La Wally	4		
Wozzeck	3	SpF, SM, SC	
	6	SC	
	8		
	9	SC	

SOPRANO, BASS

L'Amore dei tre re	2a		
	6a		

OPERA	EXCERPTS	LESSER ROLES	CHORUS
Carry Nation	4		
The Cunning Little Vixen	4		F or C
Double Trouble	2		MO
He Who Gets Slapped	2		
Lucrezia Borgia	3a		
Luisa Miller	3	S or M-S	X
Maria Golovin	1	MO	
	2	MO, C	
	4	M-S	
	5a		
Maria Stuarda	6a		
Miss Julie	2		
	3		
L'Oca del Cairo	3	S, M-S, T	
	3a		
Regina	4	S, T, 2BAR, 2SpF	
	4a		
Rusalka	1a		
Semiramide	3	T, SM	
	3a		
Tiefland	6b		
Troilus and Cressida	4d		
Il Turco in Italia	1	SF	M
	4		

2 MEZZO-SOPRANOS

OPERA	EXCERPTS	LESSER ROLES	CHORUS
L'Arlesiana	4		
La Clemenza di Tito	1b		
Il Ritorno d'Ulissse in Patria	1		
	4		

MEZZO-SOPRANO, TENOR

OPERA	EXCERPTS	LESSER ROLES	CHORUS
Adriana Lecouvreur	3		
Arlecchino	3	SpM	
	3b	SpM	
Béatrice di Tenda	1		
Béatrice et Bénédict	1		

OPERA	*EXCERPTS*	*LESSER ROLES*	*CHORUS*
I Capuleti ed i Montecchi	3		X
Christopher Columbus	3		
Edgar	3		
Idomeneo	2		
Lucrezia Borgia	4	T	M
Luisa Miller	2b		
Maria Stuarda	1b		
Le Prophète	5a	T	
Il Ritorno d'Ulisse in Patria	2		
	5a		
Roberto Devereux	3		

MEZZO-SOPRANO, BARITONE

Black Widow	1		
Carry Nation	2a	BAR	XO
	2b		
	3b		
Elegy for Young Lovers	8	SpM	
Hamlet (Thomas)	7	BS	
La Jolie fille de Perth	2		
	4		
Linda di Chamounix	1		
Oberon	6a		
Owen Wingrave	6	SM, SC	
Roberto Devereux	5		
Sir John in Love	6a		
The Wings of the Dove	2c		

MEZZO-SOPRANO, BASS

Anna Bolena	2		
Elegy for Young Lovers	1a	SF	
Hamlet (Thomas)	4a		
Semiramide	1	BS, SM	
	1a		
The Sojourner and Mollie Sinclair	2	BAR	
	2a		
L'Ultimo Selvaggio	5		

OPERA	EXCERPTS	LESSER ROLES	CHORUS
	MEZZO-SOPRANO, COUNTERTENOR		
La Calisto	5a		
	2 TENORS		
Idomeneo	2		
Il Ritorno d'Ulisse in patria	5a		
Troilus and Cressida	1c		
	TENOR, BARITONE		
L'Amore dei tre re	7	BS	XO
Death in Venice	1		XO
	2	4S, 3M-S, 2T, 2BAR, BS, 3SM, 3SF, SC	
	2a	SM	
	3	S, M-S, 3T, 3BAR, SM	
	4	S	
	6	S, T, BAR, SM, SF, SC	
Doktor Faust	2		
Guillaume Tell	1		
He Who Gets Slapped	3		
Iris	2a	M-S, SF	F
Les Mamelles de Tirésias	3		
I Masnadieri	1		
	6	SM	
Of Mice and Men	1		
	5	T, BAR	MO
School for Wives	3a		
A Tale of Two Cities	2	S, T, BS, SpM, dancers, musicians	
Die tote Stadt	1a		
The Voyage of Edgar Allan Poe	1a	SF	X opt.
	3	SM	

OPERA	*EXCERPTS*	*LESSER ROLES*	*CHORUS*
Wozzeck	1		
	2		
	TENOR, BASS		
L'Amore dei tre re	1		
Death in Venice	1		XO
	2	4S, 3M-S, 2T, 2BAR, BS, 3SM, 3SF, SC	
	2a	SM	
	3	S, M-S, 3T, 3BAR, SM	
	4	S	
	6	S, T, BAR, SM, SF, SC	
Linda di Chamounix	7		
Lucrezia Borgia	2		MO
Maria Stuarda	1a		
Markheim	1a		XO
	1c		
	1d	S	
	1e	S	SO
	2		
	2a		
	3		
I Vespri Siciliani	1b		
	3	BS	
	3a		
	2 BARITONES		
Double Trouble	4		XO
Les Mamelles de Tirésias	4		X
Of Mice and Men	3a		
	BARITONE, BASS		
L'Amore dei tre re	3	S	
Arabella	2a	SpM	
Attila	1		

OPERA	*EXCERPTS*	*LESSER ROLES*	*CHORUS*
Il Campanello di notte	2	M-S, T	
	3	T	
Doktor Faust	1	T, BAR, BS	
Double Trouble	4		XO
Ernani	3		
Hamlet (Searle)	8	BAR	
Hamlet (Thomas)	5	BS	
Iolanta	2a		
Linda di Chamounix	3		
Luisa Miller	1		
Simon Boccanegra	1		XO
Sir John in Love	6b		
L'Ultimo Selvaggio	4		
Wozzeck	4		

2 BASSES

OPERA	*EXCERPTS*	*LESSER ROLES*	*CHORUS*
Double Trouble	4		XO
I Lombardi alla Prima Crociata	3		
Luisa Miller	4a		
Il Turco in Italia	6		

3 SOPRANOS

OPERA	*EXCERPTS*	*LESSER ROLES*	*CHORUS*
Guillaume Tell	5		F
	5a		

2 SOPRANOS, MEZZO-SOPRANO

OPERA	*EXCERPTS*	*LESSER ROLES*	*CHORUS*
La Calisto	1		
Cendrillon	5	3S, 3M-S	FO
Guillaume Tell	5		F
	5a		
Owen Wingrave	3a		
Postcard from Morocco	4		
Riders to the Sea	2	M-S	F
The Sweet Bye and Bye	3		

OPERA	*EXCERPTS*	*LESSER ROLES*	*CHORUS*

SOPRANO, 2 MEZZO-SOPRANOS

OPERA	*EXCERPTS*	*LESSER ROLES*	*CHORUS*
Anna Bolena	1		X
La Clemenza di Tito	1		
Sir John in Love	5		

SOPRANO, MEZZO-SOPRANO, TENOR

OPERA	*EXCERPTS*	*LESSER ROLES*	*CHORUS*
L'Arlesiana	2a	M-S	
Béatrice di Tenda	3		X
Black Widow	5		
Esclarmonde	1		FO
	1b		
Hugh the Drover	1		
Idomeneo	4		
Jenůfa	2a		
	5		
Linda di Chamounix	2		F
Nabucco	1		
Le Prophète	5	T, SM	
Roberto Devereux	6	BAR	X
Romeo und Julia	2		

SOPRANO, MEZZO-SOPRANO, BARITONE

OPERA	*EXCERPTS*	*LESSER ROLES*	*CHORUS*
L'Arlesiana	1	M-S	
Black Widow	3		
Double Trouble	1a		XO
The Growing Castle	1	BAR	
	4	BAR	
Hamlet	6		
Linda di Chamounix	6b		
Maria Golovin	5	SM	
	6	T	
Miss Julie	4		
Nightingale	3		
Porgy and Bess	4b		
	7		X
Thaïs	5		F
Troilus and Cressida	4g		

OPERA	*EXCERPTS*	*LESSER ROLES*	*CHORUS*

SOPRANO, MEZZO-SOPRANO, BASS

OPERA	EXCERPTS	LESSER ROLES	CHORUS
I Capuleti ed i Montecchi	1		
La Clemenza di Tito	2c		
	3a		
Double Trouble	1a		XO
Elegy for Young Lovers	1	SF	
Maria Golovin	5	SM	
	6	T	
Rusalka	1		
Semiramide	5	BS	X
Troilus and Cressida	1d		MO
	4b		
La Vida Breve	2	M-S, T, 2BAR	X

SOPRANO, MEZZO-SOPRANO, COUNTERTENOR

OPERA	EXCERPTS	LESSER ROLES	CHORUS
La Calisto	5		

2 SOPRANOS, TENOR

OPERA	EXCERPTS	LESSER ROLES	CHORUS
Arabella	1a		
Cendrillon	5	3S, 3M-S	FO
Elegy for Young Lovers	3	SpM	
Idomeneo	3a		
Jenůfa	3c		
	5		
Tiefland	6a		
The Turn of the Screw	3		
La Wally	6		MO

SOPRANO, 2 TENORS

OPERA	EXCERPTS	LESSER ROLES	CHORUS
Idomeneo	4		
Doktor Faust	3		
Die tote Stadt	2	S, M-S	
Troilus and Cressida	1b	BAR	
	2b		
	4i		

OPERA	*EXCERPTS*	*LESSER ROLES*	*CHORUS*
	SOPRANO, TENOR, BARITONE		
Adriana Lecouvreur	6c	SF	
Attila	3a		XO
The Boor	3		
Capriccio	2		
The Cunning Little Vixen	9		
Ernani	1b	M-S	F
Giovanna d'Arco	1		XO
Gloriana	1	SpM or SpF	
Iolanta	3		
Iris	1	BSO	
	2	M-S	F
Luisa Miller	5a	BS, 2SM	XO
Maria Stuarda	5		
L'Oca del Cairo	2		
Porgy and Bess	1	2T, BAR	X
Roberto Devereux	4b		
Romeo und Julia auf dem Dorfe	3		
Salome	1		
The Scarf	3		
School for Wives	3		
Simon Boccanegra	4a		
Tiefland	7	S, M-S, BS	X
	7a	BS	
	SOPRANO, TENOR, BASS		
L'Amore dei tre re	2		
Anna Bolena	5	T	
Ernani	2	BAR	
	4		
Esclarmonde	4		M, FO
Fedora	1		
Hamlet (Searle)	3		
La Jolie fille de Perth	3	BS	
I Lombardi alla Prima Crociata	5		
Lucrezia Borgia	3		
Maria Stuarda	1	BAR	X

OPERA	EXCERPTS	LESSER ROLES	CHORUS
Markheim	1		XO
	1b		
Le Prophète	2b		
Simon Boccanegra	2	S or M-S, BAR	
The Sojourner and Mollie Sinclair	1		
	1a		
	1b		
I Vespri Siciliani	2		M
	6a		
2 SOPRANOS, BARITONE			
Death in Venice	5	Acrobats	
Fedora	2a		
He Who Gets Slapped	4	T, BS, 2M mimes	
Nightingale	2	T, BAR, SX	
	3		
SOPRANO, 2 BARITONES			
Les Mamelles de Tirésias	5	S, M-S, BS	X
School for Wives	2		
SOPRANO, BARITONE, BASS			
L'Amore dei tre re	6		
Antony and Cleopatra	1	SF	XO
	3a		
Maria Stuarda	6		
L'Oca del Cairo	1a		
Le Rossignol	2	3T, BS	M, F
	2a	2T, BS	M, F
La Wally	2		
2 SOPRANOS, BASS			
Death in Venice	5	Acrobats	
MEZZO-SOPRANO, 2 TENORS			
Christopher Columbus	4		

OPERA	*EXCERPTS*	*LESSER ROLES*	*CHORUS*
MEZZO-SOPRANO, TENOR, BARITONE			
Edgar	2		
	4		
The Good Soldier Schweik	4	2T, 2BAR	X
Hamlet (Searle)	1		
Maria Stuarda	5		
Oberon	6	M-S or T or SM	
L'Ormindo	1a		
	5a	SF	
MEZZO-SOPRANO, TENOR, BASS			
La Clemenza di Tito	4a		
Luisa Miller	2		X
	2a		
Maria Stuarda	1	BAR	X
MEZZO-SOPRANO, 2 BARITONES			
School for Wives	1b		
The Wings of the Dove	1a	BAR	
MEZZO-SOPRANO, BARITONE, BASS			
Arabella	2	T, SpM	
Carry Nation	2	BAR	XO
Hamlet (Searle)	6	BS	
Hamlet (Thomas)	4		
Il Turco in Italia	5		
2 TENORS, BARITONE			
Christopher Columbus	2		
The Good Soldier Schweik	2		
	3		
TENOR, 2 BARITONES			
School for Wives	1a		

OPERA	*EXCERPTS*	*LESSER ROLES*	*CHORUS*
	TENOR, BARITONE, BASS		
Béatrice et Bénédict	2		
The Cunning Little Vixen	5	T	
	6		
Guillaume Tell	3		
Hamlet (Thomas)	9		
Owen Wingrave	1		
Il Turco in Italia	2		
Wozzeck	7		
	2 TENORS, BASS		
The Love for Three Oranges	2		
I Masnadieri	5		
	TENOR, 2 BASSES		
Le Prophète	3	BAR	
	2 BARITONES, BASS		
Arlecchino	2	SpM	
Hamlet (Searle)	2		
Tiefland	4		
	BARITONE, 2 BASSES		
The Pilgrim's Progress	1	2T, BAR, BS	
Sir John in Love	4a		
	2 SOPRANOS, 2 MEZZO-SOPRANOS		
Iolanta	1	4 musicians	F
	2 SOPRANOS, MEZZO-SOPRANO, TENOR		
Idomeneo	5		
	5b		
Owen Wingrave	4	SM	

OPERA	*EXCERPTS*	*LESSER ROLES*	*CHORUS*
The Wings of the Dove	2a		
2 SOPRANOS, MEZZO-SOPRANO, BARITONE			
La Calisto	6		
Gloriana	4	BS	
Owen Wingrave	3		
Riders to the Sea	1		
2 SOPRANOS, MEZZO-SOPRANO, BASS			
Regina	5		
	5a		
SOPRANO, 2 MEZZO-SOPRANOS, TENOR			
Antony and Cleopatra	2	dancers	F
SOPRANO, 2 MEZZO-SOPRANOS, BARITONE			
Cendrillon	1	MC opt.	
The Cunning Little Vixen	2	2C	
Maria Golovin	3	T, BAR, C	
	3a		
Sir John in Love	7	3SM	
SOPRANO, 2 MEZZO-SOPRANOS, BASS			
La Clemenza di Tito	2b		
	3a	2SM	
Maria Golovin	3	T, BAR, C	
	3a		
SOPRANO, MEZZO-SOPRANO, 2 CHILDREN			
The Turn of the Screw	1b		
SOPRANO, MEZZO-SOPRANO, 2 TENORS			
Jenůfa	3		
Il Ritorno d'Ulisse in Patria	6		

OPERA	*EXCERPTS*	*LESSER ROLES*	*CHORUS*
SOPRANO, MEZZO-SOPRANO, TENOR, BARITONE			
L'Arlesiana	2	M-S	XO
Gloriana	2		
La Jolie fille de Perth	1b		
Linda di Chamounix	6		
Luisa Miller	5	BS, 2SM	F, XO
Oberon	4		
L'Ormindo	2a		
	2b		
The Pilgrim's Progress	4		
Salome	2	T or BAR, BAR or BS, SF or SM	
Thaïs	1	BAR	
Die tote Stadt	1		
Troilus and Cressida	2a	2S, 2M-S, 3SF opt.	
SOPRANO, MEZZO-SOPRANO, TENOR, BASS			
Elegy for Young Lovers	4		
Esclarmonde	5		XO
La Vida Breve	1	T	M
	1a	T	
	1d	T	M
La Wally	3		
SOPRANO, MEZZO-SOPRANO, 2 BARITONES			
The Growing Castle	2		
	5		
SOPRANO, MEZZO-SOPRANO, BARITONE, BASS			
Arabella	4	T, BAR, BS	
La Calisto	2		
	4	2T	BS or M
	4a		
Carry Nation	1	T	
The Pilgrim's Progress	2		
Signor Deluso	1a		
Troilus and Cressida	4c		MO
	4e		MO

OPERA	*EXCERPTS*	*LESSER ROLES*	*CHORUS*
SOPRANO, MEZZO-SOPRANO, 2 BASSES			
Luisa Miller	4		
	4b		
2 SOPRANOS, 2 TENORS			
Jenůfa	3		
L'Oca del Cairo	1c		
Postcard from Morocco	5	M-S, BAR, BS	
2 SOPRANOS, TENOR, BASS			
Rusalka	4		
SOPRANO, 3 TENORS			
Il Ritorno d'Ulisse in Patria	5		
SOPRANO, 2 TENORS, BARITONE			
Troilus and Cressida	4	2SM	
SOPRANO, 2 TENORS, BASS			
Romeo und Julia	1		
Troilus and Cressida	1	M-S, BAR, 2SM	
SOPRANO, TENOR, 2 BARITONES			
Porgy and Bess	4a		
Signor Deluso	2	S	
SOPRANO, TENOR, BARITONE, BASS			
Arabella	5		
Attila	3	T	X
The Cunning Little Vixen	8		F or C
Ernani	1	M-S	F, M
I Masnadieri	2		

OPERA	*EXCERPTS*	*LESSER ROLES*	*CHORUS*
L'Ormindo	6d		
Owen Wingrave	2		
Simon Boccanegra	5		
I Vespri Siciliani	5	BS	
	6		X
SOPRANO, TENOR, 2 BASSES			
Il Turco in Italia	3		
2 SOPRANOS, 2 BARITONES			
Nightingale	1	BAR	C opt. F opt.
2 SOPRANOS, BARITONE, BASS			
The Cunning Little Vixen	8		F or C
La Wally	5	T	
3 MEZZO-SOPRANOS, TENOR			
L'Ormindo	1b		
2 MEZZO-SOPRANOS, 2 TENORS			
Il Ritorno d'Ullisse in Patria	6		
2 MEZZO-SOPRANOS, TENOR, BARITONE			
L'Ormindo	5	SF	
2 MEZZO-SOPRANOS, TENOR, BASS			
La Clemenza di Tito	4	2SM	
2 MEZZO-SOPRANOS, 2 BARITONES			
The Wings of the Dove	1	BAR	
	5		
MEZZO-SOPRANO, 2 TENORS, BARITONE			
Sir John in Love	2		

OPERA	*EXCERPTS*	*LESSER ROLES*	*CHORUS*
MEZZO-SOPRANO, TENOR, 2 BARITONES			
School for Wives	1		
Sir John in Love	2		
MEZZO-SOPRANO, TENOR, BARITONE, BASS			
Sir John in Love	6		
MEZZO-SOPRANO, TENOR, BARITONE, CHILD			
The Pilgrim's Progress	4		
MEZZO-SOPRANO, TENOR, 2 BASSES			
Christopher Sly	1a		
MEZZO-SOPRANO, BARITONE, BASS, COUNTERTENOR			
La Calisto	7		
2 TENORS, BARITONE, BASS			
Le Prophète	2a		
	2c		
TENOR, 2 BARITONES, BASS			
Of Mice and Men	3b		
TENOR, BARITONE, 2 BASSES			
Hamlet (Thomas)	2		
Iolanta	2	M-S	
2 TENORS, 2 BASSES			
Love for Three Oranges	4		
2 BARITONES, 2 BASSES			
Hamlet (Searle)	4		

OPERA	*EXCERPTS*	*LESSER ROLES*	*CHORUS*
3 SOPRANOS, 2 MEZZO-SOPRANOS			
The Cunning Little Vixen	3		F or C
Tiefland	2	BAR	
3 SOPRANOS, MEZZO-SOPRANO, TENOR			
Arabella	1		
2 SOPRANOS, 2 MEZZO-SOPRANOS, BARITONE			
Cendrillon	4		
2 SOPRANOS, MEZZO-SOPRANO, TENOR, BARITONE			
Double Trouble	1		XO
Jenůfa	1	S or M-S	
Signor Deluso	3	BAR	
The Wings of the Dove	2	SM, SF	
2 SOPRANOS, MEZZO-SOPRANO, TENOR, BASS			
Christopher Columbus	1		
Double Trouble	1		XO
Idomeneo	6	2T	M, XO
Jenůfa	4	S, SF	
2 SOPRANOS, MEZZO-SOPRANO, TENOR, COUNTERTENOR			
La Calisto	3		
SOPRANO, 2 MEZZO-SOPRANOS, 2 TENORS			
The Love for Three Oranges	3	4SM	
SOPRANO, 2 MEZZO-SOPRANOS, TENOR, BASS			
Jenůfa	4	S, SF	
SOPRANO, 2 MEZZO-SOPRANOS, BARITONE, BASS			
Antony and Cleopatra	4a		

OPERA	*EXCERPTS*	*LESSER ROLES*	*CHORUS*
SOPRANO, MEZZO-SOPRANO, 2 TENORS, BARITONE			
Anna Bolena	6		X
A Tale of Two Cities	1	2BAR	
Troilus and Cressida	2	2S, 2M-S, 3SF opt.	
	4h		MO
I Vespri Siciliani	1		
SOPRANO, MEZZO-SOPRANO, TENOR, BARITONE, BASS			
I Capuleti ed i Montecchi	2		M
	2a		
SOPRANO, MEZZO-SOPRANO, TENOR, 2 BARITONES			
L'Arlesiana	3		
Porgy and Bess	4		
School for Wives	3		
SOPRANO, MEZZO-SOPRANO, TENOR, 2 CHILDREN			
The Turn of the Screw	1		
SOPRANO, MEZZO-SOPRANO, 2 BARITONES, BASS			
Sir John in Love	8		
SOPRANO, MEZZO-SOPRANO, BARITONE, 2 BASSES			
Sir John in Love	4		
L'Ultimo Selvaggio	2		
2 SOPRANOS, 2 TENORS, BASS			
Idomeneo	6	2T	M, XO
2 SOPRANOS, TENOR, 2 BARITONES			
Signor Deluso	2		
The Wings of the Dove	3		

OPERA	*EXCERPTS*	*LESSER ROLES*	*CHORUS*
2 SOPRANOS, TENOR, 2 BASSES			
Le Rossignol	1		M
SOPRANO, 2 TENORS, BARITONE, BASS			
Adriana Lecouvreur	4		
The Good Soldier Schweik	5	M or F	
Roberto Devereux	4		M
SOPRANO, TENOR, 2 BARITONES, BASS			
The Pilgrim's Progress	5a		
Simon Boccanegra	4		
2 MEZZO-SOPRANOS, 3 TENORS			
Il Ritorno d'Ulisse in Patria	7		
TENOR, 3 BARITONES, BASS			
Sir John in Love	3	SM	
2 SOPRANOS, 2 MEZZO-SOPRANOS, TENOR, BASS			
La Clemenza di Tito	2		
2 SOPRANOS, MEZZO-SOPRANO, 2 TENORS, BARITONE			
Jenůfa	2		
Die tote Stadt	3		
2 SOPRANOS, MEZZO-SOPRANO, TENOR, BARITONE, BASS			
Adriana Lecouvreur	6b	SF	
Maria Stuarda	4		
SOPRANO, 3 MEZZO-SOPRANOS, TENOR, BARITONE			
L'Ormindo	3 3a		

OPERA	*EXCERPTS*	*LESSER ROLES*	*CHORUS*
SOPRANO, 2 MEZZO-SOPRANOS, 2 TENORS, BARITONE			
The Voyage of Edgar Allan Poe	1	SF	X opt.
SOPRANO, 2 MEZZO-SOPRANOS, TENOR, BARITONE, BASS			
Anna Bolena	3		
Maria Stuarda	4		
La Vida Breve	3		
The Voyage of Edgar Allan Poe	2		X opt.
SOPRANO, MEZZO-SOPRANO, 2 TENORS, BARITONE , BASS			
Le Prophète	2		
Troilus and Cressida	4		MO
	4f		MO
SOPRANO, MEZZO-SOPRANO, TENOR, 2 BARITONES, BASS			
School for Wives	5		
SOPRANO, MEZZO-SOPRANO, TENOR, BARITONE, 2 BASSES			
La Jolie fille de Perth	1		
SOPRANO, 2 MEZZO-SOPRANOS, 2 BARITONES, BASS			
Antony and Cleopatra	5		
2 SOPRANOS, 2 TENORS, BARITONE, BASS			
L'Oca del Cairo	1		
SOPRANO, 2 TENORS, 2 BARITONES, BASS			
Of Mice and Men	3	SM	
The Pilgrim's Progress	5		

OPERA	*EXCERPTS*	*LESSER ROLES*	*CHORUS*

3 SOPRANOS, MEZZO-SOPRANO, TENOR, BARITONE, BASS

Christopher Columbus	5		
Owen Wingrave	5		

2 SOPRANOS, MEZZO-SOPRANO, 2 TENORS, BARITONE, BASS

Adriana Lecouvreur	6	SF	
Postcard from Morocco	1		
	2		
	3		
	5		

SOPRANO, 2 MEZZO-SOPRANOS, TENOR, 2 BARITONES, BASS

Antony and Cleopatra	4		
L'Ormindo	6		
	6a		

SOPRANO, 2 MEZZO-SOPRANOS, BARITONE, 3 BASSES

Antony and Cleopatra	3	SF	

SOPRANO, MEZZO-SOPRANO, 2 TENORS, BARITONE, 2 BASSES

Adriana Lecouvreur	2		

2 SOPRANOS, 2 TENORS, BARITONE, 2 BASSES

Christopher Sly	2a		

MEZZO-SOPRANO, 3 TENORS, BARITONE, 2 BASSES

Lucrezia Borgia	5a		

4 MEZZO-SOPRANOS, 2 TENORS, BARITONE

L'Ormindo	1		

2 SOPRANOS, MEZZO-SOPRANO, 2 TENORS, 2 BARITONES, BASS

Capriccio	3		

OPERA	*EXCERPTS*	*LESSER ROLES*	*CHORUS*
2 SOPRANOS, MEZZO-SOPRANO, 2 TENORS, BARITONE, 2 BASSES			
Adriana Lecouvreur	1a	SM	
SOPRANO, MEZZO-SOPRANO, 3 TENORS, BARITONE, 2 BASSES			
Lucrezia Borgia	5b	BAR	MO
3 SOPRANOS, 2 TENORS, BARITONE, 2 BASSES			
Christopher Sly	1b 2		
2 SOPRANOS, 2 MEZZO-SOPRANOS, 2 TENORS, BARITONE, 2 BASSES			
Iolanta	4		F
2 SOPRANOS, MEZZO-SOPRANO, 3 TENORS, BARITONE, 2 BASSES			
Adriana Lecouvreur	1	SM	
SOPRANO, MEZZO-SOPRANO, 3 TENORS, BARITONE, 3 BASSES			
Lucrezia Borgia	5	BAR	
2 SOPRANOS, 2 MEZZO-SOPRANOS, 2 TENORS, 2 BARITONES, 2 BASSES			
Iolanta	5		X
3 SOPRANOS, MEZZO-SOPRANO, 3 TENORS, BARITONES, 3 BASSES			
Christopher Sly	1	SM	

More Opera Scenes for Class and Stage

Adriana Lecouvreur

Francesco Cilea (1866–1950)

Paris, 1730

EXCERPT 1 SZ i, g pp. 1–46/3/2 21 min.

Adriana, the title role, requires a spinto soprano voice (C3–A♭4) and dramatic ability to suggest a great tragedienne; in fact, the acting demands of the role exceed the vocal demands. Maurizio, tenor (F2–A♭3), should have sufficient vocal weight for the verismo style of opera but is often required to sing pianissimo at the top of the range; tessitura is difficult at times. Michonnet, baritone (B1–F3), is a role requiring precise musicianship and acting ability. The supporting roles are all very important, comprising an ensemble that can be a challenge to one's musicianship. They are Mlle Jouvenot, lyric soprano; Mlle Dangeville, lyric mezzo; Poisson, tenor; Quinault, bass; Abate, tenor; and Prince, bass. The role of the Prince should project dignity, authority, and nobility. A Majordomo, silent, completes the scene.

Backstage at the Comédie-Française, Michonnet, the stage manager, complains of the demands of the actors that he do everything at once. The Prince de Bouillon and the Abate enter and greet the actors, who include Jouvenot, Dangeville, Poisson, and Quinault. The famous actress Adriana Lecouvreur enters, trying out her monologue, and in the aria "Io son l'umile ancella" acknowledges modestly the praise of her admirers. Michonnet, whom she considers her best friend, has been in love with her ever since she joined the company and starts to tell her this when they are left alone. She, however, is in love with an unknown cavalier attached to the Count of Saxony (at this point she is unaware that he is really Maurizio, the Count of Saxony, in disguise). Michonnet thus leaves her alone to keep her rendezvous with her unknown lover. As Maurizio prepares to join the audience in the theatre, Adriana gives him a small bouquet of violets for his lapel.

EXCERPT 1a SZ i, g pp. 1–27 11 min.

All of the characters in excerpt 1 except Maurizio.

EXCERPT 1b SZ i, g pp. 28–37/1/3 5 min.

Adriana and Michonnet only.

EXCERPT 1C SZ i, g pp. 36/3/1–46/3/2 6 min.

Adriana and Maurizio only.

EXCERPT 2 SZ i, g pp. 46/3/1–67/3/1 7 min.

Dangeville, Jouvenot, Poisson, Quinault, Abate, Prince, and Michonnet are all described in excerpt 1. This scene includes an aria for Michonnet, baritone, with a sustained G♭3, and an intricate sextet for the other six characters.

The Prince and the Abate enter the backstage foyer of the Comédie-Française, and the latter reads an intercepted letter from the Prince's wife, the Princess of Bouillon. She makes an assignation for eleven o'clock in the villa of the Prince's mistress, the actress Duclos, also appearing in the theatre at that time; the Prince suspects, therefore, that the letter comes from Duclos, and they plot to surprise the lovers and are overheard by the four actors who join them in a spritely ensemble. Michonnet calls places onstage; left alone, he then sings a monologue commenting on Adriana's performance, his admiration and love for her, and the behavior of the audience.

EXCERPT 3 SZ i, g pp. 79–99/2/3 10 min.

The Princess, appearing for the first time in this scene, calls for a high dramatic mezzo (B2-A4) of regal bearing. Maurizio, described in excerpt 1, sings yet another aria in this excerpt, to a sustained A3.

The Princess de Bouillon, having arranged an assignation at the villa belonging to the actress Duclos, awaits Maurizio and expresses her anxiety in an aria. Maurizio arrives, apologizing for his tardiness. Suspecting his infidelity to her, she questions the violets in his lapel, a gift from Adriana Lecouvreur, who has recently fallen in love with him. To subdue the Princess' jealousy, he presents the flowers to her, assuring her that they were meant for her. They are interrupted by the sound of her husband's carriage; she hides.

EXCERPT 4 SZ i, g pp. 99–123/2/5 11 1/2 min.

Adriana, Maurizio, Michonnet, Abate, and Prince are all described in excerpt 1. The ensemble of the four men poses some tricky musical problems, while the duet of Adriana and Maurizio has a sustained high B♭ for both soprano and tenor.

The Prince and the Abate enter the villa and are surprised to find

Maurizio alone, expecting to catch him in a rendezvous with actress Duclos. Maurizio threatens a duel, and the Abate calms the Prince and suggests that if the Prince is tired of La Duclos, why shouldn't Maurizio take her on as his mistress. Maurizio begins to understand when Adriana is introduced to him and is astonished to find that her new beau is not a retainer of the Count of Saxony but the Count Maurizio himself. Maurizio and Adriana renew their vows under his true identity. Michonnet arrives to see Duclos, and Maurizio swears to Adriana that Duclos is not there. Adriana believes him, and insists that the unknown woman's identity be kept secret, as she has promised Maurizio to help this woman escape from the villa.

EXCERPT 5 SZ i, g pp. 123/3/1–134 7 1/2 min.

Adriana and the Princess are described in excerpts 1 and 3. This confrontation scene between the two women requires dramatic but beautiful singing from both. Michonnet briefly appears at the end of the scene, does not sing, and must be accompanied by at least two servants with lanterns.

Adriana, in order to facilitate the escape referred to in Excerpt 4, extinguishes all candles during a touching orchestral interlude and then knocks at the door to the room where the Princess is hiding. The Princess plies Adriana with questions in order to learn her identity; finally when the Princess refers to Maurizio by his first name, Adriana can resist no longer, and the mood suddenly turns from one of compassion to one of passionate rivalry. The Princess, hearing the approach of her husband, quickly runs to the garden to which Adriana has given her the key. Adriana summons the servants with lanterns in order to expose the Princess but she is too late—the Princess is gone. After cursing her, Adriana falls weeping into Michonnet's arms.

EXCERPT 6 SZ i, g pp. 187–237 31 min.

Act 4 complete includes Adriana, Maurizio, Michonnet, Jouvenot, Dangeville, Poisson, and Quinault, all described in excerpt 1. A maid is silent. This includes Adriana's melodramatic death scene.

Adriana is in her home, having retired from the stage, and is desperate. Michonnet attempts to comfort her, and the four actors cheer her up momentarily as they beg her to return to the stage. As the actors prepare to leave, a small package is brought in by the maid. Adriana opens it and screams as she discovers the violets, now withered and faded. She curses the violets and Maurizio. Her aria "Poveri fiori" is an expression of her mixed emotions over the symbolism of the end of a love affair; indeed, she seems to have a premonition of death as she presses the flowers to her lips. Maurizio arrives and the two are briefly reunited in a renewed declaration of love. But it is too late; the obvious becomes clear—the Princess had poisoned the violets before returning them to Adriana. In the arms of both her love and her longtime friend, Michonnet, Adriana expires.

EXCERPT 6a SZ i, g pp. 187–99/2/4 9 1/2 min.

Adriana and Michonnet only.

EXCERPT 6b SZ i, g pp. 187–216 17 1/2 min.

Same as excerpt 6 without Maurizio, ending with Adriana's aria.

EXCERPT 6c SZ i, g pp. 212–37 17 1/2 min.

After the exit of the actors, this portion includes Adriana's aria, her duet with Maurizio, and the death scene including Michonnet in a pivotal role.

Alceste

Christoph Willibald von Gluck (1714–1787)

Thessaly, era of Greek legend

EXCERPT 1 Kal f pp. 68–82 13 min.

This first excerpt is for Alceste (Alcestis), dramatic soprano (C3–B♭4) with a majestic sound, both sustained and flexible, and the High Priest, baritone (D2–F3).

King Admetus (Admète) of Pherae is dying and the Priest has proclaimed that the King is to die unless someone is willing to take his place. His wife, Alcestis, offers herself and is accepted by the gods, ending the scene with the familiar "Divinités du Styx."

EXCERPT 2 Kal f pp. 130–56 23 min.

Alceste (see excerpt 1) is again in this scene with Admète, tenor (F2–A3), who needs strength in a rather high tessitura. An SATTB chorus is included.

King Admetus has recovered and has discovered his wife's sacrifices; however, he believes that Alcestis is abandoning him rather than saving his life, and for that reason he prefers to die himself.

EXCERPT 2a Kal f pp. 130–31; 134–43 12 1/2 min.

The cut in 2a makes the same scene possible without the chorus, and ending with Alceste's aria.

EXCERPT 3 Kal f pp. 184–206/3/1 19 1/2 min.

Alceste and Admète (described above) sing this excerpt with an invisible men's chorus.

Alcestis is at the gates of Hades when Admetus appears. She confesses that she loves him but convinces him that if she does not sacrifice her life, he will die. The scene ends in a duet.

EXCERPT 3a Kal f pp. 184–89/1/5; 190–206/3/1 18 1/2 min.

The same scene as excerpt 3 omitting the men's chorus.

L'Amore dei tre re (The Love of the Three Kings)

Italo Montemezzi (1875–1952)

Italy, tenth century

EXCERPT 1 Ric i pp. 2/5/2–23 10 min.

Flaminio, tenor (E2–A4), and Archibaldo, bass (A1–F3), are in this scene.

The blind old King Archibaldo, unable to sleep, is led by Flaminio into an open space in his castle. He tells Flaminio that he suspects the Princess Fiora of infidelity. She is married to the King's son, Manfredo, who is away on a campaign, but she had at one time been betrothed to Avito, an Italian prince.

EXCERPT 2 Ric i pp. 23/2/1–42/1/2 10 min.

An excerpt for Fiora, spinto soprano (C3–G♭4), whose part lies mostly in the middle range; Avito, tenor (F2–A♭4); and Archibaldo (described in excerpt 1).

Fiora and Avito keep their usual tryst, but Avito escapes just before Archibaldo enters. Fiora, anticipating her husband Manfredo's return, tells the King that she was eagerly awaiting Manfredo in an attempt to convince the King of her innocence.

EXCERPT 2a Ric i pp. 31/3/2–42/1/2 5 min.

Fiora and Archibaldo only are in this portion of excerpt 2.

EXCERPT 3 Ric i pp. 45/2/1–58 7 min.

Manfredo, baritone (E♭2–G♭3), sings in a rather high tessitura with Archibaldo, bass. Fiora, soprano, appears only briefly.

Manfredo returns from battle and embraces his father, Archibaldo. When Fiora appears, she remains cold and distant toward her husband in spite of his outpouring of love for her. Archibaldo cannot bear to tell Manfredo of his suspicions and, left alone, thanks God that he cannot see.

EXCERPT 4 Ric i pp. 62–78/4/2 9 1/2 min.

This is a scene for Fiora and Manfredo, both previously described.

Manfredo is about to return to war and asks Fiora to watch him from the terrace until he is out of sight. In response to his amorous phrases, she begins to feel a renewed sense of love for her husband.

EXCERPT 5 Ric i pp. 82/5/1–122; 18 1/2 min.
126/3/1–28/3/2
(G♭-major cadence)

Fiora (to B4) and Avito (to A3) have most of the singing in this excerpt. The Maid, soprano or mezzo-soprano, sings one line. There is also an offstage voice of a boy soprano or a mezzo-soprano.

After Manfredo leaves, Avito arrives, and Fiora at first tells him that she must not see him anymore. The Maid brings a gift from Manfredo; remembering her promise, Fiora takes the white scarf from the case and waves it. She continues to resist Avito's advances and asks him to leave her, but eventually capitulates; the scene ends in a passionate embrace.

EXCERPT 6 Ric i pp. 132–36; 8 1/2 min.
139–44/4/2; 145/3/3–156

A scene for Fiora, Manfredo, and Archibaldo (see descriptions above).

Archibaldo has overheard Fiora and Avito; Avito wanted to kill the blind old man but was stopped by Flaminio and allowed to escape. Archibaldo taunts Fiora; she refuses to divulge her lover's name, until her father-in-law, enraged, strangles her. Manfredo, suspecting that all is not well, returns to the castle. Archibaldo explains all that has happened. Dejected, Manfredo forgives his lifeless wife.

EXCERPT 6a Ric i pp. 132–36; 139–44/4/2 4 min.

The portion of excerpt 6 for Fiora and Archibaldo only.

EXCERPT 7 Ric i pp. 175–94 8 1/2 min.

Avito and Manfredo have most of the singing in this scene; Archibaldo appears briefly at the end, and a chorus sings offstage.

The body of Fiora is lying in the crypt of the castle. Avito returns and passionately kisses her, but Archibaldo has spread poison on her lips in order to discover her lover's identity. After Avito expires, Manfredo, who cannot bear to go on living without Fiora, kisses her and dies. When Archibaldo enters to discover the identity of the lover, he stumbles upon the body of his own son.

Anna Bolena (Anne Boleyn)

Gaetano Donizetti (1797–1848)

Windsor Castle, 1536

EXCERPT 1 Ric i pp. 10–32 15 min.
(could cut 11/1/1–14/1/1;
or 12/3/1–13/1/4)

The opening scene in the opera uses Anna (Anne Boleyn), soprano (B2–C5), who must have sustained dramatic ability in addition to agility; Giovanna (Jane Seymour), mezzo-soprano (E♭3–B♭4), who has difficult sustained and florid singing; and Smeton, mezzo-soprano (G2–G4), the page and musician of the queen, whose serenade is not difficult. There is also a chorus.

The scene takes place in Queen Anne Boleyn's apartments in Windsor Castle in the early hours of the morning. King Henry VIII has been delayed and everyone is awaiting his arrival. Rumor among the members of the court is that the King is tiring of Anne Boleyn who has not borne him a male heir. The Queen has sent for Giovanna (Jane

Seymour), one of her Maids of Honor, and after a serenade by Smeton, the Queen, unaware of the identity of her rival, confides her fear to Jane, whose conscience disturbs her.

EXCERPT 2 Ric i pp. 33–49/1/3; 50/4/3–51 13 1/2 min.

A scene between Giovanna (Jane Seymour), mezzo-soprano (see excerpt 1), and Enrico (Henry VIII), bass (F1–E3). Enrico needs flexibility throughout the range.

Jane, alone in the chamber, voices her fear that the Queen may suspect her guilty secret, but she knows it cannot be so because Anne has been so kind to her. There is a knock and Jane, unfastening a secret door, admits the King. In a long duet, Jane tells Henry of her remorse and that this must be their last secret meeting. The King insists that their marriage is being arranged and that he will dispose of Anne. Jane's ambition outweighs her loyalty to Anne and she consents, but she begs the King not to use means which are too barbarous.

EXCERPT 3 Ric i pp. 91–96/3/4; 99/2/1–115/1/3; 116/4/2–161 28 min.

This excerpt begins with mezzo-soprano Smeton's aria (5 1/2 min.) and also includes Anna, Giovanna, and Enrico (described in excerpts 1 and 2), and Lord Richard Percy, tenor (F2–B♭4), who has considerable high tessitura, and Lord Rochefort, baritone (A1–F3).

Smeton has arrived early, hoping the Queen will ask him to sing. At the close of his aria, Anne enters with her brother Lord Rochefort, and Lord Richard Percy enters. Smeton hides behind a curtain and listens. Anne tells Percy, her former suitor, that she is not happy and that the King no longer loves her but she begs Percy to be careful. He says that if he cannot have Anne, he cares not what happens to him, and she begs him to leave. Smeton steps forward to keep Percy from stabbing himself. They are interrupted by the King, who arrests Anne, Percy, and Rochefort. Their fate is sealed because Anne will not admit guilt and so save herself.

EXCERPT 3a Ric i pp. 101–15/1/3; 116/4/2–119/1/2 12 min.

The portion of excerpt 3 with Anna and Percy; Rochefort has only one phrase.

EXCERPT 4 Ric i pp. 168–87 13 1/2 min.

Anna and Giovanna sing this scene (see descriptions above).

This is the confrontation scene between Queen Anne and Jane Seymour. Jane has come to beg Anne to leave and save her life. Anne is shocked that Jane should counsel this course of action and asks who her rival may be. When Jane finally confesses to Anne her love for the King, Anne is outraged but soon forgives her rival.

EXCERPT 5 Ric i pp. 194/2/4–215/4/6; 219/2/3–222 13 min.

Anna, Percy, and Enrico have leads in this excerpt with a great deal of trio singing. Sir Hervey, tenor (E♭2–E♭3), official of the King, appears in a minor role.

This is the scene in which Henry condemns Anne and Percy to death.

EXCERPT 6 Ric i pp. 260–82/2/3; 283/3/2–283/3/5 17 min.

The characters, all described in previous excerpts, are Anna, Smeton, Percy, Rochefort, and Hervey. There is also a chorus in this scene.

The final scene of the opera includes Anne's "mad scene." As she is lead to her death along with Smeton, Percy, and Rochefort, proclamation of Jane Seymour as new Queen is heard in the distance.

Antony and Cleopatra

Samuel Barber (1910–1981)

Egypt, B.C.

EXCERPT 1 GS (rev.) e pp. 16/1/3–31 8 min.

The role of Cleopatra calls for a lyric-spinto soprano (C3–B♭4) with a high pianissimo. Antony is a dramatic baritone (C2–G♭3, with lower options), and Enobarbus is a bass (C2–E♭3). Charmian and Iras, servants, are silent in this scene. A mixed chorus has a few lines in the manner of a Greek chorus.

Antony confides to his friend Enobarbus that he intends to break off his affair with Cleopatra, the Egyptian queen. Having learned of Antony's intention to return to Rome, Cleopatra enters, first ignoring him, then bitterly telling him to leave. In spite of this, she yields to his caresses in a tender farewell.

EXCERPT 2 GS (rev.) e pp. 49–78 12 1/2 min.

Cleopatra's attendants are both mezzos: Charmian (C3–G4), and Iras (F2–E4); the Messenger is a tenor (B♭2–G♯3). Cleopatra is attended by a chorus of female slaves (very little singing), some of whom should be able to dance if a troupe of dancers is not available.

In her palace in Alexandria, Cleopatra longs for Antony and asks for a draught of mandragora in order to sleep out his absence. A Messenger arrives. When Cleopatra reads his message, she whips him furiously; Antony has married Caesar's sister, Octavia. Crestfallen, she bids her attendants lead her to her chamber.

EXCERPT 3 GS (rev.) e pp. 118–37/2/2 7 min.

Antony, Cleopatra, Enobarbus, Charmian, and Iras are described in previous excerpts. Alexas and the Soothsayer are also basses, the Soothsayer being the lower of the two parts. Other slaves (silent) are in attendance.

Near a pool in Cleopatra's garden, Charmian and Iras tease the chief eunuch, Alexas, and the Soothsayer predicts the future to the two handmaidens. Antony and Cleopatra enter, but their renewed declaration of love is interrupted by Enobarbus bringing news that the Roman legions are drawing near. Cleopatra declares that together with her army she wishes to share the fate of her love.

EXCERPT 3a GS (rev.) e pp. 127/2/1–37/2/2 3 1/2 min.

The final portion of excerpt 3, with Cleopatra, Antony, and Enobarbus.

EXCERPT 4 GS (rev.) e pp. 216–45 13 min.

This scene contains a great deal of ensemble for the women's voices. Cleopatra, Charmian, Iras, Antony, and Alexas have all been previously described. Caesar, dramatic tenor (D♯2–B♭3) and Dolabella, baritone, complete the scene along with a chorus of soldiers who sing only a few lines.

Antony, mortally wounded, has been brought to his tomb. On a platform above the tomb, Cleopatra and her attendants mourn his impending death. After Antony bids farewell and dies, Caesar and his retinue appear; Caesar comforts Cleopatra, offering to take her to Rome. He then sings his own tribute to Antony.

EXCERPT 4a GS (rev.) e pp. 216–36 8 1/2 min.

The first portion of excerpt 4: Cleopatra, Charmian, Iras, Antony, and Alexas.

EXCERPT 5 GS (rev.) e 249–78/2/1 10 1/2 min.

Cleopatra has the most extensive singing in this scene. She is attended by Charmian, Iras, Dolabella, a Guardsman (baritone), and a Rustic (bass).

Inside Antony's monument, a throne stands in the middle. The Rustic brings in a basket of figs to Cleopatra in which has been smuggled a poisonous asp. First Iras, then Cleopatra ascending the throne, and finally Charmian apply the asp and all three succumb to its poison.

Arabella

Richard Strauss (1868–1949)

Vienna, 1860

EXCERPT 1 B&H g pp. 5–49/1/1 18 min.

The two leading ladies of the opera are Zdenka, high lyric soprano (C♯3–C5), who is disguised as a boy most of the time, and Arabella (C3–A4), who should have a darker timbre in contrast but still be capable of the subtleties typical of the music of Richard Strauss. A smaller soprano role is that of a Fortune-teller (D3–G4). Adelaide, mezzo-soprano (B2–G4), and Matteo, tenor (D2–B♭3), complete the cast. The leading tenor role demands a somewhat dramatic voice with some difficult high phrases. Bill collectors and Arabella's chaperone are referred to in this scene, but it can be staged so that they remain outside the door.

Count and Countess Waldner, in a financial crisis because of his gambling, seek to marry off his eldest daughter, Arabella, to a wealthy suitor. In order to accomplish this, Arabella is to be presented to society at a ball in Vienna. Her younger sister, Zdenka, must remain disguised as a boy until Arabella is suitably wed. The Fortune-teller predicts a wealthy suitor for Arabella—a tall, dark, handsome stranger. Matteo arrives, finds that Arabella is out for a walk, and complains to "Zdenko" that Arabella has reacted coldly to him. He threatens to kill himself if he cannot win her. Zdenka, secretly in love with Matteo, is determined to prevent Matteo's suicide until Arabella is married to someone else and Zdenka can reveal her own identity. After Matteo leaves, Arabella returns and the two sisters have a bit of an argument but then pledge devotion to each other in a beautiful duet.

EXCERPT 1a B&H g pp. 22/2/1–49/1/1 12 min.

The portion of excerpt 1 with Matteo, Zdenka, and Arabella.

EXCERPT 1b B&H g pp. 31/1/3–49/1/1 8 1/2 min.

The entrance of Arabella through her duet with Zdenka.

EXCERPT 2 B&H g pp. 72–111/2/1 18 min.

Adelaide, mezzo (G2–G4), has wide skips and must possess power at extremes of range. Mandryka is a somewhat dramatic baritone (A♭1–G♭3) who has the most taxing role in this excerpt. Waldner is a bass-baritone (G1–E3). A Servant (tenor) and Mandryka's servant, Welko (speaking role), complete the scene.

Count Waldner tells his wife, Adelaide, that he has written to a wealthy regimental comrade of his by the name of Mandryka and has sent a picture of his daughter Arabella. When a servant announces Mandryka, Waldner is astonished to find that his old army buddy has passed away and Arabella's picture has fallen into the hands of his nephew and heir by the same name. Young Mandryka has fallen in love with the picture and has sold a portion of his inheritance in order to make the trip to Vienna in hopes of winning Arabella.

EXCERPT 2a B&H g pp. 83/2/3–111/2/1 13 min.

The portion of the scene with Mandryka and Waldner only. The servant, Welko, has one spoken line.

EXCERPT 3 B&H g pp. 120/3/2–134 7 1/2 min.

Of the two sopranos, Arabella (B♭2–A♭4), has the major role in this scene. Zdenka, a light lyric soprano (E3–G4), has only a few lines.

Arabella is horrified at the thought of marrying Count Elemer, one of her four suitors. She finishes her aria, anticipating becoming queen of the ball; she and Zdenka leave together to meet Count Elemer.

EXCERPT 4 B&H g pp. 135–68/3/1 14 min.

Arabella (C3–B4) has many high passages in this scene. Mandryka, baritone (A1–F♯3), likewise must possess strength in the upper register. Adelaide (mezzo-soprano) and Waldner (bass-baritone) appear in this scene, and brief supporting roles are sung by Elemer (tenor), Dominik (baritone), and Lamoral (bass).

As Arabella descends the staircase of the ballroom, she meets Mandryka and they are immediately attracted to each other. He talks about a brief first marriage to a woman who died, and how he wishes Arabella would share his lands on the Danube with him. After refusing offers to dance with three other suitors who interrupt from time to time, Arabella pledges her love to Mandryka.

EXCERPT 4a B&H g pp. 154–68/3/1 7 1/2 min.

The final portion of excerpt 4, with Arabella and Mandryka only.

EXCERPT 5 B&H g 189/4/4–205/4/2 6 1/2 min.

Arabella (B♭2–B♭4); Elemer (E2–B♭3), short but difficult part with high tessitura; Dominik, baritone, shortest of the roles in this scene; Lamoral, bass (C♯2–D♯3), some sustained singing.

A lighthearted scene in waltz time, this is where Arabella, having fallen in love with Mandryka, bids farewell to three other suitors by giving them each a turn to waltz with her at the ball.

EXCERPT 6 B&H g pp. 265–86/2/3 7 min.

Arabella (A2–B♭4) and Matteo, tenor who must sustain a B3, are described in excerpt 1.

Zdenka has given Matteo a key to a room where he believes he will meet Arabella in a quarter of an hour. Instead, Zdenka keeps the nocturnal rendezvous, undetected by the ardent Matteo. When Matteo goes to his room to put on his uniform and reappears, he is astonished to see Arabella in full dress, as he was under the impression that he had been making love to her. Likewise, she cannot understand why he tells her he has already promised to leave her alone and now wishes to look in her eyes once more as he could not do in the dark.

EXCERPT 7 B&H g pp. 348/3/1–365 10 min.

Arabella and Mandryka are described in previous excerpts. Welko, Mandryka's servant, is silent in this scene.

The night before at the ball, Mandryka has indulged in some rather jealous and drunken behavior and now realizes how foolishly he acted, as it was Zdenka, not Arabella, who arranged the assignation and actually kept the rendezvous. Disguises removed and the plot unraveled, Matteo has decided it is Zdenka, not Arabella, whom he loves and wishes to marry. When Arabella appears descending the staircase, she is carrying a glass of water to present to Mandryka in the custom of his homeland—a symbol of her betrothal to him. Ecstatically, they fall into each other's arms; she then runs up the stairs while he looks longingly after her.

Arlecchino

Ferruccio Busoni (1866–1924)

Bergamo, about the eighteenth century

EXCERPT 1	Brei	g, e	pp. 10–23	6 min.
	AMP	g	pp. 6–18	

The opening scene of the opera is sung by Ser Matteo, baritone (G1–E3), with Arlecchino speaking his lines except for his offstage exit, which could be sung by him or by a tenor (F♯2–A3). Ser Matteo's wife, Annunziata, is a mute role. All of the roles require expressive acting in the manner of a theatrical caprice, and Arlecchino must have a trained speaking voice. A tambourine could well be used to accompany the end of this excerpt, and portions of the opening and closing narrations could be used with the scenes being presented.

Ser Matteo, a tailor, has set up a portable workshop in front of his house and is sewing at a cloak while reading a volume of Dante. At the window right above his head, Arlecchino and Ser Matteo's pretty young wife peep slyly out. As the scene progresses, Arlecchino jumps from the window to stand in front of the tailor and to frighten him into the house with talk of an invasion by barbarians.

EXCERPT 2 Brei g, e pp. 24–46 15 1/2 min.
AMP g pp. 19–40

This excerpt includes the Abbot Cospieno, high baritone (B1–F3), and Doctor Bombasto, bass (F♯1–E♭3), and later Matteo, baritone (G1–E♭3), first as a duet and then as a trio.

The Abbot and the Doctor are walking toward Matteo's residence and are involved in conversation. When they get to his house, they notice that the shutters are closed and they call to him to find out what is the matter. He opens the window slightly and repeats the fabricated story Arlecchino has told him. The Abbot and the Doctor agree to find out more about the invasion as they leave for a short visit to the wine house.

EXCERPT 3 Brei g, e pp. 54–87 13 min.
AMP g pp. 47–77/1/5

Colombina is a mezzo-soprano (D3–B♭4) who has the opening of this scene with her husband, Arlecchino, an actor. When Arlecchino leaves, Leandro, tenor (C2–B♭3), approaches and sings of his love for Colombina. The tenor role requires a fine voice secure in a high tessitura. Some duet singing with Colombina and Leandro is included.

Colombina finds Arlecchino on the street and berates him for his adultery. He quarrels with her, but when she changes her tone of voice and begins to nestle up to him, he cannot stand it and runs away. When he has left, Leandro enters and overcomes Colombina with his song of love, but when Arlecchino returns and confronts them, he forces Leandro to hurl away his lute, knocks Leandro's sword from his hand, and tries to stab him. Leandro falls, as if dead.

EXCERPT 3a Brei g, e pp. 54–64 4 min.
AMP g pp. 47–56

The portion of excerpt 3 with only Colombina and Arlecchino.

EXCERPT 3b Brei g, e pp. 65–74 8 min.
AMP g pp. 57–77/1/5

The portion of excerpt 3 using Colombina and Leandro plus Arlecchino in a short appearance at the closing of the scene.

L'Arlesiana (The Maid of Arles)

Francesco Cilea (1866–1950)

Provence, nineteenth century

EXCERPT 1 SZ i, g pp. 5–29 12 min.

Baldassare, the old shepherd, is a baritone (B1–G♯3) whose upper range is important. Mamma Rosa is a full-voiced mezzo-soprano (C♭3–G4) and Vivetta, a lyric soprano (D3–G♯4). The role of the young boy, known as L'Innocente, can be taken by a mezzo-soprano, who has only one line to sing in this scene.

An old shepherd, Baldassare, is telling a story to Rosa's younger son, L'Innocente, who is slightly retarded. Rosa enters, worried about her elder son, Federico, who has met a girl from Arles whom he wants to marry. Vivetta, Rosa's goddaughter, in love with Federico herself, is distraught as Rosa tries to explain how her son and the young lady met, voicing her concern.

EXCERPT 2 SZ i, g pp. 63–110 27 min.

In addition to the characters in excerpt 1, the entire second act of the opera includes Federico, tenor (E2–A3, opt. B3). Vivetta has a sustained B♭4 in this scene. Again, L'Innocente has only a few important lines, and a mixed chorus sings briefly offstage.

Beside a pond, Rosa and Vivetta look for Federico, who has left home. Baldassare finds him; he and L'Innocente urge Federico to consider his mother's grief and return home. Rosa, however, realizes her son's misery and tells Federico she is prepared to welcome the girl into her home. Federico is unable to accept this; he resolves to forget the girl from Arles and marry Vivetta; moved to tears, his mother warmly embraces him.

EXCERPT 2a SZ i, g pp. 83/1/3–102/2/1 13 1/2 min.

Vivetta, Rosa, Federico, and L'Innocente.

EXCERPT 2b SZ i, g pp. 83/1/3–97/4/1 10 min.

Federico's lament and duet with Vivetta (includes L'Innocente).

EXCERPT 3 SZ i, g pp. 139/2/1–162/5/3 10 1/2 min.

Vivetta, soprano, has a sustained C5 in this scene, as well as some high pianissimo singing. Federico has an optional C4. Of the two baritones, Baldassare has a higher line than Metifio in a rather difficult quartet. Rosa, mezzo-soprano, appears only briefly at the end of the scene and sings one very important line to A4.

In the farmhouse, Federico, about to marry Vivetta, assures her that he is completely over his infatuation with the girl from Arles, who has been the mistress of Metifio. Metifio has arrived to collect the letters showing that the parents of the girl approved of the liaison with him; Baldassare has in fact returned the letters, but Metifio has been in Arles and has not received them. When Metifio declares he has decided not to give up the girl, Federico attacks him with a hammer. His mother, Rosa, with Baldassare's help, breaks up the fight and takes Federico to his room.

EXCERPT 3a SZ i, g pp. 139/2/1–145/3/4 5 min.

The opening duet from excerpt 3.

EXCERPT 4 SZ i, g pp. 167–78/2/1 9 min.

Rosa, dramatic mezzo (B2–A4), sings the aria "Esser madre è un inferno." She is joined in the scene by her young son, L'Innocente, also sung by a mezzo (E♭3–G4), the lighter and less difficult of the two roles.

Rosa, alone, laments the madness of her son Federico and prays to God that he will come to his senses. The younger son, L'Innocente, comes from his room trying to comfort her; in vain he offers to stay up and watch over his older brother so that his mother may sleep.

Attila

Giuseppe Verdi (1813–1901)

Italy, 452 A.D.

EXCERPT 1 Kal i pp. 27/4/1–39 7 1/2 min.

Attila, bass (C2–F3), and Ezio, baritone (C2–G3), are in this excerpt from the prologue.

Attila, leader of the Huns, invades Italy and captures the city of Aquileia. Ezio, envoy of the Roman Empire, who has defeated Attila the previous year in the battle of Chalons, bargains unsuccessfully with him for Italy's deliverance.

EXCERPT 2 Kal i pp. 63–80/2/3; 82/4/1–83 13 min.

Odabella, a dramatic soprano (C3–C5), has a lyric aria requiring flexibility in this excerpt with Foresto, tenor (G2–A3), whose singing is in a high tessitura.

In a wood near Attila's camp, Odabella mourns her father and her beloved Foresto, whom she believes has also been killed. Foresto, disguised as a barbarian, appears before her; he accuses her of treachery. Odabella convinces him of her innocence and her determination to have revenge. Foresto begs her forgiveness as they embrace.

EXCERPT 3 Kal i pp. 174–201 14 min.

Odabella, Ezio, Attila, and Foresto, who has an aria in this scene, have been described in excerpts 1 and 2. Others in the excerpt are Uldino, tenor, an onstage men's chorus and an offstage mixed chorus.

In previous action, Foresto has offered Attila a cup of poisoned wine, thus cheating Odabella out of the chance to avenge her father's murder. She saves Attila's life; in return, Attila has sworn to make her his queen. When excerpt 3 opens, Foresto is waiting to hear from Uldino when the wedding will take place, and he laments the fact that Odabella has betrayed him. Ezio hurries in and tells Foresto that his men are about to attack the Huns, while the wedding march is heard in the distance. Odabella pleads with the ghost of her father for forgiveness in marrying the man who killed him; she confesses that she always loved Foresto. Finding the three of them together, Attila accuses them all of ingratitude and treachery. Each answers him with hatred, and Odabella stabs Attila as the Romans defeat the Huns.

EXCERPT 3a Kal i pp. 175/5/1–188 8 min.

A portion of excerpt 3 with Odabella, Foresto, Ezio, and an offstage chorus.

Beatrice di Tenda (Beatrice of Tenda)

Vincenzo Bellini (1801–1835)

Castle of Binasco, 1418

EXCERPT 1 Kal i pp. 27–41 9 min.

Agnese, mezzo-soprano (E♭2–A4), flexibility required in a high tessitura, and Orombello, lyric-dramatic tenor (E2–A3) requiring flexibility, are in this scene from act 1.

Agnese is impatiently waiting for Orombello, Lord of Ventimiglia, to whom she has sent an anonymous letter of assignation. When Orombello arrives, he is amazed, for he imagined the letter to come from Beatrice with whom he is really in love. Agnese hints that there is someone (meaning herself) who longs for him, but Orombello, believing she is talking about Beatrice, admits his love for Beatrice. Agnese is shocked, displays her jealousy, and Orombello realizes the truth too late. He pleads with Agnese to spare the life and good name of his beloved Beatrice.

EXCERPT 2 Kal i pp. 43/3/4–72/2/5; 75/1/6–77 26 1/2 min.

Beatrice, a spinto soprano (D3–B4), needs both dramatic and coloratura ability in a high tessitura when she sings with Filippo, dramatic baritone (B♭1–F3), who also has a high tessitura and needs some flexibility. Rizzardo, tenor, has a lesser role in this scene, and there is a chorus of women.

In a solitary grove on the grounds of the ducal palace, Beatrice is strolling with her ladies and bemoaning the neglect of her husband, Filippo, Duke of Milan. They leave the scene shortly before Filippo arrives with his confidant, Rizzardo, Agnese's brother. He dispatches Rizzardo in search of Beatrice; when she reappears, Filippo accuses her of jealousy and intrigue; she defends herself and demands justice.

EXCERPT 2a Kal i pp. 56/4/1–72/2/5; 75/1/6–77 14 1/2 min.

This the same as excerpt 2, eliminating the women's chorus, Beatrice's aria, and the minor role of Rizzardo.

EXCERPT 3 Kal i pp. 197–211 12 1/2 min.

Beatrice, spinto soprano (B♭2–opt. C5), Agnese, and Orombello (see excerpts 1 and 2), and a chorus.

Beatrice has been condemned to death and, in a vestibule leading to the scaffold, her ladies and friends have gathered to comfort her and bid her a last farewell. As she swears vengeance upon Filippo and the unknown informer who has falsely accused her to the Duke, Agnese appears, falls at Beatrice's feet and begs forgiveness. At first, Beatrice coldly bids Agnese keep silent, but just then, Orombello's voice is heard, forgiving Agnese; Beatrice, too, forgives, before walking bravely to her death.

Béatrice et Bénédict (Beatrice and Benedict)

Hector Berlioz (1803–1869)

Messina, Sicily, sixteenth century

EXCERPT 1 Kal f pp. 50 (dialogue)–68 7 min.

Both Béatrice, mezzo-soprano (C♯3–A4), and Bénédict, tenor (C♯2–A3), require strength in the middle range in this opera based on *Much Ado about Nothing.*

Bénédict returns from the war with his friend, Claudio, who is betrothed to Béatrice's cousin, Hero. Béatrice's uncle is determined to find a husband for her as well and believes Bénédict an ideal choice. The two young people in question, however, have quite different ideas, which are expressed in this amusing, quarrelsome duet.

EXCERPT 2 Kal f pp. 69–89 7 1/2 min.

Bénédict, tenor, described in excerpt 1, has a B3 in this scene. Claudio, baritone, and Don Pedro, bass, have no special range problems.

Both Claudio and Don Pedro urge Bénédict to marry Béatrice; Bénédict mocks them and continues to fight his urges to fall in love.

EXCERPT 3 Kal f pp. 119–32 10 min.

Hero, soprano (C♯3–G♯4), should have a lyric voice, for elsewhere in the opera she has high coloratura singing. Ursula, contralto or mezzo-soprano (G♯2–E4), should have a voice of darker timbre than Béatrice.

Hero, anticipating her marriage with both joy and melancholy, is joined by her attendant, Ursula, in a ravishing nocturne, some of the most beautiful music Berlioz ever wrote.

EXCERPT 4 Kal f pp. 156–85 18 min.

Béatrice has a bravura aria to B♭4 in this scene; she is joined by Hero and Ursula in a trio (see excerpt 3 for description).

Béatrice reflects upon her own mixed feelings about Bénédict and the prospect of marriage. When Hero and Ursula find her in this mood, they are somewhat surprised. At first, Béatrice does not want to listen to their admonitions, but in the reprise of their trio, she joins them harmoniously, indicating that she is beginning to weaken from her earlier resolve not to marry Bénédict.

Black Widow

Thomas Pasatieri (1945–)

A Spanish town, early twentieth century

EXCERPT 1 Bel e pp. 1–18 11 1/2 min.

This is the opening scene of the opera between Raquel, a beautiful young Spanish widow, mezzo-soprano (G2–A4), and Juan, a wealthy young man, baritone (C2–E3), who has become her lover. Raquel's role is extremely demanding both lyrically and dramatically; Juan has a difficult role dramatically and should be a good actor.

Raquel refuses Juan's proposal of marriage because as a religious Spanish woman she feels her purpose in life must be to bear children, and she cannot. His despair leads Raquel to reveal her plan: Juan should marry Berta and give Raquel their firstborn child. Juan is at first aghast at the idea, and then, unable to resist Raquel's tenderness, he begins to give in.

EXCERPT 2 Bel e pp. 31–42/2/4 7 1/2 min.

This excerpt, scene 3 of the opera, is between Juan (see description in excerpt 1) and Berta, soprano (C♯3–B♭4), who has loved Juan since childhood.

Juan comes to propose to Berta, who has waited all her life for him. He asks that she help him free himself of Raquel, and she cannot resist his proposal, but when she has accepted, both she and Juan feel a fear of the future.

EXCERPT 3 Bel e pp. 73–88 9 1/2 min.

A scene for Raquel, Berta, and Juan (all previously described).

Raquel is playing with a rag doll in anticipation of the day when she will have Juan and Berta's child. Berta enters, trying courageously to face her rival, and Raquel takes advantage of her visit by telling her that the way to win back her husband is to make him a father. Berta leaves, convinced of Raquel's sincerity. When Juan comes, Raquel refuses to make love to him, and when he asks if he may return, she says he should not until he brings word of Berta's pregnancy.

EXCERPT 3a Bel e pp. 73–84/3/1 7 min.

The portion of excerpt 3 for the two women only.

EXCERPT 4 Bel e pp. 89–98/2/5 6 min.

A scene between Berta, soprano, and Juan, baritone, as described in previous excerpts.

As the scene opens, Berta is praying before a statue of the Blessed Mother and her prayer reveals she is expecting a child. Juan enters and finally, at the peak of Berta's emotions, understands what she is telling him. He says that he must go, and Berta realizes that he is going to Raquel. In a wild outburst, she orders him to go and to tell Raquel that she, Berta, has won.

EXCERPT 5 Bel e pp. 134–53 10 min.

This is an excerpt featuring Berta and her mother, Marta, mezzo-soprano (B♭2–G4), and her father, Pedro, tenor (E2–A♭3).

Raquel has moved in with Juan and Berta and has taken over their child. Now Berta, dressed like a little girl with her hair in ribbons, has decided to return home where she was once loved. Her father is sympathetic but her mother, Marta, says that Berta should live in the streets rather than hide like a coward. An emotional trio provides the climax of this scene.

The Boor

Dominick Argento (1927–)

Widow's house in the country, 1890

EXCERPT 1 B&H e pp. 1–17 9 min.

This fifty-five-minute opera uses only three characters. In this excerpt, the old Servant, tenor (E♭2–F♯3), and the young and pretty Widow, soprano (B2–A4), have a duet, and the Widow has an aria.

The young Widow, whose husband has died a year before, refuses to be consoled and remains dressed in black, fasting and weeping, with no desire to go outside even though it is now a lovely April day.

EXCERPT 2 B&H e pp. 18–35 8 min.

The Servant, tenor (F♯2–E3), the Boor, a middle-aged bass-baritone (G1–F♯3), and the Widow, soprano (C3–F4), are all included in this excerpt. The major portion of the singing is for the Boor and is quite dramatic, calling for a mature voice with good control at the top of the range.

The Boor, a neighbor, has come to the Widow's home to demand that she pay for oats that her husband bought from him and that were not paid for when her husband died. She promises to pay the bill "day after tomorrow."

EXCERPT 2a B&H e pp. 20–28 3 1/2 min.

The portion of excerpt 2 that includes only the conversation between the Boor and the Widow without the Boor's aria.

EXCERPT 2b B&H e pp. 20–35 7 min.

This includes the conversation between the Boor and the Widow, and the Boor's continuing aria.

EXCERPT 3 B&H e pp. 71–105 9 1/2 min.

The Servant (F♯2–A3) has a small part in this scene but must have some strength at the top of the range. The Boor (C2–F♯3, opt. F1) and the Widow (C♯3–G4) are included in this scene.

The Boor has decided not to leave the house until he gets the money owed him by the Widow's deceased husband. The Servant tries in vain to get him to leave before the Widow returns to face a duel with the Boor. When the Widow appears with the guns, she asks the Boor to show her how to use a gun, and in the ensuing duet in which they sing about love and spring, he tries to show her but at the same time falls in love with her.

EXCERPT 3a B&H e pp. 76–105 7 min.

The Servant could be excluded by beginning on p. 76 and also cutting his entrance and exit (104/2/1–105/2/1) but not cutting the music.

La Calisto

Francesco Cavalli (1602–1676)

Pelasgia in the Peloponnese

EXCERPT 1 Fab i, e, g pp. 2–12 5 min.

In this very early opera realized by Raymond Leppard, the prologue is sung by Nature, mezzo-soprano; Eternity, soprano; and Destiny, soprano. None of the roles have any special problems except the difficulty of the seventeenth-century style. A women's chorus (behind the scenes) is optional.

The prologue asks for Calisto to be immortalized.

EXCERPT 2 Fab i, e, g pp. 13–48/2/5 20 min.

Jove, bass (A1–D3); Mercury, baritone (C2–G3); and Calisto, soprano (D3–G4), are heard in this excerpt. When Jove is masquerading as Diana, his role is sung by the same mezzo-soprano (C♯3–D4) who sings the role of Diana later on.

In a parched forest, Calisto, the daughter of Lycaon, King of Pelasgia, bemoans the fact that the shady woodlands are gone, the flowers withered, and no water is in the fountain. Jove, overcome by Calisto's loveliness, commands water to gush from the spring, but Calisto is fearful. Mercury suggests that Jove take the form of his daughter, Goddess Diana, and Calisto will submit to the embraces of a goddess. Jove decides to try, and Calisto promises Goddess Diana whatever she desires, she may have. As Diana (Jove) and Calisto leave, Mercury says it is the cheating lover who will enjoy Calisto.

EXCERPT 3 Fab i, e, g pp. 48/3/1–78 19 min.

This scene features countertenor Endymion (A2–D3), a shepherd in love with Diana; the Virgin Goddess Diana, mezzo-soprano (D3–G4); Linfea, a follower of Diana, which is a travesty role sung by a tenor (C2–G3); Satirino, a satyr, soprano (D3–F4); and Calisto, soprano (described in excerpt 2).

Endymion enters exclaiming that the trees are now green again and the drought is over. Then he sees his love Diana who is sad because all of the animals fled when there was no water, and there is no hunting. When Endymion and Diana meet, Linfea will not let him stay and forces them to part in spite of their love for each other. Then Calisto enters and does not realize that it was Jove, disguised as Diana, who kissed her so passionately; she expects Diana to remember and does not understand why Diana thinks she is obscene and immodest. Linfea then says she has watched others and she does not think she wants to be a virgin, but when the young Satirino offers himself, Linfea sends him away.

EXCERPT 4 Fab i, e, g pp. 79–94 7 1/2 min.

Diana and Satirino (described in earlier excerpts); Pan, god of shepherds, bass (B1–D3); and Sylvano, god of the woods, bass-baritone (E1–D3), sing in this excerpt. There is a short section for a three-part men's chorus that could be sung instead by a trio.

Pan tries to make Diana consent to marry him, but she will hear nothing of it, calling him a coarse, barbarous mortal. Satirino and Sylvano agree always with Pan, and when Diana rejects him, they try to comfort him.

EXCERPT 4a Fab i, e, g pp. 79–91/1/3 6 min.

The same scene as excerpt 4 without the men's chorus.

EXCERPT 5 Fab i, e, g pp. 95–109 8 1/2 min.

Countertenor Endimione, mezzo-soprano Diana, and Satirino, played by a soprano (all previously described), are in this scene.

At the summit of Mount Latmos, Endimione and Diana meet and sing of their love while Satirino watches and cannot understand why Diana ignores Pan but throws herself in the arms of the shepherd Endimione.

EXCERPT 5a Fab i, e, g pp. 95–106 7 min.

The portion of Excerpt 5 with Diana and Endimione only.

EXCERPT 6 Fab i, e, g pp. 110–43 11 1/2 min.

Giunone, consort of Jove, soprano (C3–A4), opens this scene that also uses Jove, disguised as Diana, mezzo-soprano; Calisto and Mercury (see earlier excerpts).

Giunone knows that Jove is being unfaithful to her, and when Calisto tells her how Diana first made love to her and then rejected her, Giunone realizes that it was probably Jove impersonating Diana who made love to Calisto. Giunone then confronts Jove, telling him she knows of his philandering, and then Jove and Mercury discuss his escapades.

EXCERPT 7 Fab i, e, g pp. 165/2/1–167/3/1 (D-major cadence); 169/1/1–179/2/5 6 1/2 min.

Endymion, Pan, Diana, and Sylvano (all described in previous excerpts) sing in this final scene.

Endymion tells Pan that he would rather die than renounce his love for Diana. When Diana enters, Pan asks her why she disdains the man she has been seen embracing. She admits that if she loves, she loves only the virtues of a noble shepherd. Then, Diana and Endymion, left alone, express their love in a duet.

Il Campanello di notte (The Night Bell)

Gaetano Donizetti (1797–1848)

Foria, a suburb of Naples, about 1835

EXCERPT 1 Ric i pp. 35–50 9 min.
Int i, e pp. 37–54

There are no range problems for Serafina, soprano (C♯3–G4, opt. A4), and Enrico, baritone (C♯2–E3), in this scene but flexibility is required.

Serafina has just become the bride of an old pharmacist, Don Annibale, much to the dismay of her cousin, Enrico. After the wedding ceremony, the two are dancing together when suddenly Enrico stops, protesting her marrying without his permission. In the amusing duet that follows, Enrico plots the method he will use to get even with the old man.

EXCERPT 2 Ric i pp. 74/2/1–109 13 1/2 min.
Int i, e pp. 78/2/1–113

Enrico, baritone, must vocalize from G1–B♭3 in falsetto, while Don Annibale, bass, has a range of B1–E3. Lesser roles are sung by Madame Rosa, mezzo-soprano, and Spiridione, tenor.

Enrico, carrying out his plot to get back at Don Annibale, decides to keep him out of his bridal chamber on his wedding night. First, the night bell rings; when Spiridione answers, it is a messenger with an edict declaring that all pharmacists are to dispense their prescriptions in person. The next time the bell rings, it is Enrico disguised as a Frenchman, seeking a cure for indigestion. While Don Annibale is preparing the prescription, Enrico rearranges the furniture and then leaves. No sooner has Don Annibale put everything back in order (after a few minor accidents), than the bell rings again. This time Enrico pretends to be an opera singer about to make his local debut, suddenly stricken with laryngitis. After Don Annibale administers a remedy, Enrico vocalizes and then sings a serenade that, unbeknownst to Don Annibale, is directed at Serafina. His voice cracks again; he is given more pills, and the duet ends hilariously as Enrico regains his voice and shows off while Don Annibale impatiently tries to get rid of him.

EXCERPT 3 Ric i pp. 110–32 7 min.
Int i, e pp. 114–36

Enrico, baritone, and Don Annibale, bass, both described earlier, are in this scene with a lesser role for Spiridione, tenor.

The night bell rings one more time; now Enrico arrives dressed as an old man in a nightgown and cap, with a long list of his wife's ailments and the prescribed medications. In this extremely wordy duet, Enrico rattles off all these medications, leaving Don Annibale dumbfounded. As he leaves, Enrico says he will return the next noon to pick up the supplies. (Of course, this will keep Don Annibale up all night preparing prescriptions.)

Capriccio

Richard Strauss (1868–1949)

Paris, 1775

EXCERPT 1 B&H g pp. 34/4/1–48/3/1 5 1/2 min.

The Countess Madeleine is a lyric-spinto soprano (D3–A4) and the Count is a baritone (C2–F♯3).

The Countess is holding a salon discussion on operatic reform—which comes first, the words or the music? Her brother, the Count, shows only an indirect interest in the subject because his eye is on the actress Clairon.

EXCERPT 2 B&H g pp. 64/3/2–90/2/3 11 1/2 min.

This is the Countess' discussion with Flamand, tenor (F♯2–G♯3), and Olivier, baritone (C2–G3).

Olivier has written a sonnet that in this scene is sung by Flamand, a composer. It appears that the two professionals involved in the discussion of opera are also rivals for the affections of the Countess.

EXCERPT 3 B&H g pp. 107/4/2–243/1/2 45 min.

This is the major ensemble involving all the leading characters. In addition to the Countess, the Count, Flamand, and Olivier (previously described) are Clairon, mezzo-soprano (B♭2–A♭4); LaRoche, the theatre director, bass-baritone (E♭1–F3), who has a rather difficult part; and two Italian singers, soprano (E3–C5) and tenor (E2–C4), both requiring great flexibility in a high tessitura.

As the discussion continues, Strauss uses various musical and dance forms to illustrate the text, including a fugue and an Italian-style duet (in Italian). This duet builds into an ensemble of all eight principals. The argument is stopped by the theatre director, who launches into a monologue extolling the virtues of the theatre.

EXCERPT 4 B&H g pp. 305–32 19 min.

The final scene is for the Countess (see description above) with a short part for the Majordomo, bass.

The guests have left, and Madeleine has a long soliloquy in which she repeats the sonnet from act 1 to her own harp accompaniment. It has been agreed that Olivier is to write a libretto, which Flamand will set to music, and that the Countess will decide by the next morning between the two rivals. When the Majordomo announces that supper is served, she goes out rather lightheartedly, her mind still not made up.

I Capuleti ed i Montecchi (The Capulets and the Montagues)

Vincenzo Bellini (1801–1835)

Verona, thirteenth century

EXCERPT 1 Kal i pp. 41–61 23 min.

Giulietta, lyric-coloratura soprano, sings the opera's best-known selection, "Oh! quante volte," in this excerpt; her range is D3–C5, with the option of E♭5 in the cadenza of her cavatina. Romeo, in this opera, is a trouser role for mezzo-soprano (A♭2–A4; B♭4 or C5 may be interpolated). Occasionally, for credibility's sake, the role is sung by a tenor, but it is generally considered a *tour de force* for mezzo, requiring great flexibility. Lorenzo, bass, sings only in the recitative.

Based loosely on Shakespeare's *Romeo and Juliet*, the opera differs from the play in that Lorenzo is the Capulet family doctor rather than a priest, and Tebaldo is betrothed to Juliet as opposed to being her cousin. In this excerpt, we find Giulietta alone in her room, despairing of her impending marriage to Tebaldo, as she is secretly in love with Romeo. Lorenzo, sympathetic with her plight, announces Romeo's arrival; in the duet that follows, Romeo pleads with Giulietta to elope with him; she hesitates and Romeo escapes by means of a secret exit in order not to be seen by Giulietta's father.

EXCERPT 2 Kal i pp. 62–96 18 min.

All five principal singers appear in this scene; Romeo and Giulietta are described in excerpt 1. Tebaldo, tenor (A♭1–A♭3), is doubled in the low passages; therefore, the tessitura is not particularly difficult. Capellio, baritone (C2–E♭3), and Lorenzo, bass (A♭1–E♭3), as well as a chorus of men, complete the cast.

As the wedding guests arrive at the Capulet palace for Giulietta's marriage to Tebaldo, her secret lover, Romeo, leader of the enemy Montague family, mingles among the guests in disguise. After exchanging a few words of love with Giulietta, Romeo is discovered by her father, Capellio, and boldly confronts both him and Tebaldo. Romeo declares his love for Giulietta, but his attempt to abduct her has been foiled.

EXCERPT 2a Kal i pp. 67–82/1/7 11 min.

The portion of the above in which the male chorus sings off stage only.

EXCERPT 3 Kal i pp. 108/5/1–124/4/8 13 min.

The characters in this scene are Romeo, mezzo-soprano (B♭2–B♭4), and Tebaldo, tenor (D2–B♭3), both requiring agility at extremes of range. A mixed chorus appears briefly.

Romeo, in love with Giulietta, has challenged his rival, Tebaldo, to a duel. Their fighting is interrupted by a funeral procession; believing Guilietta dead, both men are filled with grief and cease their combat.

EXCERPT 4 Kal i pp. 124/5/1–136 19 min.

In performance, this excerpt is often replaced by the final scene from Vaccai's *Guiletta e Romeo*; however, for purposes of this book, we include only the Bellini selection.

Giulietta and Romeo are described in excerpt 1; Romeo has a sustained aria in this scene. Lorenzo and Capellio, along with a men's chorus, appear only briefly.

Giulietta has been given a sleeping potion by Lorenzo, who has been intercepted, preventing him from telling Romeo of the plot by which the two lovers can escape together. Arriving at Capulets' tomb, Romeo, believing Giulietta dead, poisons himself. Just then, Giulietta awakens from her sleep to renew her love with the dying Romeo; as he expires, Giulietta collapses with grief. The Montagues enter to discover the lifeless couple, and with Lorenzo, they denounce Giulietta's father for his responsibility for the tragedy.

EXCERPT 4a Kal i pp. 129/3/5–135/5/2; 136/3/4–4/7 11 min.

The portion of excerpt 4 with Romeo and Giulietta only; by means of a cut, the curtain falls without the final entrance of the Montagues.

Carry Nation

Douglas Moore (1893–1969)

Kansas and Missouri, mid-nineteenth century

EXCERPT 1 Gal e pp. 20–47 16 1/2 min.

The first scene in this historic opera about Carry Nation who led the crusade for prohibition has Carry, mezzo-soprano (B♭2–G♭4); her Father, bass-baritone (B♭1–E♭3); her Mother, soprano (E3–G4); and Dr. Charles Gloyd, baritone (D♯2–E3), whom she later marries. Ben, the livery man, is a tenor but has very little singing in this scene.

An afternoon in late spring 1865, Father is reading the Bible while Carry is cleaning the room. When Mother enters, she is dismayed because Carry is doing work that the "darkies" did before the Civil War, and she wishes her daughter to be a lady. The cleaning is in preparation for welcoming a boarder, Dr. Charles Gloyd, who has just been discharged from the army and will be living with them. He enters and the introductions take place, ending in a quartet.

EXCERPT 2 Gal e pp. 48–74 13 1/2 min.

This excerpt calls for an offstage Preacher, baritone (E2–D3), and offstage chorus, while onstage Charles and Carry have a love scene followed by a confrontation between Charles and Carry's Father (all described in excerpt 1).

In the churchyard, Charles is bemoaning the preaching of the day, but when Carry arrives, he proposes to her, and they have a short love duet interrupted by Carry's Father who accuses Charles of improprieties and demands that he leave.

EXCERPT 2a Gal e pp. 48–63/2/4 9 1/2 min.

The opening of excerpt 2 using all of the characters except the Father and ending with Charles and Carry's love duet.

EXCERPT 2b Gal e pp. 55/3/3–63/2/4 4 1/2 min.

Charles and Carry's duet only.

EXCERPT 3 Gal e pp. 108–33 15 min.

This is the first scene of act 2 and it uses Carry and a four-part women's chorus with a soloist. The women leave when Charles arrives home. (See excerpt 1 for descriptions of Carry and Charles.)

In Charles and Carry's home in Holden, Missouri, in 1867, Carry is entertaining the Ladies Auxiliary. The women are sewing curtains, braiding rugs, making quilts, etc., while one woman is reading to the group. Charles arrives, the women leave abruptly, and Carry attempts to make him pledge to give up drinking, as she is going to have a baby.

EXCERPT 3a Gal e pp. 108–20/3/3 7 min.

A short scene for the women in excerpt 3.

EXCERPT 3b Gal e pp. 120/4/4–133 8 min.

Duet for Carry and Charles.

EXCERPT 4 Gal e pp. 134–46 7 min.

An excerpt with most of the singing for the Mother, soprano (E3–C♯5), and a short portion for the Father, bass-baritone (B1–E3).

It is evening, and the Mother is in her bedroom in a nightdress with her hair flowing. She clasps a doll dressed as a bride. The Father enters and reads the letter she has received, which says that Carry is going to have a baby and that she needs money because there have been many problems. The Father decides to leave immediately by train to get Carry and bring her home.

EXCERPT 5 Gal e pp. 169–91 11 1/2 min.

The Caretaker of the Belton Church, baritone (C2–D3), sings in this last scene. Also included are Carry and Father and a chorus, although the chorus could be unseen. Mother is present but has no singing.

It is Easter Monday in the churchyard at Belton, where the Caretaker is placing Easter flowers on the graves. Carry, wheeling a baby carriage, comes in with her mother and tells how excited she is to have the letter from Charles that she is reading. The Father has entered and is listening before telling her that Charles has died the night before. Then the Father leads the Mother and baby off, while Carry sinks to her knees and prays with the chorus in the background. As she rises, she has shed her cape and stands dressed in black with a Bible in one hand and a hatchet in the other, the way she was always pictured during the years she crusaded for prohibition.

Cendrillon (Cinderella)

Jules Massenet (1842–1912)

Period of Louis XIII

EXCERPT 1 Heu f, e pp. 52/2/3–75/2/1 4 min.

This is the final segment of the opening scene of the opera and uses Noemié, soprano (C3–C5); Dorothée, mezzo-soprano (C3–A4); Mme de la Haltière, contralto or mezzo-soprano (B2–F4); and Pandolfe, baritone (C2–F3).

Pandolfe has married into a noble family; his wife and her two daughters are preparing to go to the Prince's ball. Pandolfe feels guilty that his own beloved daughter from a previous marriage, Lucette (known as Cendrillon), must stay behind.

EXCERPT 2 Heu f, e pp. 75/2/2–141 20 min.

This scene between Cendrillon, lyric soprano (D3–B4), and her Fairy Godmother, coloratura soprano (B2–D5), also needs six Spirits (female voices of all ranges), who could be supplemented by dancers and/or children.

Cendrillon appears for the first time in the opera, singing a simple folk song as she goes about her work. Eventually, she falls asleep near the fire, whereupon the Fairy Godmother appears to her in a dream. She and her Spirits go about transforming Cendrillon into an elegant young lady; when she awakens, she is ready to go to the ball and assured that no one in her family will recognize her. The one condition is that she return home by midnight.

EXCERPT 3 Heu f, e pp. 199/4/1–213 8 min.

This is a duet for Cendrillon, soprano (D3–B♭4), and Prince Charming, trouser role for a mezzo-soprano (C♯3–A4). Sometimes the role of the Prince is sung by a tenor, in which case the tessitura lies rather low.

Cendrillon and Prince Charming meet at the ball, but she keeps her identity unknown to him and suddenly disappears as the clock strikes midnight.

EXCERPT 4 Heu f, e pp. 214–68/2/1 21 1/2 min.

Cendrillon, Noemié, Dorothée, Mme de la Haltière, and Pandolfe, all previously described, are in this excerpt.

Cendrillon returns home, reflecting on her adventure at the ball and the handsome prince she has met. Mme de la Haltière and her two daughters enter, arguing with Pandolfe about the identity of the mysterious young lady they have seen at the ball. Pandolfe tries to defend himself and Cendrillon but is overwhelmed by the three women. Eventually, he does fend them off; left alone with Cendrillon, he sings tenderly to her and they talk of returning to their former life and happiness. Once left alone, however, Cendrillon suddenly decides to seek the Fairy Godmother's help in finding Prince Charming.

EXCERPT 4a Heu f, e pp. 250/2/1–268/2/1 10 1/2 min.

From excerpt 4, the duet for Cendrillon and Pandolfe, and Cendrillon's monologue.

EXCERPT 5 Heu f, e pp. 268/2/2–308 16 min.

Cendrillon, Prince Charming, Fairy Godmother, six Spirits, invisible chorus, and dancers take part in excerpt 5. Problems include some difficult offstage chorus work and the fact that Cendrillon and the Prince appear onstage and must sing together (often in unison) without seeing each other.

The Fairy Godmother and her Spirits cast a spell on Cendrillon and Prince Charming that they may not see each other. Cendrillon tells the Prince her name is Lucette, and they both beg the Fairy Godmother to let them see each other. The spell is broken.

Christopher Columbus

Jacques Offenbach (1819–1880)

In Spain and America, 1492, without regard for credibility

EXCERPT 1 JW e pp. 26–69 14 min.

The first excerpt of this *opéra bouffe* uses a trio of wives—Rosa, mezzo-soprano or contralto (G2–F#4); Fleurette, soprano (D#3–A4); and Gretel, soprano (D#3–D5)—who sing with the Waiter, tenor (D2–F3), and the Tourist, bass-baritone (C#2–E3). The women have two lines solo sections as well as trio and quintet music.

The scene takes place in the square of Cordova and the set and action could be as sparse or as elaborate as the director wishes.

EXCERPT 2 JW e pp. 70–80 4 1/2 min.

A short scene that also takes place in the square of Cordova and is between Luis de Torres, president of the Round Earth Society, who is a baritone (D2–F3); Columbus, tenor (D2–G3); and the Waiter, described in excerpt 1.

EXCERPT 3 JW e pp. 124/3/1–144 9 1/2 min.

This is Columbus' plea to Isabella, mezzo-soprano (B2–A4), which is an imaginary love affair between the two.

EXCERPT 4 JW e pp. 145–53 5 1/2 min.

A scene for Isabella, Columbus, and Ferdinand (tenor), concluding with Isabella's Jewel Song.

EXCERPT 5 JW e pp. 188–243 18 min.
(storm music may be shortened to accommodate the action)

Again, the scene includes Gretel; Fleurette; Rosa; the Waiter and the Tourist (see excerpt 1); Beatriz, Christopher Columbus' fiancée, soprano (C3–B4); and the Chief of Police, baritone (B1–F♯3).

This excerpt takes place aboard the *Santa Maria* and includes a storm at sea and the decision to throw Columbus overboard.

Christopher Sly

Dominick Argento (1927–)

Rural England, sixteenth century

EXCERPT 1 B&H e pp. 2–64 20 1/2 min.

Peter Turph, tenor (E2–B♭3), and Henry Pimpernell, bass-baritone (F♯1–E3), are searching for Christopher Sly, bass-baritone (A♭1–F♯3), and find him as he is thrown out of the alehouse by Marion Hacket, mezzo-soprano (A2–A♭3). A Lord, tenor (C2–A3), with an optional B♭3; two Ladies, both sopranos; three Huntsmen—baritone, tenor, and bass; a Page, soprano; and an Officer of the Law, nonsinging role, are included.

When Peter Turph, tailor, and Henry Pimpernell, smith, come up the street calling for Christopher Sly, a tinker, Sly manages to sneak into the alehouse, but he is soon thrown out by Marion Hacket, the hostess of the alehouse. Christopher Sly owes all three of these people and they wish their money. Because Sly will not respond to their demands, they leave to get a policeman.

At the entrance of the hunting party, Sly is found, and when it has been determined that he is drunk and not dying, the Lord decides to take Sly back to the manor, bathe and dress him in fine clothes, and lay him on the Lord's bed. Then a page will masquerade as Sly's wife and persuade him that he is really a nobleman. The party leaves taking the still insensible Sly with them, so that when the three creditors return with a young policeman, they believe Sly has escaped.

EXCERPT 1a B&H e pp. 2–26/3/4 7 1/2 min.

The portion of excerpt 1 using only Turph, Pimpernell, Hacket, and Christopher Sly. The excerpt should end on an F-major chord.

EXCERPT 1b B&H e pp. 27/5/2–63 12 min.

This scene begins with the entrance of the hunting party and continues until just before the creditors return looking for Sly.

It features the two Ladies, the Page, the Lord, Christopher Sly, and the three Huntsmen.

EXCERPT 2 B&H e pp. 71–123/2/6 19 min.

Christopher Sly, three Servants (the same as the three Huntsmen), the Lord and his two mistresses, and the Page, all described in excerpt 1. Both Sly and the Lord have considerable singing in this excerpt.

Christopher Sly wakes up from his stupor waited on by the Servants and very surprised at his surroundings. Then his "wife" is brought in (the Page), and he continues to be confused until finally he decides all this must be the truth, and he asks everyone except his wife to leave.

EXCERPT 2a B&H e pp. 71–102 11 1/2 min.

This scene starts at the opening of excerpt 2 but ends before the Page is brought in as Sly's wife.

La Clemenza di Tito (The Mercy of Titus)

Wolfgang Amadeus Mozart (1756–1791)

Ancient Rome

EXCERPT 1	Int	i	pp. 6–25	14 1/2 min.
	Pet	i, g	pp. 8–23/1/4	

Vitellia, lyric-spinto soprano (A2–B4), has considerable florid singing and requires strength in extremes of range. Sesto (Sextus), trouser role, should be a high mezzo-soprano (C3–G4) with flexibility. A less difficult trouser role is Annio (Annius), mezzo-soprano (C3–E4).

Vitellia, daughter of the deceased emperor of the Roman Empire, plans revenge on her father's successor, Titus, for his refusal to marry her. She persuades Sextus, who is in love with her, to kill Titus and burn the capitol. Annius, a close friend of Sextus, arrives to tell Vitellia that Titus' intended bride has been dismissed because the marriage would not have pleased his subjects. Thus, she orders Sextus to postpone the enactment of the plot, believing she still may have a chance to become Titus' empress. Left alone with Sextus, Annius asks his permission to marry Servilia, Sextus' sister. Sextus readily consents, and the two young men pledge their friendship in a short but charming duet.

EXCERPT 1a	Int	i	pp. 6–15/2/4	6 min.
	Pet	i, g	pp. 8–23/1/4	

The opening recitative and duet for Vitellia and Sesto.

EXCERPT 1b	Int	i	pp. 24–25	2 min.
	Pet	i, g	pp. 36–38	

The duet for Sesto and Annio.

EXCERPT 2	Int	i	pp. 47–79/3/6	24 1/2 min.
	Pet	i, g	pp. 66–123	

The entire cast of principals appear in this scene. Servilia, lyric soprano (E3–A4), sings a duet with Annio, trouser role for mezzo-soprano (A2–F♯4). Tito (Titus), tenor (F♯2–A3), requires some flexibility. Publio, bass (B1–E3), sings a trio with Vitellia (see excerpt 1), whose part lies in a high tessitura (F3–D4) in this excerpt, and

Annio. A highlight of this scene is the aria "Parto, parto, ma tu ben mio" sung by Sesto, mezzo-soprano (C3–B♭4), and requiring extreme flexibility.

Annius, in love with Servilia, has the difficult task of telling her that she has been chosen as a bride for Emperor Titus. Heartbroken and perplexed, the couple sing of their love in the duet "Ah perdona al primo affetto." When Titus arrives, Servilia confesses her love for Annius, and the Emperor is deeply moved by her sincerity. Meanwhile, Vitellia, once more embittered by Titus' indifference to her, orders Sextus to carry out the plot to burn the capitol. After Sextus has sung his farewell aria to her, Vitellia is confounded when Publius enters with news that Titus has decided to marry Vitellia after all. She calls after Sextus, but it is too late to stop him; her confusion and elation are expressed in a trio with Annius and Publius.

EXCERPT 2a Int i pp. 45–51 4 min.
Pet i, g pp. 66–74/2/4

From excerpt 2, the duet between Servilia and Annio.

EXCERPT 2b Int i pp. 59/5/1–79/3/6 12 1/2 min.
Pet i, g pp. 88/4/1–123

Sesto's aria and the trio from excerpt 2.

EXCERPT 2c Int i pp. 72–79/3/6 3 1/2 min.
Pet i, g pp. 109–23

The final trio only from excerpt 2.

EXCERPT 3 Int i pp. 98–112/2/7 9 1/2 min.
Pet i, g pp. 154–78

An aria for Annio, mezzo-soprano (D3–G4); and a trio for Vitellia, lyric-spinto soprano (B♭2–A♭4); Sesto, mezzo-soprano (C3–G4); and Publio, bass (B♭1–F3). Two guards (silent) complete the scene.

Annius urges Sextus to go to Emperor Titus and confess his assassination attempt. Vitellia, on the other hand, urges Sextus to flee; Sextus, however, vows to stand trial for his crime and keep secret Vitellia's part in the conspiracy. Publius arrives with his guards to summon Sextus to court.

EXCERPT 3a	Int	i	pp. 103/2/1–112/2/7	5 1/2 min.
	Pet	i, g	pp. 163–78	

The same as excerpt 3 without Annio.

EXCERPT 4	Int	i	pp. 116/2/1–160/2/4	29 min.
	Pet	i, g	pp. 185–254	

A scene for the four male characters of the opera, two of them sung by mezzo-sopranos. Sesto (C3–A♭4) and Annio (F3–A4) have an aria each; Publius, bass (B1–E3), has a short but important aria; while Tito, tenor (F2–B♭3), sings the famous bravura aria "Se all'impero." Two silent guards complete the scene.

It has been revealed that Sextus has committed the crime of arson in an attempt to assassinate Emperor Titus. However, Titus cannot believe his friend Sextus could be so disloyal and agrees to give him a hearing. Unsatisfied with Sextus' explanations, Titus signs the decree ordering Sextus thrown into the arena with the beasts.

EXCERPT 4a	Int	i	pp. 126–60/2/4	22 min.
	Pet	i, g	pp. 201/3/1–254	

From excerpt 4, Tito's recitative, the trio, and the arias of Sesto and Tito.

EXCERPT 5	Int	i	pp. 161–76/2/4	12 min.
	Pet	i, g	pp. 256/2/1–282/2/3	

This excerpt centers around two soprano arias, the resplendently lyric "S'altro che lagrime" for Servilia (F♯3–A4) and the difficult rondo "Non piu di fiori" of Vitellia (G2–A4), which requires considerable strength at the extremes of range. Annio, mezzo-soprano, sings briefly in the recitative.

Servilia and Annius lament the fate of Sextus who has been condemned to die; they urge Vitellia, who is to marry Emperor Titus, to plead with Titus for Sextus' pardon. Left alone, Vitellia expresses guilt for her part in the conspiracy against the Emperor, with which Sextus has been charged, and her affection for Sextus. Knowing she must confess her guilt to the Emperor, her hopes of a royal marriage are now destroyed.

The Cunning Little Vixen (Příhody Lišky Bystroušky)

Leoš Janáček (1854–1928)

A fairy-tale forest

EXCERPT 1 UE cz, g pp. 8–19/2/2 5 1/2 min.

The Gamekeeper, baritone (F♯1–F♯3), has considerable high tessitura, in this scene with the Cricket, Grasshopper, Mosquito, Frog, and the young Vixen. The insects and the young Vixen can all be children who have a small amount of singing with action and dancing.

The Gamekeeper enters with his gun on his shoulder, puffing and sighing, and lies down to doze off. The insects play around him, and when the Frog awakens him, he sees the young Vixen, Sharpears, catches her, and takes her home.

EXCERPT 2 UE cz, g pp. 24/3/1–35/4/1 5 1/2 min.

The Gamekeeper (described in excerpt 1); his Wife, mezzo-soprano (E3–A4); the Vixen, now a soprano (D♭3–B♭4); the Dog, mezzo-soprano; and two children, Pepik and Frantik, are in this excerpt.

Installed at the Gamekeeper's, the Vixen exchanges stories with the Dog and defends herself both against his sexual advances and against the children's baiting, for which she is tied up.

EXCERPT 3 UE cz, g pp. 36/5/1–50 5 1/2 min.

The Vixen (see excerpt 1), the Dog, and the Gamekeeper's wife (described in excerpt 2) are again in this scene with the Rooster, soprano; the Hen, soprano; other hens (sopranos and altos); and a Crested Fowl, mezzo-soprano.

The Vixen's plans to entice the hens into her range start with political demagoguery; when this fails she threatens to bury herself alive in disgust at their conservatism. The Rooster is sent to investigate and is soon dispatched, as are all the hens in turn. Fearing retribution at the hands of the Gamekeeper and his wife, the Vixen bites through her leash and escapes into the forest.

EXCERPT 4 UE cz, g pp. 51–58/4/3 3 min.

The Vixen, described in excerpt 2, is again in this excerpt with the Badger, bass (D2–E♭3), and other animals (sopranos and altos).

In this scene in the forest, the Vixen ruthlessly evicts the Badger and takes over his comfortable home.

EXCERPT 5 UE cz, g pp. 60/6/2–72 6 min.

The Gamekeeper (see excerpt 1) sings with the Priest, bass (A♭1–F♭3), and the Schoolmaster, tenor (E♭2–A3). The Innkeeper, tenor, has a very small part, while the chorus is optional.

The Gamekeeper is playing cards and drinking with the Schoolmaster, and the Priest, who resembles the Badger. The Gamekeeper teases the Schoolmaster about his inactivity as a lover; the Schoolmaster, in turn, teases the Gamekeeper about the escape of the Vixen.

EXCERPT 6 UE cz, g pp. 72/4/1–87 7 min.

This scene includes the Schoolmaster, the Priest, and the Gamekeeper, all of whom have been previously described.

The Schoolmaster, tipsy, has trouble finding his way home and mistakes the Vixen for his distant beloved. The Priest, separately winding his way home, lets his thoughts wander back to an incident in his youth when he was wrongly accused of seducing a girl. Both men are startled when the Gamekeeper fires two shots after the Vixen.

EXCERPT 7 UE cz, g pp. 89/2/3–116/4/2 13 min.

The Vixen (see excerpt 2) and the Fox, tenor (D♯2–B3) or soprano (D♯3–B4), sing together in this scene.

The Vixen meets a handsome Fox; she tells him how she was brought up at the Gamekeeper's and later escaped. They fall in love and she is soon obliged to marry.

EXCERPT 8 UE cz, g pp. 133/2/1–159/1/3 11 1/2 min.

In this excerpt the Gamekeeper, the Vixen, and the Fox again appear, as do Harašta, bass, and children costumed as Fox Cubs.

Harašta, a poultry dealer, is heard approaching; he is accosted by the Gamekeeper, who thinks he has been poaching. Harašta tells him that he is about to marry Terynka. The Gamekeeper leaves a trap for the Vixen. She and her mate and her litter make fun of the trap. The Vixen and her mate contemplate their growing family and possible additions. Harašta returns and the Vixen lures him into the forest, where he trips and falls. While he is nursing his injuries, the Vixen and her family demolish the chickens. Harašta, in his anger, shoots the Vixen.

EXCERPT 9 UE cz, g pp. 162/4/1–170/4/1 5 1/2 min.

The Gamekeeper and Schoolmaster (see excerpts above) and the Innkeeper's wife, soprano, sing in this excerpt.

In the inn, the Schoolmaster is tearful at the news of Terynka's marriage to Harašta, and both he and the Gamekeeper regret the absence of the Priest. The Gamekeeper, feeling his age, sets off for home through the forest.

Death in Venice

Benjamin Britten (1913–1976)

In Munich and later in Venice, mid-nineteenth century

EXCERPT 1 Fab e, g pp. 1–18/3/1 11 min.

Gustav von Aschenbach, a novelist, is the main character in this difficult opera. He is a tenor (B1–G♯3) and sings with the bass-baritone (A1–D♯3), who sings many different characters. In this scene the bass-baritone is the Traveller. There is also an offstage chorus. The accompaniment, very difficult for one pianist, might be divided for two pianos.

Aschenbach is walking in the suburbs of Munich on a spring evening. He stops before the entrance to a cemetery and notices the texts on the façade of the mortuary chapel, where suddenly he is aware of the Traveller who urges Aschenbach to travel to the South.

EXCERPT 2 Fab e, g pp. 52–76/1/5 13 min.

This scene is between Aschenbach, tenor, and the Hotel Manager, again sung by the bass-baritone (see excerpt 1 for voice ranges.) In the second half of the scene, they are joined by a group of twelve hotel guests who all have singing parts: four sopranos (English lady, Danish lady, French girl, Russian mother), three mezzos (French and German mothers, Russian nanny), two tenors (two Americans), two baritones (German father, Pole), and one bass (Russian father). In addition, a waiter and a porter sing in unison (male voices, middle range), while numerous children appear along with the Polish family consisting of the mother, two girls, a governess, and Tadzio (fourteen-year-old boy, preferably a dancer), all of whom have very important mime parts. This is an excellent scene for a large workshop in which there are two fine male singers but others who may be more adept at dancing, acting, etc., than singing.

As the Hotel Porter brings Aschenbach and his luggage into the hotel, Aschenbach is greeted by the Hotel Manager who points out the amenities of the establishment. As the hotel guests and their children proceed to the dining room, Aschenbach notices the Polish family, particularly the young boy Tadzio. As the family bow to Aschenbach and move into the dining room, Aschenbach, left alone, comments on the striking beauty of Tadzio. (His infatuation with Tadzio needs to be handled with utmost discretion, stressing the symbolism thereof and at all costs avoiding cheap sensationalism.)

EXCERPT 2a Fab e, g pp. 52–65/1/1 8 min.

This is the early portion of excerpt 2 with Aschenbach and the Hotel Manager only.

EXCERPT 3 Fab e, g pp. 96–116 14 min.

Again, Aschenbach and the Hotel Manager are the leading characters (see excerpts 1 and 2); however, this time the supporting characters have lines of a more solo nature. They include Lace Seller (soprano); Beggar Woman (mezzo); Gondolier, Glassmaker, Porter (tenors); Gondolier, Guide, and Waiter (baritones). Again, Tadzio is silent and is accompanied by some other boys at the end of the scene.

This scene takes place in a gondola, back and forth between the Lido and Venice, creating a production problem that would require some imagination. Aschenbach crosses to Venice in a gondola; as he disembarks, he begins to wander unhappily through the streets, where vendors and beggars call to him from all sides. Disenchanted, he gets back into the gondola and returns to his hotel at the Lido, where he speaks a few words to Tadzio, who glances back at him. He once more gets into the gondola returning to Venice, where he intends to get on a train to go home but suddenly finds he cannot do this. Returning to the Lido in the gondola, he notices Tadzio and his friends playing on the beach in the distance and admits to himself it was Tadzio who made it difficult for him to leave.

EXCERPT 4 Fab e, g pp. 160–71/2/1; 176–80/3/4 10 1/2 min.

Aschenbach, tenor, has this excerpt with the Hotel Barber, another role for the bass-baritone. Then, at the cut, a Newspaper Seller, soprano (C3–F4), has a few lines.

Aschenbach is getting his hair cut in the hotel barbershop when he senses that the Hotel Barber is referring to illness in Venice. When he reads the German newspaper, he finds that German citizens are urged to return home because of cases of cholera, which the Venetian city fathers refuse to admit.

EXCERPT 5 Fab e, g 198/1/3–204/3/3 3 1/2 min.

This scene for the Strolling Players can be staged without an onstage audience, if desired. It should include a boy and a girl, treble voices with choreographed action, two acrobats who mime the instruments (flute and guitar), and the Leader of the Players, the same bass-baritone mentioned in earlier excerpts, who enters when an acrobat mimes a trumpet.

EXCERPT 6 Fab e, g 240/2/1–260/2/1 12 1/2 min.

An excerpt including the Hotel Barber, bass-baritone, and Aschenbach, tenor (see excerpt 3). It includes a very short part for the Strawberry Seller, soprano (G3–F4), and portions for the Hotel Manager, bass-baritone, and the Hotel Porter, tenor (E#2–F#3). Tadzio and family are silent in this scene. If only one bass-baritone is used, he could make a costume change during the time when Aschenbach is talking to the Strawberry Seller.

Again Aschenbach is in the hotel barbershop with the Barber cutting his hair. It seems unnecessary for Aschenbach to get into a gondola but he should continue the text. He sees the Polish family; Tadzio detaches himself from his family to look at Aschenbach for a moment. Aschenbach buys strawberries from the Strawberry Girl. The Hotel Manager and Hotel Porter remark that all of the hotel guests are departing now at the end of the season, but when when Aschenbach enters, he goes to his usual chair and gets up no more.

Doktor Faust (Doctor Faust)

Ferruccio Busoni (1866–1924)

Wittenberg, Germany, sixteenth century

EXCERPT 1 Brei g pp. 13–30 10 min.

In this excerpt Faust, baritone (B♭1–G♭3); Wagner, bass (F♯1–C3); and three students, tenor, baritone, and bass, are heard.

In Faust's study, Wagner tells him that three students are asking to see him and have with them a remarkable book called *Clavis Astartis Magica*. Faust is excited; this is perhaps the book that will give the power he has wanted for so long. The three students, dressed in black, enter and announce themselves as students from Cracau. Faust is reminded of his youth. The students give him the book and a key with which to unlock it and a letter that makes it his property. He offers them hospitality, but they decline and leave. Wagner returns and when Faust asks him why he did not show the students out, he says he saw no one, and Faust begins to understand the identity of the visitors.

EXCERPT 2 Brei g pp. 66/2/1–81 8 min.

Another scene for Faust, baritone, with Mephistopheles, tenor (E2–B♭3).

When Mephistopheles enters, Faust makes an unusual demand. He wishes to understand the actions of mankind and to have his every wish granted so that he will have freedom. But Faust has gone beyond the magic circle, and Mephistopheles will only agree to serve him at a price. After he has done Faust's bidding, Faust must serve him forever.

EXCERPT 3 Brei g pp. 182/5/2–194 10 min.

The Duchess of Parma is a soprano (B2–B4) capable of singing a high pianissimo, who sings with Mephistopeles, tenor, and the Duke of Parma, also a tenor (F2–F♯3), in this scene.

When the Duchess appears in this excerpt, she is convinced that Faust is calling her. She sings of her love for him and then goes slowly out, still calling from offstage. It is suddenly daylight and the Duke of Parma is in conversation with his Chaplain, who tells him that the Duchess has eloped with Faust. It would be best to hush up everything and marry the sister of the Duke of Ferrara, who otherwise threatens war. The Duke accepts the Chaplain's counsel and as the scene ends, the hand raised in blessing turns to a claw as it emerges from the sleeve. The Chaplain is Mephistolpheles in disguise.

Double Trouble

Richard Mohaupt (1904–1957)

A Mediterranean island street

EXCERPT 1 AMP e, g pp. 16–48 12 min.

The chorus in this opera need not be costumed but may be seated at the side or in the pit in order to comment on the story and the action. The style of acting for the principals is commedia dell'arte, with masks, and could prove to be an excellent teaching tool for this style. The first excerpt includes Hocus, bass-baritone (A1–F♯3), who needs a trill; the courtesan Erotia, a flashy, seductive, coloratura soprano (D3–B♭4), who also needs a trill; and Naggia, mezzo-soprano (A♭2–A♭4), the shrewish wife of Hocus. Cynthia, daughter of Hocus and Naggia, a soprano (D3–A4), and her lover, Lucio, tenor (D2–A3), are also in this scene. The chorus has a few comments.

Hocus and Pocus, twin sons of Docus and Crocus, have been separated in youth, when Docus took Hocus on a "business" trip and lost him. Hocus has grown up, married Naggia, and is involved with the courtesan Erotia.

As the scene opens, Hocus enters from his own house with a fur coat and a diamond necklace stolen from his wealthy wife to give to Erotia. He walks over to Erotia's house just as she is opening her window. He offers her the coat and the diamond, and she invites him to come in. Just then we hear Naggia screaming from inside her house. She has missed the coat that Erotia by now has taken from Hocus and has quickly closed her window. Naggia and Hocus quarrel bitterly until she slams the window with a bang.

Hocus starts toward Erotia's when he sees his daughter, Cynthia, and Lucio. He vehemently forbids them to marry and then exits while they finish with a love duet.

EXCERPT 1a AMP e, g pp. 16–38 8 min.

The opening of Excerpt 1 until Hocus is left alone on the stage.

EXCERPT 1b AMP e, g pp. 39–48 4 1/2 min.

From the entrance of Cynthia and Lucio until they exit after their love duet.

EXCERPT 2 AMP e, g pp. 51/1/2–67 6 1/2 min.

Pocus, twin brother of Hocus, is also a bass-baritone (G1–E3). Erotia is described in excerpt 1.

Pocus enters singing a sea chantey, with a little punctuation by the men of the offstage chorus. Erotia listens and appears at the house door with the fur coat that Hocus has given her. She thinks Pocus is Hocus and lures him into her house.

EXCERPT 3 AMP e, g pp. 109/3/2–123 5 1/2 min.

Characters in this scene have all been described in earlier excerpts—Pocus, Erotia, Cynthia, and Lucio.

Cynthia and Lucio are in the shadows and watch Erotia bid Pocus good-bye. Erotia thinks it is Hocus, and Cynthia and Lucio do, too. Cynthia upbraids Pocus, who she thinks is her father; Pocus, to get out of the situation, agrees that she may marry Lucio.

EXCERPT 4 AMP e, g pp. 171–79 3 1/2 min.

A very short excerpt for Hocus and Pocus, but it could be used for teaching young singers "mirror" action.

Pocus has been taken in and chained by Naggia, who thinks he is Hocus, her unfaithful husband. As Pocus escapes, he meets Hocus and they realize that they are twin brothers.

Edgar

Giacomo Puccini (1858–1924)

Flanders, 1302

EXCERPT 1 Ric i pp. 6/2/1–14/2/2 4 1/2 min.

A duet for Fidelia, soprano (C3–B4), and Edgar, tenor, with no particular vocal difficulties.

Edgar is torn between pure love for Fidelia and sensual attraction for Tigrana, a negress abandoned as a baby by gypsies and brought up by Fidelia's father. In this scene, Fidelia appears at her balcony, sings lovingly to Edgar, and throws a flower to him, begging him not to leave her.

EXCERPT 2 Ric i pp. 16–32/2/4 8 min.

This scene calls for Tigrana, mezzo-soprano (C3–G4); Edgar, tenor (to Ab3); and Frank, baritone (D2–F3), who sings a beautiful lyric aria in this scene.

Tigrana attempts to seduce Edgar, who flees from her. When she attempts to run after him, she is blocked by Frank, who is in love with her; she does not return his love. Left alone, he sings of his unrequited love.

EXCERPT 3 Ric i pp. 83/4/1–99/2/2 9 min.

Tigrana and Edgar (see descriptions above) are in this scene.

Edgar and Tigrana have eloped, but Edgar longs for the pure love of Fidelia. Tigrana once more seduces him with feminine wiles.

EXCERPT 4 Ric i pp. 168/2/2–183/2/5 7 min.

Tigrana, Edgar, and Frank are again in this excerpt.

Edgar is believed to have been killed in battle but has instead become a monk. Tigrana approaches, and when she recognizes Edgar, she wants him to love her again. Frank, however, continues to give presents to Tigrana, hoping to win her favor.

Elegie für junge Liebende (Elegy for Young Lovers)

Hans Werner Henze (1926–)

Austria, early twentieth century

EXCERPT 1 Sch g, e pp. 1–42 15 min.

Hilda, white-haired woman in her sixties, is a coloratura soprano (G♯2–B♭3) who opens this scene with an aria. Then Carolina Grafin von Kirschstetten, contralto (B♭2–A4), is introduced with Dr. Wilhelm Reischmann, bass (G1–G3), and they continue their singing, ending in a short duet. The music, especially the piano reduction, is very difficult and might require two pianos; the vocal line is also difficult but melodious. There is some spoken dialogue and some singing speech on three pitch levels. A silent maid is included in this excerpt.

Hilda Mack, a sixty-year-old widow, is dressed as a young woman of the 1870s. She is sitting on the terrace and telling of the death of her husband on Mt. Hammerhorn forty years before. His death has driven her mad and every year Gregor Mittenhofer, a self-centered poet, returns to this Alpine inn to observe her visions and incorporate them into his poems. He has brought with him Carolina, a middle-aged secretary, and Dr. Wilhelm Reischmann, his physician. In this scene, while reading reviews of Mittenhofer's poetry, the two describe the current situation well and set the story.

EXCERPT 1a Sch g, e pp. 9–42 12 min.

The portion of the scene with Carolina and Dr. Reischmann only.

EXCERPT 2 Sch g, e pp. 43–100/2/2 19 1/2 min.

The second scene includes Hilda, Dr. Reischmann, and Carolina, all of whom have appeared in excerpt 1, and introduces Dr. Reischmann's son, Toni, lyric tenor (C♯2–G♯3); Gregor Mittenhofer, the poet, baritone (G1–F♯3); and his young mistress, Elisabeth Zimmer, soprano (F♯3–F4). Hilda and Mittenhofer have the majority of the singing in this scene. A servant and a maid are mute.

Dr. Reischmann, Carolina, and Hilda are onstage when Toni enters carrying a small valise. He has a certain sullen reticence that encourages the idea that those present make him uncomfortable. When Gregor Mittenhofer and his beautiful, young mistress enter, Carolina and Dr. Reischmann play their roles by rushing to their master; Toni rises slowly and Hilda continues to knit. Hilda then drops her knitting and cries out in her madness while the others remain frozen. During the sextet that follows, Carolina quietly shepherds the others away and Mittenhofer seats himself near Hilda, occasionally taking notes. When Hilda breaks off and moves from Mittenhofer, Carolina enters with the reviews, and during Mittenhofer's tirade that follows, she faints. Mittenhofer calls for Dr. Reischmann, who puts Carolina to bed so that Mittenhofer may resume his writing.

EXCERPT 2a Sch g, e pp. 43–72/2/1 12 min.

This is the portion of excerpt 2 before Hilda leaves the scene.

EXCERPT 3 Sch g, e pp. 115–43 11 1/2 min.

This excerpt includes the above-described Hilda, Elisabeth, and Toni, in singing roles, plus Mittenhofer in a very short speaking appearance.

The body of Hilda's husband, who disappeared forty years earlier, has been discovered in a glacier, and Elisabeth has been designated to break the news to Hilda. In order to make Hilda understand, Elisabeth must tell her very carefully and then have Hilda repeat everything, ending the conversation in a short duet. Toni has watched from a distance and is touched by the unexpected story and by Elisabeth's warmth as she communicates with Hilda. When Mittenhofer comes to get Elisabeth to go for a walk, Toni sings of his own past, and Hilda joins in as her sanity begins to return.

EXCERPT 3a Sch g, e pp. 115–30 5 min.

This is the portion of excerpt 3 with only Hilda and Elisabeth. It should end with Hilda's speech on p. 130.

EXCERPT 3b Sch g, e pp. 131–43 6 min.

The portion of excerpt 3 for Toni and Hilda.

EXCERPT 4 Sch g, e pp. 144–74/1/3 8 1/2 min.

This is a love scene between Toni and Elisabeth who are interrupted by Carolina and Dr. Reischmann (all earlier described).

Toni and Elisabeth have had several days to become acquainted and have fallen in love with each other. While they are singing a love duet, Carolina enters and finds them. She immediately calls Dr. Reischmann, Toni's father, and together they upbraid the young couple.

EXCERPT 4a Sch g, e pp. 144–55/3/1 4 1/2 min.

Excerpt 4 has this scene for Toni and Elisabeth. It should end with the singing on p. 154 but continue with orchestra only through the arpeggiated chord at 155/3/1.

EXCERPT 5 Sch g, e pp. 189/3/2–210/3/3 8 min.

Mittenhofer has a long aria in this excerpt, which is sung with short interruptions by Elisabeth.

EXCERPT 6 Sch g, e pp. 212–41 8 1/2 min.

Mittenhofer has the most singing in this scene, although Toni, Elisabeth, Carolina, and Dr. Reischmann, all previously described, are very important. Toni needs a strong B♭3 for this excerpt.

Toni wanted Elisabeth to tell Mittenhofer that she no longer wished to be his mistress, but Elisabeth was unable to do so. Now Toni has resolved that he will tell Mittenhofer himself.

EXCERPT 7 Sch g, e pp. 242–92 15 min.

A scene for Hilda, coloratura soprano, who must have an E4 in this excerpt, and Elisabeth, Toni, Dr. Reischmann, and Mittenhofer, baritone, who sings in a high tessitura and needs a G3 in this scene.

Hilda enters with Mauer, an Alpine guide. She is slightly tipsy and holds a cowbell in one hand and an enormous cigarette holder in the other. Elisabeth speaks to Hilda while the others are trying to get rid of her and then tells Toni she will marry him. Mittenhofer gives his consent and suggests a trip for Elisabeth and Toni into the mountains to seek a certain flower he wishes.

EXCERPT 7a Sch g, e pp. 242–58 5 1/2 min.

This portion of excerpt 7 uses all of the characters, but most of the singing is Hilda's.

EXCERPT 7b Sch g, e pp. 270–92 6 min.

After Dr. Reischmann places Toni's hand into Elisabeth's hand, displaying a father's blessing on the couple, Mittenhofer asks the couple to go into the mountains to seek the flower.

EXCERPT 8 Sch g, e pp. 307/2/1–380/2/1 22 min.

A scene for Mittenhofer, baritone, and Carolina, contralto, with a short interlude when Mauer speaks.

Mittenhofer is attempting to get back to his writing, while Carolina is concerned that he has lost his mistress to a younger man, even though she feels he needs to be alone in order to write. When Mauer, the guide, enters, he tells them a severe blizzard is on its way and if there is anyone out, he should get them right away or they will be lost in the storm. Mittenhofer says he knows of no one out in the storm, and Carolina is shocked that he did not tell Mauer that he had sent Toni and Elisabeth out.

EXCERPT 9 Sch g, e pp. 406–31/2/3 10 min.

An excerpt for Elisabeth, soprano, and Toni, tenor, both described earlier.

Elisabeth and Toni, caught in the storm on Hammerhorn and too exhausted to go on, stop under the shelf of a rock and sing of the life they can imagine they might have lived. In the final duet of the scene, they ask God's forgiveness for their sins.

Ernani

Giuseppe Verdi (1813–1901)

Aragon, Aix-la-Chapelle, Saragossa, 1519

EXCERPT 1 Ric, Kal i pp. 32–41/2/3; 44/3/1–63/1/2; 66/2/4–67/3/4; 68/2/1–75/3/2; 78/2/3–79 21 min.

Elvira, spinto soprano, opens the scene with her famous aria, "Ernani, involami" (B♭2–C5), requiring considerable flexibility throughout the range. She then sings a duet with Don Carlo, baritone (C2–G3), requiring strength in the upper register; they are joined by Ernani, tenor (E2–A3). Silva, bass (G1–F3), closes the scene with a demanding aria, "Infelice! e tuo credevi!" and its cabaletta, "Infin che un brando vindice." Female and male choruses appear separately; the cast is completed with the brief mezzo role of Giovanna.

Elvira, alone in her chamber in the castle of Aragon, broods over her forthcoming marriage to the elderly grandee Don Ruy Gomez de Silva. She is thinking only of the man she really loves, Don Juan of Aragon, who, in exile, has become known as Ernani. Don Carlos, King of Castile, also in love with Elvira, enters the room to woo her; just as he is about to force her to flee with him, a secret panel opens and Ernani steps forth. During the ensuing quarrel between the two men, Elvira tries to defend Ernani. Suddenly, the door flies open and Silva appears, astonished to find two men fighting over his bride. After brooding upon his wounded pride in an aria, he calls in his soldiers, swearing revenge.

EXCERPT 1a Ric, Kal i pp. 32–41/2/3; 44/3/1–56 13 1/2 min.

The opening portion of excerpt 1 with Elvira, Don Carlo, Giovanna, and women's chorus only.

EXCERPT 1b Ric, Kal i pp. 32–41/2/3; 44/3/1–63/1/2; 66/2/4–67/3/4; 68/2/1–68/3/6 16 min.

Continuation of excerpt 1a through the trio with Ernani.

EXCERPT 2 Ric, Kal i pp. 142/1/3–163/2/3; 166/2/6–169 11 min.

Elvira, Ernani, and Silva are all described in excerpt 1. This trio is less demanding for Elvira and Silva than their arias from excerpt 1, while the tenor part of Ernani is somewhat more taxing. Jago, baritone, sings only a few lines.

In the great hall of Silva's castle, wedding guests have just celebrated the impending marriage of Silva and Elvira. As they retire to another room, a holy man arrives seeking hospitality in the castle. Silva admits him, but as Elvira appears in her bridal gown, the pilgrim immediately throws off his disguise and reveals himself as the bandit Ernani. He demands to be turned over to the King, preferring death to life without his beloved Elvira. Silva, however, fearing that the King might succeed in taking Elvira away from him, determines to conceal his guest when told of the King's forthcoming arrival.

EXCERPT 3 Ric, Kal i pp. 170–80/2/2 5 1/2 min.

This scene, which immediately follows excerpt 2, is basically an aria for Don Carlo, baritone (C2–F♯3), requiring strength and flexibility, supported by the important role of Silva, bass.

King Carlos enters, suspecting that Silva is concealing the bandit Ernani in his castle, and demands that Ernani be surrendered to him, which Silva adamantly refuses to do.

EXCERPT 4 Ric, Kal i pp. 275/2/2–297 12 1/2 min.

The final trio includes Elvira, Ernani, and Silva, who are described in excerpt 1; this scene poses a vocal and dramatic challenge for all three.

Don Carlos, in an act of magnanimity, has listened to Elvira's plea and has freed those who had conspired to assassinate him, including Ernani. In addition, he has renounced his own love for Elvira and has given her and her true love Ernani his blessings. On the terrace of the palace, the couple is rapturous in newly found happiness, when suddenly a horn sounds. It is the horn Ernani had given Silva, also a rival for Elvira's love, with the oath that he would kill himself. Silva has never forgiven Ernani his misdeeds nor forgotten their rivalry; he approaches, demanding that the oath be fulfilled. Deaf to Elvira's pleas for her husband's life, Silva offers a dagger or a cup of poison. Ernani bids farewell to his beloved Elvira and stabs himself; Elvira faints over his body, and Silva triumphs sinisterly upon his revenge.

Esclarmonde

Jules Massenet (1842–1912)

Byzantium and Blois, Middle Ages

EXCERPT 1 Kal f pp. 20–70 21 1/2 min.

A scene for Esclarmonde, lyric soprano with upper extension (C3–D5); Parseïs, mezzo-soprano (B2–A4); and Énéas, tenor (E2–G3). A chorus of Invisible Spirits (sopranos) completes the scene.

Phorcas, the Emperor of Byzantium, is abdicating his throne to his daughter Esclarmonde, to whom he has taught the art of sorcery. She will retain her powers only if her face is veiled from all men until her twentieth birthday, when the victor of a great tournament will win her as his wife. Esclarmonde mourns her fate, as she is in love with the knight Roland whom she has seen once in passing. Her sister, Parseïs, suggests she use her magic powers to guide Roland to Byzantium. Énéas returns from battle to tell them that King Cleomer of Blois has promised his daughter's hand in marriage to Roland. In an effort to prevent this marriage, Esclarmonde conjures up the spirits of air, sea, and fire to cause Roland to be led to an enchanted island. Mounting a griffin-drawn chariot, she flies off to join him.

EXCERPT 1a Kal f pp. 20–36/2/1 8 1/2 min.

Esclarmonde's opening aria and first duet with Parseïs.

EXCERPT 1b Kal f pp. 20–56 17 min.

Esclarmonde, Parseïs, and Énéas, with the Invisible Spirits, concluding with Esclarmonde's "Esprits de l'air!"

EXCERPT 1c Kal f pp. 52/3/2–70 7 min.

After Énéas' exit, with Esclarmonde, Parseïs, and Spirits.

EXCERPT 2 Kal f pp. 82/3/1–104/5/3 12 min.

A duet for Esclarmonde (see excerpt 1) and Roland, tenor (E♭2–A♭3), with the Invisible Spirits.

Roland wonders how he came to be borne to the enchanted island. Esclarmonde enters, keeping her face veiled the entire time, and confesses her love for Roland. Then they give full expression to their passion.

EXCERPT 3 Kal f pp. 106–16/3/1 7 min.

This is another duet for Esclarmonde and Roland (to B♭3). Esclarmonde tells Roland that he must keep their marriage a secret; she gives him a magic sword so that he can go and defend his countrymen; the sword will be invincible as long as he keeps his vow to her.

EXCERPT 4 Kal f pp. 191–225 19 1/2 min.

A scene for Esclarmonde, soprano (to E♭5, opt G5); Roland, tenor; and the Bishop of Blois, bass-baritone (C2–F3). A chorus of Priests and the Invisible Spirits complete the scene.

In King Cleomer's palace, the Bishop demands that Roland confess to God his secret, and in desperation, he does so. Esclarmonde appears, and the Bishop begins the rite of exorcism. The veil is snatched from Esclarmonde's face; she accuses Roland of having betrayed her. When the Bishop and Priests are about to seize her, she calls upon the spirit world to defend her. But when Roland tries to defend her with the magic sword, the blade breaks and Esclarmonde disappears, leaving a dejected Roland, while the Priests chant the rite of exorcism.

EXCERPT 5 Kal f pp. 232/5/1–272 18 min.

Esclarmonde, Parseïs, Énéas, and Phorcas, bass (C2–E3) are in this excerpt with the chorus of Spirits, this time a mixed chorus.

In the forest of Ardennes, Parseïs and Énéas seek Phorcas, who is told of Esclarmonde's secret meetings with Roland and is outraged at his daughter's disobedience. He calls upon the Spirits to return Esclarmonde to him; she appears. He and the Spirits proclaim that Roland must die, and that she must renounce her love for him in order to retain the throne and her magic powers. In desperation she agrees.

Fedora

Umberto Giordano (1867–1948)

St. Petersburg, Paris, and Switzerland, late nineteenth century

EXCERPT 1 SZ i, g pp. 114/3/1–192 17 1/2 min.

This scene calls for Fedora, a dramatic soprano and tragic actress of the grand tradition (D3–C5); Loris, tenor (E2–A3), with a strong middle register as well as brilliance in the high range; and Grech, bass (top D♭3), a short but important acting role.

At a party in Paris, Princess Fedora Romanoff believes she has found the man responsible for killing her fiancé, the late Count Vladimir Andrejevich. Count Loris Ipanov has declared his love for Fedora, as well as his part in Count Vladimir's death, but insists he is innocent of the murder and can prove his innocence with certain documents that he can obtain. While he is gone, Fedora summons Grech, a police officer, confirming that he and his men are to kidnap Loris. Loris arrives; upon being accused of revolutionary political leanings as well as murder, he explains to Fedora that her fiancé was in fact carrying on a clandestine affair with Loris' late wife, Wanda. He had caught the guilty pair together, whereupon he was shot at and wounded by Vladimir and in turn inflicted a mortal wound on his enemy. Loris says he is pursued by an unknown adversary who will not let him live out his exile in peace. Fedora, too overcome to admit that she herself is his enemy, returns his love by persuading him to stay with her rather than face his kidnappers.

EXCERPT 1a SZ i, g pp. 121/2/2–154 13 1/2 min.

After Grech's exit, the portion with Fedora and Loris only.

EXCERPT 2 SZ i, g pp. 159/4/1–192 10 1/2 min.

Loris and Fedora (see excerpt 1) appear in this scene, along with Olga, lyric soprano or soubrette (D♯3–A4), and DeSiriex, baritone (C2–F♯3).

Fedora and Loris are living, happily married, in Switzerland. Fedora's friend, Olga, appears, and when Loris goes to collect his mail, Count DeSiriex arrives on a bicycle. There is some conversation over tea about Olga's friend, the pianist, which sends Olga into hysterics; DeSiriex, noticing another bicycle propped up against the wall, calms Olga by suggesting a bicycle ride together. When Olga goes off to change into riding gear, DeSiriex tells Fedora that Loris' brother, Valerian, was put in prison on the banks of the Neva, where he was drowned by the suddenly rising tide, which so much shocked his aged mother that she fell ill and died. Fedora feels terribly distressed and guilty over this news. As Olga and DeSiriex gaily ride off into the countryside, they bid her a tender farewell.

EXCERPT 2a SZ i, g pp. 167/1/3–192 7 1/2 min.

After Loris' exit, the portion of the scene with DeSiriex and the two ladies.

EXCERPT 3 SZ i, g pp. 193–234 17 min.

Another demanding duet for Fedora and Loris, with a young boy (M-S or treble) heard offstage.

Fedora prays that Loris may be spared the trap into which he has fallen because of her suspicions over the death of her former fiancé. Loris enters with a telegram telling him he has been pardoned and is free to return to Russia, but at the same time he has heard of his brother's and mother's deaths. Guilt-ridden, Fedora listens to Loris' cries of anguish and pleas for comfort. She can no longer hide the fact that she is the guilty one, and as he rushes at her in fury, she drinks the poison concealed in her Byzantine crucifix. As she dies, telling Loris how much she loved him, he forgives her. The scene ends as it began, with the haunting folk melody sung by the offstage voice.

Giovanna d'Arco (Joan of Arc)

Giuseppe Verdi (1813–1901)

France, fifteenth century

EXCERPT 1 Kal i pp. 49–81 19 1/2 min.

This scene uses Giovanna, lyric or lyric-spinto soprano (D♯3–C5 with opt. D5), a role that requires considerable flexibility; Carlo, tenor (G2–A3); Giacomo, baritone (C2–G3); and an offstage chorus.

In the final portion of the prologue, Giacomo, father of Giovanna, hides in a cave when he sees his daughter arriving in the forest. Giovanna prays for the chance to fight for France and then falls asleep on a rock. The voices of demons and angels speak to her in a dream. Carlo, King of France, gives Giovanna the weapons she needs, much to the dismay of her father.

EXCERPT 2 Kal i pp. 107–24/2/1 11 1/2 min.

Giovanna, soprano (D3–B4), is in this scene with Carlo, tenor (D2–A♭3), and an offstage women's chorus.

In a garden in the Court of Reims, Giovanna thinks of giving up her military campaign to return to her home and her father. When King Carlo approaches, he and Giovanna declare their love for each other. The voices of the angels are heard by Giovanna, and Carlo, who cannot hear them, wonders why Giovanna trembles. She bids him leave her to her destiny.

EXCERPT 3 Kal i pp. 203/2/4–220 8 1/2 min.

Giovanna and Giacomo (described in excerpt 1) are heard in this scene.

Giovanna has been taken prisoner in the English camp, and her father comes to rescue her, assuring her of her innocence.

Gloriana

Benjamin Britten (1913–1976)

England, in later years of Elizabeth I's reign (1558–1603)

EXCERPT 1 B&H e pp. 49/3/3–76 18 min.

Queen Elizabeth I, dramatic soprano with flexibility (B2–G4), is alone with Sir Robert Cecil, baritone (B1–F3), when the second scene of the opera opens. After the Queen's Song, Cecil sings his Song of Government. Robert Devereux's page enters followed by Devereux, the Earl of Essex, tenor (E2–A3) who needs flexibility and dramatic tension in a high tessitura. He sings two Lute Songs and a duet with the Queen before he exits. The excerpt concludes with Elizabeth's Soliloquy and Prayer.

Essex and Mountjoy have been fighting in boisterous rivalry and Elizabeth asks Cecil about it. When the Queen admits she favors

Essex, Cecil advises her to be careful, saying: "The art of government is in procrastination, silence, and delay." Essex pleads his suit to Elizabeth and she, much taken by Essex, prays to retain her will and honor as a monarch and to subdue her womanly impulses.

EXCERPT 1a B&H e pp. 49/3/3–58/1/1 5 1/2 min.

This is the opening of excerpt 1 with Elizabeth and Cecil only.

EXCERPT 1b B&H e pp. 58–76 12 1/2 min.

This is the section of excerpt 1 beginning with the entrance of the Earl of Essex and concluding with Elizabeth's Soliloquy and Prayer.

EXCERPT 2 B&H e pp. 100–119 8 1/2 min.

This excerpt has Charles Blount, Lord Mountjoy, who is a baritone (B1–F3); Penelope, Lady Rich, sister of the Earl of Essex, soprano (B2–G4); Frances, the Countess of Essex, mezzo-soprano (B♭2–E4); and the Earl of Essex, tenor (C2–A3). There is a quartet as well as duet and solo singing in this scene.

Mountjoy and Lady Rich, Essex's sister, meet in the garden of Essex House, and soon after, Essex and Lady Essex appear, but they do not see Mountjoy and Lady Rich, so for a portion of the scene there is a double duet and later a quartet with Lady Essex, warning the others to be cautious in their plans to rule the land.

EXCERPT 3 B&H e pp. 158/5/2–184 16 min.

This scene opens with the Lady-in-Waiting, soprano (E3–B4), and the Maids of Honor, a two-part women's chorus, until the entrance of Essex, who then has a duet with Elizabeth. After Essex leaves, the Maids sing as they dress Elizabeth before Cecil enters. (The leading characters are described in excerpt 1.)

The Queen is sitting at her dressing table in an old robe when Essex, to whom she has given the desired Irish command, breaks in on her to tell her of his defeat. On Cecil's advice, Elizabeth decides to proclaim Essex a traitor.

EXCERPT 3a B&H e pp. 163/4/1–175/3/3 7 1/2 min.

This is the duet between Elizabeth and Essex; the Lady-in-Waiting has a few lines but the Maids do not have to sing in this scene.

EXCERPT 4 B&H e pp. 212/2/1–224/1/1 7 1/2 min.

This scene begins with a solo by Queen Elizabeth I and continues with Lady Essex, Penelope Rich, and Mountjoy, all previously described. Sir Walter Raleigh, bass, has a few lines.

The Queen is pacing up and down, grieving that she must sign the death warrant for the Earl of Essex. Penelope, Lady Essex, and Lord Mountjoy enter to plead for Essex in a trio, and then Penelope, alone, pleads for her brother. As the others leave at the end of this excerpt, the Queen signs the warrant and hands it back to Sir Walter Raleigh. The Queen is left alone onstage as the spotlight fades.

The Good Soldier Schweik

Robert Kurka (1921–1958)

Bohemia, before and during World War I

EXCERPT 1 Wei e pp. 15–22/1/5 3 1/2 min.

Josef Schweik, buffo tenor (A1–B3), is the leading character in the opera and must have excellent command of the voice and good acting ability. Mrs. Muller, also in this scene, is a soprano (C3–G4).

The excerpt takes place in Schweik's flat on June 28, 1914. Among other pictures on the wall is one of Emperor Franz Josef. Mrs. Muller, the landlady, enters and they discuss the assassination of the Archduke Ferdinand.

EXCERPT 2 Wei e pp. 22/2/1–36 6 min.

Schweik (see description in excerpt 1) sings in this excerpt with Bretschneider, tenor (D2–C♯4), and Palivec, baritone (B1–C♯3).

In the tavern, The Flagon, Palivec, the tavern owner, is at the bar; the plainclothes policeman, Bretschneider, on secret service work, is drinking a glass of beer; and Schweik is seated at a table looking through newspapers. Bretschneider arrests Schweik for harmless political remarks.

EXCERPT 3 Wei e pp. 82–89 5 1/2 min.

Schweik (see previous excerpts) is joined by two doctors, tenor and baritone, for this scene. He sings his aria, "Who will go to the war when it comes?"

The two doctors are examining Schweik who is in an insane asylum. Schweik is thoroughly happy there, but he is accused of malingering and thrown out.

EXCERPT 4 Wei e pp. 101/3/2–120/3/5 10 1/2 min.

Schweik, tenor; Doctor, baritone (G♯1–F3); Malingerers, two tenors and two baritones; a Baroness, mezzo-soprano (B2–G♭4); and a chorus are the characters for this excerpt.

Schweik, even though suffering from rheumatism, has reported for army duty. In the infirmary the Army Doctor attempts to convert him and other suspected Malingerers to patriotism by prescribing an enema three times a day. The Baroness von Botzenheim comes to see Schweik, whose gesture in reporting for the draft in a wheelchair has aroused wide acclaim. The Baroness and her retinue give gifts and food to Schweik and the other Malingerers, but the Doctor objects and throws Schweik and the others into the guardhouse.

EXCERPT 5 Wei e pp. 130–152/3/3 8 1/2 min.

Act 2, scene 3, needs Schweik, buffo tenor (see above); Lukash, baritone (G1–F3); Katy, soprano (F3–C5); Wendler, tenor (E#2–C4); Zillergut, bass (G1–C3); a Dog, played by a male or female musician who can "bark" on cue.

The chaplain has picked Schweik as an orderly but has lost him to Lieutenant Lukash in a poker game. Schweik complicates his master's life by bringing in a stolen Dog and by arranging an embarrassing meeting between Lukash, his mistress, and her husband.

Goyescas

Enrique Granados (1867–1916)

Madrid, about 1800

EXCERPT 1 GS sp, e pp. 124–51 17 min.

Rosario (B♭2–A4, opt. B4) should be a full-voiced lyric soprano capable of some high pianissimo singing. Fernando, tenor (C♯2–B♭3), requires a robust sound, but the tessitura is not particularly high. Paquiro, a bullfighter, appears silently in this scene.

Paquiro has made advances to Fernando's sweetheart Rosario, a lady of rank. During the preceding candlelight ball, Fernando, driven to madness, has challenged Paquiro to a duel. Rosario is now in her garden, listening to the song of the nightingale and replying with her own love song. Then she slowly enters the house. Fernando appears at her window, and the two sing a passionate love duet. The fatal hour sounds; the figure of Paquiro is seen passing in the background. Fernando rushes out; hesitant at first, Rosario follows him. Offstage screams are heard—one from Fernando, mortally wounded by Paquiro; the other from Rosario. Once again the sinister figure of Paquiro is seen crossing in the background.

EXCERPT 2 GS sp, e pp. 152–65 9 1/2 min.

This scene is a continuation of the previous excerpt; the two may be performed either together or separately. Fernando's role is considerably shorter in this excerpt; Rosario's a bit more dramatic than in excerpt 1.

Rosario supports her lover, Fernando, who has been mortally wounded in a duel with a rival for Rosario's affection. She leads him to a bench in her garden, where earlier she sang her love song in harmony with the nightingale. As he dies in her arms, she pours out her thoughts about love and death while the theme of her aria with the nightingale is heard once more.

The Growing Castle

Malcolm Williamson (1931–)

Sweden, about 1900

EXCERPT 1 JW e pp. 1–28/1/4 13 min.

Based on Strindberg's *A Dream Play,* the twenty-eight roles of the opera are performed by four singers: soprano, mezzo-soprano, and two baritones. The first scene features Agnes, a daughter of the gods, who is a soprano (C3–B♭4); an Officer, baritone II (G1–E3); the Mother, mezzo-soprano (G♯2–F4); and a Billsticker, baritone I, who has little in this scene and could be cut. There is the possibility of using other instruments (harpsichord, bells, tambourines, etc.) with piano when these excerpts are presented.

Agnes, a daughter of the god Indra, comes down from the heavens to experience for herself the trials and tribulations of life on earth. Her first encounters are with the Officer and with the Mother, a dying old lady.

EXCERPT 2 JW e pp. 26/3/3–65/2/2 13 1/2 min.

The second scene of the opera uses all four singers whose ranges are not unusual. Agnes, soprano; the Officer, baritone; and the Billsticker, baritone I (B♭1–F♯3); and this time the mezzo-soprano sings the role of the Janitress. (See excerpt 1 for explanation.) There is quartet singing in this scene.

Agnes has her second encounter with the Janitress, who at one time was a prima ballerina, but who has lost her lover and no longer dances. Each time Agnes questions and listens to one of the other characters, she experiences emotional conflicts of her own.

EXCERPT 3 JW e pp. 65/4/3–101 15 1/2 min.

This excerpt is for the Lawyer, baritone I, and Agnes, soprano. The Officer, baritone II, and the mezzo-soprano have little to sing in this scene except for the offstage ensembles.

The meeting of Agnes and the Lawyer at the Lawyer's home results in their vowing to love one another in spite of the Lawyer's deficiencies. A portion of this scene takes place in a church.

EXCERPT 4 JW e pp. 102/3/1–130 8 1/2 min.

The last scene of the first act of the opera uses the Lawyer, baritone I, and Agnes, soprano. The mezzo-soprano plays the role of Kristina, the maid, in this scene. All three have solo and ensemble singing, and the Officer, baritone II, enters near the end of the excerpt.

Kristina, the maid, appears pasting up the crevasses on the walls, the windows, and the floor. In this excerpt Agnes feels love turn to hate as she and the Lawyer quarrel until she is finally led away by the Officer.

EXCERPT 5 JW e pp. 131–166/4/1 12 1/2 min.

The four singers (see excerpt 1) begin with a quartet. Later Agnes, soprano, and the Officer, baritone II, meet the Schoolmaster and the Lawyer, both sung by baritone I, and Ugly Edith, the mezzo-soprano.

Now Agnes is in Foulstrand, a gray darkness with sulphurous patches on the ground, with the Officer, who says he is to be a teacher in Fairhaven. The Schoolmaster enters and finally snatches and destroys the Officer's laurel crown and drags him away. Then Ugly Edith enters, unhappy because she is ugly and not asked to dance. The Lawyer (see excerpt 3), with cloak and glasses, enters. He is evidently blind and Agnes does not recognize him except that his voice seems familiar. When he reveals himself and demands that she come back to her household duties, she will not.

EXCERPT 6 JW e pp. 167/1/2–198 11 1/2 min.

Agnes is alone onstage when the Poet, mezzo-soprano, enters. The Officer has a very short part that could easily be omitted, and both baritones sing as the offstage sailors.

In this scene at Fingal's Cave, Agnes finds a Poet. The Poet is a pure Orphic youth, enjoying the early sunlight. Agnes admits to the Poet that she has stayed on earth too long and her thoughts can no longer fly. She longs for the ship to take her home.

EXCERPT 7 JW e pp. 221–38 9 min.

The final scene of the opera is for the soprano and the mezzo-soprano only.

Agnes and the Poet are involved in this climactic scene in which Agnes sings her farewell to the Poet, who questions Agnes and then sinks slowly to her knees while Agnes recedes from sight with her final "Farewell."

Guillaume Tell (William Tell)

Gioacchino Rossini (1792–1868)

Switzerland, thirteenth century

EXCERPT 1 Kal f, e pp. 48/1/3–68 10 1/2 min.

This excerpt features Arnold, tenor with high tessitura to C4, and William Tell, baritone (B♭1–G3). Arnold is a Swiss patriot who has saved Mathilde, daughter of the Austrian tyrant Gessler, from drowning.

As the scene opens, Arnold, who has fallen in love with Princess Mathilde, is singing of his love for her. When he hears Gessler's guards approaching, he knows he will see Mathilde again, and because Gessler is an enemy of the Swiss, he is frightened. William Tell questions Arnold, and when he realizes that Arnold is torn between loving his homeland and loving Mathilde, Tell joins Arnold in a duet.

EXCERPT 2 Kal f, e pp. 176–97; 200/1/5–201 18 min.

Mathilde, soprano (C3–B♭4), must be capable of very florid singing and needs a trill. In this scene she sings with Arnold, tenor (G2–C4) who also needs a dramatic but flexible voice.

In a valley by a lake, Arnold and Mathilde meet and again pledge their love. This scene includes Mathilde's aria, "Sombre forêt," and ends with a duet.

EXCERPT 3 Kal f, e pp. 203/1/3–228 12 min.

This excerpt uses the three men, William Tell, baritone (A1–F3); Arnold, tenor (E2–B3); and Walter Furst, bass (F♯1–E3); all with powerful, dramatic voices.

When Arnold learns from Tell and Walter that his father has been slain by Gessler's order, his thoughts turn to vengeance. The three men bind themselves by oath to free Switzerland.

EXCERPT 4 Kal f, e pp. 266–79 9 min.

In the interior of a ruined chapel, Mathilde and Arnold meet (see excerpt 2 for voice descriptions).

Arnold tells Mathilde that he must leave her to avenge the death of his father whom Gessler had ordered slain. This is followed by a tearful farewell duet.

EXCERPT 5 Kal f, e pp. 388–404/1/1 11 1/2 min.

An excerpt for three sopranos: Hedwige and Jemmy, Tell's wife and son, and Mathilde. In the trio, Mathilde generally has the highest part, with Jemmy singing the middle range, and Hedwige's part being quite low with optional notes given. The role of Hedwige could be sung by a mezzo-soprano. Also included is a women's chorus of short duration.

Hedwige, fearful for the life of her husband and child, is begged by the women to stay, but she says she must go to Gessler even if he kills her, for he has taken her husband and her child. Just then Mathilde enters with Jemmy and they rejoice that the child has been saved.

EXCERPT 5a Kal f, e pp. 389–96 6 min.

The portion of excerpt 5 omitting the women's chorus.

Hamlet

Humphrey Searle (1915–1982)

Denmark, 1600

EXCERPT 1 Fab e, g pp. 7/2/3–21/1/4 7 1/2 min.

A scene for Hamlet, dramatic baritone (A♭1–F3); the King, dramatic tenor (D♯2–G♯3); and the Queen, mezzo-soprano (C3–F4). The music is in the contemporary twelve-tone idiom, and the libretto follows the Shakespeare text fairly accurately.

Hamlet confronts his mother, Queen Gertrude, and his uncle Claudius for the first time since the death of his father. King Claudius begs Hamlet not to go back to the University of Wittenberg but to remain at court.

EXCERPT 2 Fab e, g pp. 15/4/3–31/1/3 8 1/2 min.

Hamlet (see excerpt 1) is joined by Horatio, baritone (A1–D♭3), and Marcellus, bass (G♯1–C3).

This scene begins with Hamlet's monologue from excerpt 1 and continues through the entrance of Horatio and Marcellus, who report they have seen the ghost of Hamlet's father.

EXCERPT 3 Fab e, g pp. 31/2/1–41/2/2 4 1/2 min.

Ophelia is a soprano (C♯3–F♯4); Laertes, a tenor (C♯2–G3); and Polonius a bass (F♯1–D3).

Ophelia, who has been courted some by Hamlet, receives advice from both her brother and her father not to take Hamlet too seriously.

EXCERPT 4 Fab e, g pp. 42–65/2/1 12 min.

Hamlet, Horatio, and Marcellus (see excerpts 1 and 2) are in this scene with the Ghost, bass (F4–C3), the tessitura of whose role lies very low. A men's chorus sings offstage but could be omitted.

Horatio and Marcellus are keeping the night watch; Hamlet joins them hoping to see the ghost of his father. The Ghost appears but will not speak to Hamlet until they move away from the other men; then he tells Hamlet how he was murdered by his brother, Claudius, who has now taken the throne and his wife from him; he advises Hamlet to avenge the murder but not to harm his mother.

EXCERPT 5 Fab e, g pp. 122–36 9 min.

A scene for Hamlet, who is described above, and Ophelia, who has a dramatic monologue climaxing on a B♭4.

This excerpt begins with Hamlet's soliloquy and continues through his confrontation with Ophelia in which he goes mad and repeats the words "Get thee to a nunnery!"

EXCERPT 6 Fab e, g pp. 172/2/1–193/3/3 10 1/2 min.

The famous "closet scene" for Hamlet, the Queen, and Polonius, as described above. The Queen has several A♭4 and A4's in this excerpt. The Ghost appears briefly.

Polonius has advised the Queen how to deal with Hamlet, and then hides behind the arras. Hamlet confronts his mother, but when he sees a moving figure, he believes it to be Claudius and stabs him in an attempt to avenge his father's murder. The victim turns out to be Polonius. The argument between mother and son continues until the Ghost appears. The Queen cannot see or hear the Ghost and therefore believes Hamlet has gone mad. The scene ends as Hamlet exits, dragging Polonius' body, while the Queen falls onto the couch, sobbing.

EXCERPT 7 Fab e, g pp. 224–34/1/2 5 1/2 min.

A scene in which most of the singing is done by Ophelia and Laertes (see excerpt 2), with the King and Queen in supporting roles.

Ophelia, having lost her father and being rejected by Hamlet, has gone mad. In this excerpt, she offers flowers to the King and Queen and her brother, Laertes, each flower having a special significance.

EXCERPT 8 Fab e, g pp. 250–58/2/1 4 min.

Hamlet, previously described, with a Gravedigger, bass (F1–B♭2), who sings in a low tessitura similar to that of the Ghost (excerpt 4). Horatio is included in a supporting role.

The Gravedigger is singing a song; Hamlet comes to question him about the grave being dug. The Gravedigger presents Hamlet with a skull—that of Yorick, the court jester.

Hamlet

Ambroise Thomas (1811–1896)

Denmark, 1600

EXCERPT 1 Heu f, e pp. 24/3/4–46 7 1/2 min.

Hamlet is a typically French lyric baritone with many high notes, yet must be able to project the dramatic intensity of this Shakespearean tragic hero; in this scene his range is D♭2–F3. Ophelia is a lyric soprano with considerable flexibility in the top (D3–C5).

Hamlet, left alone, broods on the death of his father, the King, and the fact that his mother has so soon after her husband's death taken his father's brother as her husband, and that he has become the successor to the throne ("O frailty, thy name is woman"). The scene differs from the play in that Ophelia enters at this point. Their dialogue turns into a duet based on Hamlet's letter, "Doubt that the stars are fire," in which he pledges his love to her.

EXCERPT 2 Heu f, e pp. 64–76 11 1/2 min.

Hamlet (C♯2–G3) is described in excerpt 1; his singing is more dramatic in this excerpt. Marcellus is a comprimario tenor (C♯2–F3), and Horatio a bass (B♭1–C♯3). The Ghost, bass, must be capable of strong sustained singing on only a few pitches in the middle range (D2–B♭2).

Keeping watch at the castle, Marcellus and Horatio tell Hamlet of their vision of the ghost of Hamlet's father. The Ghost appears, makes a signal for Marcellus and Horatio to leave, then speaks to Hamlet, bidding him to avenge his father's murder committed by his father's brother but to spare his mother any evil.

EXCERPT 3 Heu f, e 85–106/3/4 13 min.
(if 91/5/3–97 is cut) 9 1/2 min.

Ophelia, lyric soprano (E♭3–C♯5), has a bravura aria, which is often cut; otherwise, this excerpt is not particularly difficult. Queen Gertrude is a high mezzo-soprano (C3–A♭4), who has an aria in this scene. Hamlet appears only silently.

Ophelia is troubled because Hamlet has avoided her for the past two days. She pretends to read a book as he enters; he is silent. The Queen enters and comforts Ophelia while admitting her own fears regarding her son's strange behavior.

EXCERPT 4 Heu f, e pp. 107–24 9 min.

This scene is a rather dramatic confrontation between Queen Gertrude, mezzo (B2–B♭4), and King Claudius, bass (B♭1–E♭3), joined later by Hamlet, baritone (D2–G3).

The Queen, frightened by Hamlet's madness, confides her own sense of guilt to the King, who assures her that the dead (referring to his late brother, her first husband) are indeed dead and will appear no more. Hamlet enters, greets them rather coldly, but does tell them of the preparations for the evening's festivities (which will include a play alluding to his father's murder).

EXCERPT 4a Heu f, e pp. 107–17/3/3 4 1/2 min.

Same as above without Hamlet.

EXCERPT 5 Heu f, e pp. 185–202 11 min.

See earlier excerpts for description of Hamlet, baritone (D2–E♭3). The King, bass, sings an aria with a wide range (G1–E♭3, opt. E♭1–G3). Polonius, bass, is a minor character in this scene.

Hamlet sings a soliloquy based on "To be or not to be." His uncle, the King, appears and sings a prayer, during which Hamlet hesitates to strike the fatal blow to avenge his father's murder. Polonius, father of Ophelia, appears briefly, and it is then that Hamlet discovers to his dismay that his beloved Ophelia's father has been an accomplice in the murder and Claudius' succession to the throne.

EXCERPT 6 Heu f, e pp. 203–16/4/3 7 min.

A trio for Ophelia, lyric soprano (C♯3–B4), Gertrude, mezzo-soprano (A2–G♯4, opt. B4), and Hamlet, baritone (C2–F♯3, opt. G♯3).

Queen Gertrude bids Hamlet marry Ophelia. Distraught by the realization that Ophelia's father was an accomplice in the royal murder, Hamlet spurns Ophelia ("Get thee to a nunnery"). Each of the three characters expresses his/her feelings in a trio.

EXCERPT 7 Heu f, e pp. 217–40 11 1/2 min.

A dramatic scene for the Queen, mezzo-soprano (C3–A4, opt. B♭4) and Hamlet, baritone (B1–E3). The Ghost, bass, appears only briefly and sings only a few lines.

Hamlet confronts his mother with her guilt of having married his uncle so soon after his father's death. The Ghost appears to Hamlet, once again reminding him to spare his mother; not seeing the ghost herself, she believes her son to be mad. His anger subsides as he bids her goodnight.

EXCERPT 8 Heu f, e pp. 285–300 9 1/2 min.
add 304–12 13 min.

This is the best-known portion of the opera, Ophelia's mad scene (D3–C♯5, opt. E5). It is essential that she have a great deal of flexibility, particularly in the upper register. The role of the chorus is minimal as far as singing is concerned; dramatically, they serve an important purpose.

Ophelia, having lost her reason because of Hamlet's rejection, sings a passage based on her "flower" speech in Shakespeare's tragedy, then a folk ballad alluding to the *wilis,* women who have died after being betrayed by their lovers. As the chorus hums in the background, Ophelia slowly wanders to the river and drowns herself.

EXCERPT 9 Heu f, e pp. 313–24 7 min.

Hamlet, baritone (C♯2–F♯3), has some dramatic passages in this short excerpt, while the music of two Gravediggers, tenor (E♭2–A3) and bass (A2–E3), poses no particular difficulties.

The two Gravediggers sing a drinking song, whereupon Hamlet approaches. They do not tell him that it is Ophelia's grave that is being dug; nevertheless, Hamlet seems to have a premonition of her tragedy as his thoughts turn to her and her alleged madness.

He Who Gets Slapped

Robert Ward (1917-)

Paris, 1910

EXCERPT 1 Gal e, g pp. 48/4/2–62/1/3 5 min.

The set is the combined office, rehearsal room, and lounging room of a small circus featuring Zinida and Her Lions plus Consuelo, the Bareback Tango Queen. This excerpt features the ringmaster's wife, Zinida, dramatic soprano (D3–B♭4), and Bezano, equestrian and Consuelo's trainer.

While Zinida's husband is showing the new recruit Pantaloon around the circus, Zinida has asked that Bezano, whose attention she has been trying to get, be sent to her. She throws herself at him as if she were taming one of her lions and he forcibly rejects her.

EXCERPT 2 Gal e, g pp. 63/4/1–75 6 min.

A scene for Consuelo, soprano (D3–B4), and Baron Regnard, bass-baritone (C2–E3).

Consuelo's father, Mancini, is trying to arrange a match between Consuelo and Baron Regnard. Consuelo refuses to go to lunch with him, and this scene is one in which she accepts his gift of a string of pearls but rejects his lecherous advances.

EXCERPT 3 Gal e, g pp. 108/2/4–121 5 min.

The characters in this excerpt are Mancini, tenor (D♭2–G3, opt. A3), a buffo part lying mostly in the middle range, and Pantaloon, baritone (A1–E♭3).

Mancini tells Pantaloon that he needs money to buy off his latest mistress; Pantaloon takes this chance to ask Mancini about his ancestry. Pantaloon is able to gather that Mancini is a fraudulent Count and that Consuelo is not really his daughter, but Mancini keeps insisting that Consuelo will marry Baron Regnard.

EXCERPT 4 Gal e, g pp. 128/2/1–173 20 min.

A scene for Consuelo, Zinida, Pantaloon (described above), and Briquet, bass-baritone, who appears briefly. Bezano and two clowns make their entrance with Zinida.

Zinida's recklessness with her lions has gone to her head; in her madness she claims that her red lion really loves her and that she is capable of being loved, her words being directed at Bezano. Consuelo remains alone with Pantaloon, puzzled about Zinida's unrequited love and her own anxiety over her forthcoming marriage to Baron Regnard. Pantaloon's response is both serious and playful; he reads her palm and tells her that, like Venus, she rose from the sea, and that he himself is the sea-god come to take her back; he attempts to kiss her. She slaps him (after all he is Pantaloon, "He Who Gets Slapped"). They are interrupted by Zinida, who has been witnessing this scene and, in her madness, bitterly mocks Pantaloon.

EXCERPT 4a Gal e, g pp. 134/2/3–159/2/3 12 min.

From excerpt 4, the scene between Consuelo and Pantaloon only.

EXCERPT 5 Gal e, g pp. 248/2/1–259/2/3 5 1/2 min.

A duet for Consuelo and Bezano (described in previous excerpts).

Mancini has confessed his frauds and left his daughter, Consuelo, in the hands of the circus troupe. Consuelo is desolate until she and Bezano realize they are free to love each other. The scene ends happily in a tango love duet.

Hugh the Drover

Ralph Vaughan Williams (1872–1958)

England, early nineteenth century

EXCERPT 1 Cur e pp. 40/4/8–62/3/4 (G-major cadence) 20 min.

An excerpt for Mary, soprano (B2–B♭4); Aunt Jane, mezzo-soprano (C3–E♭4); and Hugh, tenor (D2–B♭3).

Mary has fallen in love with Hugh against the wishes of her father, who wishes her to marry the rich but oafish John the Butcher. Aunt Jane rushes off in alarm at what is happening and Hugh sings of his love for the open road; Mary pledges her love to him.

EXCERPT 1a Cur e pp. 40/4/8–45/3/3 4 min.

The opening of excerpt 1 using only Mary and Aunt Jane.

EXCERPT 1b Cur e pp. 56/2/3–62/3/4 (G-major cadence) 8 1/2 min.

This portion of excerpt 1 is for Mary and Hugh only.

EXCERPT 2 Cur e pp. 132/1/3–137; 139/2/2–146/1/5 8 1/2 min.

This duet is for Mary and Hugh (see description in excerpt 1).

Hugh has won a boxing match with John for the love of Mary; however, John has accused Hugh of being a Napoleonic spy and Hugh has been locked into the village stocks. In this scene, Mary appears with her father's keys to the stocks and unlocks them. Just as they are about to make their escape, they hear the sound of people coming; Mary has no choice but to get into the stocks next to Hugh.

EXCERPT 3 Cur e pp. 187–96/3/3 5 1/2 min.

This is another duet for Mary and Hugh (see description above).

Hugh has been released; he and Mary set off happily for the open road.

Idomeneo

Wolfgang Amadeus Mozart (1756–1791)

Crete, about 1200 B.C.

EXCERPT 1 Int i pp. 5/6/1–27 17 1/2 min.
Kal i, g

This excerpt features Ilia, lyric soprano (E3–A4), and Idamante, castrato role sung today by either a mezzo-soprano (F3–A4) or tenor (F2–A3); each sings an aria in this opening scene. The International edition contains the original scoring; when it is used, the ensembles are best done with the part of Idamante sung by a mezzo.

Ilia, daughter of King Priam of Troy, reveals that her love for Idamante, son of King Idomeneo of Crete, far outweighs her hatred for the conquerors of Troy who have brought her to Crete as a prisoner. Idamante arrives and tells Ilia that he has set the other prisoners free, and that he is very much in love with her. She hesitates to tell him of her similar feelings.

EXCERPT 2 Int i pp. 52/2/2–74 15 1/2 min.
Kal i, g

Idomeneo, tenor requiring authority and strength throughout range (E2–G3), and Idamante, mezzo-soprano (E3–G4) or tenor (E2–G3), sing individual arias in this excerpt; if two tenors are used, it is preferable that Idamante be the lighter of the two voices.

Idomeneo, King of Crete, returning from a victorious war against Troy, has encountered great storms on the sea and has vowed to offer Neptune the sacrifice of the first person he encounters upon landing safely in Crete. His son, Idamante, appears, but because of their separation since the son's infancy, they do not immediately recognize each other. When the recognition finally does occur, Idamante is puzzled by his father's anxiety and coldness.

EXCERPT 3 Int i pp. 94–134/3/4 29 min.
Kal i, g

This scene links together four arias, one by each of the leading characters: Ilia, lyric soprano (E♭3–B♭4); Electra, dramatic coloratura (G3–A4), whose aria in this scene is quite lyric and florid; Idomeneo, tenor (D2–G3), requiring agility for a bravura aria ("Fuor del mar"); and Arbace, tenor (D2–A3).

Idomeneo confides in Arbace the dilemma that he was faced with upon his return to Crete (see excerpt 2). Arbace suggests to the King that he send his son, Idamante, abroad on the pretext of escorting Electra to her native Grecian homeland. Ilia confides that she has found a father figure in Idomeneo and loves Idamante, adding to Idomeneo's anxiety the realization that his decision will break her heart as well. Meanwhile, Electra, seeing in Idomeneo's decision the prospect of her requited love for Idamante, expresses her hope in the aria "Idol mio."

EXCERPT 3a Int i pp. 106–34/3/4 23 min.
Kal i, g

Ilia, Electra, and Idomeneo only.

EXCERPT 3b Int i pp. 106–26/2/4 15 min.
Kal i, g

Ilia and Idomeneo.

EXCERPT 3c Int i pp. 114/3/1–134/3/4 14 min.
Kal i, g

Idomeneo and Electra.

EXCERPT 4 Int i pp. 142/2/1–151/1/3 4 1/2 min.
Kal i, g

A moderately easy trio for Electra, soprano (E3–A4); Idamante, mezzo-soprano or tenor (E2/3–G3/4); and Idomeneo, tenor (F2–G3).

King Idomeneo bids his son, Idamante, leave Crete and escort

Electra back to her native Argos. Idamante tearfully bids his father farewell and laments having to leave behind his beloved Ilia.

EXCERPT 5 Int i pp. 167–99 19 1/2 min.
Kal i, g

This excerpt includes the aria "Zeffiretti lusinghieri" for Ilia, lyric soprano; a duet for Ilia and Idamante; and a quartet for Ilia, Electra, Idamante, and Idomeneo (see vocal descriptions in previous scenes).

In a garden, Ilia longs for Idamante, who appears and tells her he will fight the monster sent by Neptune to ravage the land. They exchange words of love in the duet "Spiegarti non poss'io."

This outrages Electra who swears vengeance on Idamante. Idamante, still perplexed by the aloofness of his father, Idomeneo, sadly takes his leave.

EXCERPT 5a Int i pp. 167–83 13 min.
Kal i, g

Ilia's aria and the duet for Ilia and Idamante.

EXCERPT 5b Int i pp. 184–99 6 1/2 min.
Kal i, g

The quartet portion of excerpt 5.

EXCERPT 6 Int i pp. 224–62 25 min.
Kal i, g

The major characters in this scene are Ilia, Electra (whose aria "D'Oreste, d'Ajace" is a display of vocal fireworks to C5), Idamante, Idomeneo, and the voice of Neptune, bass (D2–D3). A chorus of priests sing in unison onstage and a mixed chorus sings very briefly offstage. Arbace and the High Priest (tenors) sing only a few lines.

Idamante realizes that he must be his father's sacrifice to Neptune. Ilia intervenes, offering herself as a sacrifice instead. Just then the voice of Neptune declares that Idomeneo must renounce the throne in favor of his son, with Ilia as Queen. Everyone is relieved except for the enraged Electra, who invokes the furies and collapses at the end of the scene.

Iolanta

Peter Ilyitch Tchaikovsky (1840–1893)

Southern France, fifteenth century

EXCERPT 1	Bel (Kal 6758)	r	pp. 6–42/2/5	14 min.
	SMP-Moscow	r	pp. 4–39/2/3	

The opening scene in the opera uses Iolanta, lyric soprano (D3–G4); Marta, contralto (G♯2–F4); Brigetta, soprano (C♯3–A4); and Laura, mezzo-soprano (C3–F♯4). There is also a two-part chorus of women servants and four fifteenth-century musicians playing their instruments briefly.

Iolanta, the young, beautiful daughter of the King of Provence, was blinded so early in life by a narrow escape from a fire that she does not realize her infirmity. Her father has kept her isolated, with her nurse, Marta, companions Brigetta and Laura, and her servants until the time comes for her to marry Robert, the young Duke of Burgundy, as per a contract made between the two fathers. Her blindness and lonely existence are illustrated in this scene.

EXCERPT 2	Bel	r	pp. 49/4/2–77	13 min.
	SMP	r	pp. 46–71	

Bertrand, bass (A♭1–D3); Almerick, tenor (E♭2–F3); King René, bass (F1–F3); and Ibn-Hakia, baritone (D2–F♯3), are heard in this excerpt. Marta (see excerpt 1) sings briefly.

Bertrand, retainer of King René, welcomes Almerick to the castle where Iolanta lives. Almerick tells Bertrand that the King will soon arrive and bring a famous Moorish doctor, Ibn-Hakia, who he hopes will be able to restore Iolanta's eyesight. When they do arrive, Ibn-Hakia tells the King that he cannot begin treatment until Iolanta knows about her blindness and yearns to be cured, but the King threatens to kill anyone who tells Iolanta the secret.

EXCERPT 2a	Bel	r	pp. 66–77	6 min.
	SMP	r	pp. 59–71	

King René and Ibn-Hakia only.

EXCERPT 3 Bel r pp. 78–144 29 1/2 min.
SMP r pp. 72–135

An excerpt for Robert, baritone (C♯2–F♯3); Count Vaudemont, tenor (E2–A3), each of whom has an aria; and Iolanta, lyric soprano (D3–B4).

When Robert and Vaudemont enter Iolanta's palace, they see Iolanta, and Robert, who is in love with Countess Matilde, sees only a young girl and wants to leave, while Vaudemont thinks Iolanta is a pure and beautiful image. When Iolanta hears them, she goes to get some wine and Robert quickly leaves. Vaudemont stays, only to discover that he and Iolanta have a strong bond of sympathy and affection, even after he realizes she is blind. Vaudemont reveals this to Iolanta and the scene ends in a duet.

EXCERPT 3a Bel r pp. 113/3/1–144 15 1/2 min.
SMP r pp. 104/3/1–135

The duet for Iolanta and Vaudemont only.

EXCERPT 4 Bel r pp. 145–79 10 1/2 min.
SMP r pp. 136–68

The King, Ibn-Hakia, Iolanta, Marta, Laura, Brigetta, Bertrand, Vaudemont, Almerick (all previously described), and the servants (two-part women's chorus) are in this scene.

King René tells his daughter that he has brought a doctor who can bring back her sight. She does not really understand what sight is, and she says she will obey her father. The doctor doubts he can cure her because she seems to have no strong desire for sight. The King condemns Vaudemont for having told Iolanta that she was handicapped and swears he will die if the treatment does not work. Iolanta says she will do anything necessary to save Vaudemont's life, and the doctor realizes she now possesses both the knowledge of her blindness and the motivation to see again, and is ready to begin the treatment.

EXCERPT 5 Bel r 180–229 14 min.
SMP r 169–219

Included in this final scene of the opera are Robert, King René, Vaudemont, Marta, Laura, Brigitta, the servants and Robert's retinue, Iolanta, Ibn-Hakia, Almerick, and Bertrand, all described in earlier excerpts.

Robert enters and explains to the King that he is in love with the Princess Matilda, but that he will marry Iolanta as promised. The King willingly releases Robert and accepts Vaudemont as his son-in-law, while all praise the miracle of sight returned to Iolanta's eyes.

Iris

Pietro Mascagni (1863–1945)

Japan, nineteenth century

EXCERPT 1 Ric i pp. 25–39/1/5 7 1/2 min.

Iris is a soprano (D3–B♭4) and has the most singing in the excerpt. Osaka, tenor (E2–A3), and Kyoto, baritone (E2–E3), have some singing, and Il Cieco, bass, has one offstage line.

Iris, a young and beautiful girl, comes to the door of her cottage. She has dreamed that monsters sought to injure her doll, asleep under a rosebush. With the coming of the sun the monsters have fled, and she sings about the beauty of nature. Iris is desired by Osaka, a wealthy rake, and Kyoto, keeper of a questionable resort, plots to obtain her for him. Iris loves only her blind father, Il Cieco.

EXCERPT 2 Ric i pp. 125–68 20 min.

The scene opens with one of the geisha girls, mezzo-soprano, humming while another plays a Japanese samisen, and others play gongs. Kyoto, baritone (D2–E3), Osaka, tenor (F♯2–A3), and Iris, soprano (D♯3–B♭4), have arias in this scene.

In the interior of the Green House in Yoshiwara, the geisha girls are playing instruments, and one is humming while Iris sleeps. Kyoto and Osaka enter and regard the sleeping Iris. When she awakens, she at first thinks it is an awakening after death, but death would bring paradise, and she is unhappy.

EXCERPT 2a Ric i pp. 125–150/1/5 10 min.

Excerpt 2 using the geisha girls, the sleeping Iris, Kyoto, and Osaka.

EXCERPT 3 Ric i pp. 170/2/4–206 17 min.

Iris, soprano, and Osaka, tenor (see earlier descriptions), are in this excerpt.

Osaka, a rich young man, has placed jewels beside Iris while she was sleeping, and now he comes to woo her, vainly seeking to arouse her emotions. In her innocence she does not recognize the significance of his words and caresses. His brilliant attire leads her to mistake him for Jor, the sun-god, but he tells her he is Pleasure. That frightens her because a priest has told her that pleasure and death were one. Osaka embraces her in a last effort to win her love. Then, weary of her innocence, he leaves her.

Jenůfa (Její Pastorkyňa) (Her Stepdaughter)

Leos Janáček (1854–1928)

Moravia, nineteenth century

EXCERPT 1 UE cz, g pp. 3–35 18 min.
HM cz pp. 11–47

Included in excerpt 1 are Grandmother Buryja, mezzo-soprano (E3–F4); Jenůfa, soprano (C3–B4) with some high tessitura; Laca, dramatic tenor (E2–B♭3), also with a high tessitura; Jano, shepherd boy, soprano (F♯3–A♭4); Foreman, baritone (D2–E3); and Kostelnička, soprano or dramatic mezzo, a pivotal character who sings only one line in this scene.

Of two stepbrothers, Števa and Laca, who are grandsons of Grandmother Buryja, Laca is secretly in love with Jenůfa, foster daughter of Kostelnička. Jenůfa, meanwhile, has formed an attachment to Števa, is carrying his child, and wonders if he will be drafted into the army. Jano, the shepherd boy, joyfully announces that he really can read now, thanks to Jenůfa's tutelage. The old foreman enters with the news that Števa has been deferred from the draft and will be home soon. Kostelnička suggests that everyone go to the mill, but Jenufa begs to be left alone to meet Števa when he returns.

EXCERPT 2 UE cz, g pp. 71/2/3–93 19 min.
HM cz pp. 84/1/4–109

A scene for Jenůfa, soprano, and Števa, tenor (E♭2–B♭3). They are later joined by Barena, a young girl, soprano (E♭3–A4), Grandmother, Laca, and the Foreman (previously described).

Jenůfa and Števa are alone and Jenůfa pleads her love for him and her fear that people will find out she is bearing his child. Števa answers crossly and practically accuses Jenůfa and her foster-mother of nagging at him, so that Jenůfa loses her patience and shakes him vigorously. Even when he partially pulls himself together, his answers are not reassuring. When Laca enters, Jenůfa is alone in her misery; Laca's remarks about Števa only provoke Jenůfa to take Števa's side even more firmly. Laca starts as if to embrace Jenůfa and then slashes her across the cheek with a knife. She runs into the house and Laca laments his actions. The servant Barena suggests it was an accident, but after Grandmother Buryja has gone, the Foreman accuses Laca of having done it on purpose.

EXCERPT 2a	UE	cz, g	pp. 71/2/3–81	5 min.
	HM	cz	pp. 84/1/4–96/3/5	

The portion of excerpt 2 with Jenůfa, Števa, and Grandmother only.

EXCERPT 3	UE	cz, g	pp. 74–177	40 min.
	HM	cz	pp. 113/1/3–209	

Act 2 features Jenůfa and Kostelnička, mezzo-soprano or dramatic soprano (B♭2–B4) and later Števa and Laca (see excerpts 1 and 2 for descriptions).

Kostelnička and Jenůfa are sewing, the wound on Jenůfa's face still visible (see excerpt 2). They are talking about Jenůfa's secret; the baby has been born, but Jenůfa has not seen Števa, the father, for weeks. Jenůfa thinks she hears her baby call, but he is sleeping peacefully. Kostelnička gives Jenůfa a drink with a narcotic in it to let her sleep and Jenůfa goes into the inner room. Kostelnička has sent for Števa. When Števa comes, she pleads with him to see his child, and he finally breaks down but persists in his refusal to marry Jenůfa.

Laca enters, angry that Števa was there, and still eager to win Jenůfa's love. He is horrified when he finds out about Jenůfa's baby; Kostelnička, realizing Laca's feelings, tells him the baby is dead. When Laca leaves, Kostelnička, in great agony, takes the child wrapped in a shawl and leaves. When she returns, she tells Jenůfa that she has been unconscious and delirious for two days, and during that time the child has died and been buried. She also tells her that Števa has been there and has steadfastly refused to marry her. Laca comes in and asks Jenůfa if they cannot finish their lives together. Jenůfa cannot hide her tender feelings for Laca. Just then, the window blows open, and the icy blast brings a horrible sense of foreboding and disaster.

EXCERPT 3a UE cz, g pp. 97–114 8 1/2 min.
HM cz pp. 113/1/3–132

The opening portion of excerpt 3 for Jenůfa and Kostelnička only.

EXCERPT 3b UE cz, g pp. 139–65/2/5 16 min.
HM cz pp. 162–97/2/1

This scene is between Kostelnička and Jenůfa, when Jenůfa awakens and Kostelnička tells her the baby is dead, and that Števa has been there and refuses to marry her so she must forget him.

EXCERPT 3c UE cz, g pp. 139–77 21 min.
HM cz pp. 162–209

The balance of act 2 uses Kostelnička, Jenůfa, and Laca.

EXCERPT 4 UE cz, g pp. 181/5/2–196 8 1/2 min.
HM cz pp. 213/6/3–233/1/3

Jenůfa, Laca, and Kostelnička, all previously described, are in this excerpt, with the Mayor, bass, and the Mayor's Wife, mezzo-soprano. The Maid, soprano, is a lesser role, and Grandmother Buryja, who is there, is silent.

Jenůfa, now looking much better, is preparing for the wedding, and Laca sits by her side. Kostelnička, looking haggard and worn, is pacing up and down. When the Mayor and his Wife come to offer congratulations, Kostelnička takes them all in to see the trousseau she has made for Jenůfa. When the bride and bridegroom are left alone, Laca gives Jenůfa the flowers he has brought her, and she pins them to her dress. He cannot stop reproaching himself for what he has done to her. At Jenůfa's insistence, Laca has been reconciled to Števa and has even invited him to the wedding.

EXCERPT 4a UE cz, g pp. 191/4/4–196 3 1/2 min.
HM cz pp. 227/1/4–233/1/3

The portion of excerpt 4 for Jenůfa and Laca begins when the others leave the room to look at the trousseau.

EXCERPT 5 UE cz, g pp. 238–251 6 min.
HM cz pp. 276/3/1–290

Again, the singers are Jenůfa, Kostelnička, and Laca, all previously described.

Kostelnička has admitted drowning the baby in an effort to do good, and Jenůfa's act of foregiveness toward Kostelnička somehow redeems the crime from its sordidness. Kostelnička thinks of killing herself but then realizes that she will be needed to be a witness if Jenůfa is not to suffer for something of which she is guiltless, and she goes out with the Mayor. Laca and Jenůfa at last find understanding through their suffering.

La Jolie fille de Perth (The Fair Maid of Perth)

Georges Bizet (1838–1875)

Scotland, fourteenth century

EXCERPT 1 Kal f pp. 15–62 10 1/2 min.

Six principals appear in this scene: Catherine, soprano (C3–D♭5); Mab, mezzo-soprano (B♭2–G4); Smith, tenor (F2–B♭3); the Duke, baritone (C2–A♭3 with lower options); Glover and Ralph, bass-baritones.

Smith, the armorer, is in love with Catherine Glover, but has given refuge to a gypsy woman, Mab, in his shop. When Catherine arrives, Mab has been hidden. The Duke of Rothsay comes in and begins to flirt with Catherine, provoking a fight with Smith, which is stopped by Mab. Catherine begins to suspect Smith and throws to the ground a gold enameled rose he had made for her. Just then her father, Glover, and his apprentice, Ralph, arrive with provisions for a carnival supper and are astonished to see the two strangers. But Glover recognizes the Duke and invites him to the feast; the Duke declines and takes his leave after complimenting Glover on the beauty of his daughter.

EXCERPT 1a Kal f pp. 15–29 8 min.

This is the opening portion of excerpt 1 with Catherine and Smith only.

EXCERPT 1b Kal f pp. 15–52 16 1/2 min.

Excerpt 1 concluding before the entrance of Glover and Ralph.

EXCERPT 2 Kal f pp. 88–96 4 1/2 min.

This scene is a duet for Mab and the Duke (see description in excerpt 1).

The Duke accosts Mab and entices her to aid him in his plan to abduct Catherine. She agrees, seeing the possibility of making a fool of the Duke.

EXCERPT 3 Kal f pp. 102/3/3–122 11 min.

A scene for Catherine, Smith, and Ralph, bass (B1–E3). A Laborer and a Majordomo could be played by the same person (bass). Mab appears but is silent.

Smith sings a serenade to his beloved Catherine, but she does not open the window. Ralph then arrives and drunkenly serenades Catherine before falling asleep. The Majordomo escorts Mab, masked and wearing Catherine's clothes, toward the Duke's palace, much to Ralph's amazement. Smith reappears, and just as the two of them are about to run off to pursue the masked lady, Catherine opens her window and repeats a verse of Smith's earlier serenade.

EXCERPT 4 Kal f pp. 133–41 5 min.

This is another duet for Mab and the Duke (see descriptions above).

The Duke is left alone with the masked lady, thinking she is Catherine; she still refuses to unmask for him. She does, however, give him the enameled rose that she has picked up after Catherine discarded it. She escapes his embrace and leaves the room.

EXCERPT 5 Kal f pp. 196/2/1–205 5 1/2 min.

This excerpt is a duet for Catherine and Smith (see excerpt 1 for descriptions).

Smith, still not convinced of Catherine's innocence, has allowed Ralph to challenge him to a duel. Catherine appears and begs Smith to love her as before; eventually he is convinced, and to prove her innocence, is willing to die for her.

Linda di Chamounix (Linda of Chamounix)

Gaetano Donizetti (1797–1848)

Haute-Savoie and Paris, 1760

EXCERPT 1 Kal i pp. 14/1/6–21/2/1 6 1/2 min.

This is a scene for Maddalena, mezzo (D3–F♯4), and Antonio, baritone (C2–E3).

Antonio, tenant farmer, and his wife, Maddalena, are worried they will be evicted from their farm. They are delighted that their landlord's brother, the Marquis of Boisfleury, has offered to educate their daughter, Linda, at his château; obviously they are unaware of the Marquis' less than honorable intentions.

EXCERPT 2 Kal i pp. 47/2/1–77/2/4 20 min.

Linda, coloratura soprano (C3–C5, opt. D5 or higher) sings her aria, "O luce di quest'anima," at the opening of this scene, followed by two songs for Pierrotto, mezzo-soprano (trouser role) (A2–G4) with women's chorus, and a duet for Linda and Carlo, tenor (F2–A3).

Linda, returning from Mass, is eagerly awaiting Carlo, a painter from another village, when Pierrotto arrives to amuse Linda with a song. Eventually Carlo also arrives; he and Linda are very much in love, but he refuses to reveal that he is the nephew of the Marquis of Boisfleury.

EXCERPT 2a Kal i pp. 47/2/1–64/1/1 12 1/2 min.

Linda's and Pierrotto's arias with the women's chorus.

EXCERPT 2b Kal i pp. 65–77/2/4 7 min.

The duet for Linda and Carlo from excerpt 2.

EXCERPT 3 Kal i pp. 77/3/1–90/3/5 10 min.

A duet for Antonio, baritone (to G♭3, opt A♭3), and the Prefect, bass-baritone (A♭1–G♭3).

The Prefect advises Antonio not to permit Linda to stay at the château of the Marquis; he offers instead the protection of his own brother in Paris.

EXCERPT 4 Kal i pp. 110–19/2/3 8 min.

This is a duet between Linda and Pierrotto, both described in excerpt 2.

After the death of the Prefect's brother, Linda is staying in an apartment belonging to Carlo in Paris and appears to be very wealthy. Carlo would like to marry her, but his mother opposes the match. In this scene, Pierrotto is heard singing in the street; Linda recognizes his voice and invites him in; together they sing of their happy reunion.

EXCERPT 5 Kal i pp. 119/1/2–138/1/8 11 min.

A duet for Linda, soprano (excerpt 2) and the Marquis, baritone (C♯2–F♯3), requiring rapid articulation.

The Marquis has discovered Linda's retreat, not knowing it is paid for by his nephew, and chooses this moment to force his unwelcome advances upon her. An amusing duet follows as Linda orders him to leave.

EXCERPT 6 Kal i pp. 138/2/1–171 28 min.

This excerpt includes Linda, Carlo, Pierrotto, and Antonio, all described in previous excerpts.

Carlo enters the apartment, and we learn from his aria that his mother has selected a wife for him and expects him to give up Linda. He has come to explain this to Linda and to part from her temporarily, as he still hopes to become free from the arranged marriage. As he leaves, her father arrives as a beggar, pleading for the intercession of the Viscount of Sirval, who he does not realize is the same person as Carlo, Linda's beau. Linda recognizes her father, though he does not recognize her right away. When he goes to kiss her hand, she reveals her identity. Outraged at seeing her in such lavish surroundings, he hurls at her feet the money she has just given him and storms off. Pierrotto arrives to announce the wedding of Carlo. Linda, rejected by both father and lover, begins to lose her reason, and Pierrotto attempts to comfort her as act 2 ends.

EXCERPT 6a Kal i pp. 138/2/1–153 14 min.

Carlo's aria and duet with Linda from excerpt 6.

EXCERPT 6b Kal i pp. 153/3/3–171 13 1/2 min.

The portion of excerpt 6 with Linda, Antonio and Pierrotto.

EXCERPT 7 Kal i pp. 186–98/2/6 9 1/2 min.

Carlo and the Prefect are described in earlier excerpts.

Carlo returns to Chamounix in search of his beloved Linda, whom he has finally persuaded his mother to permit him to marry. The Prefect informs Carlo that she has been disowned by her parents and believed seduced by a wealthy suitor. Carlo feels guilty for having abandoned her and resolves to find her.

I Lombardi alla Prima Crociata (The Lombards in the First Crusade)

Giuseppe Verdi (1813–1901)

Milan and the Holy Land, late eleventh century

EXCERPT 1 Kal i pp. 83–89 5 min.

This excerpt uses Giselda, soprano (C♯3–B♭4); Viclinda, mezzo-soprano, although the score says soprano (C3–D4); and Arvino, tenor, who has a lesser role.

Even though Arvino, leader of the Crusaders in Milan, has just reconciled with his brother, Pagano, he is still fearful that all is not well between them, Pagano having once been in love with Arvino's wife, Viclinda. When she confesses her misgivings to their daughter, Giselda, the two kneel in prayer.

EXCERPT 2 Kal i pp. 146–54 or 146–50; 155–61 7 1/2 min.

Sofia, soprano (C3–F♯4, opt. A♭4 or B♭4), sings with Oronte, tenor (E♭2–A3), in this scene. If the second cabaletta is used in place of the original, a C4 is required of Oronte in a difficult aria with high tessitura.

The Crusaders have now reached Antioch, where Giselda has fallen in love with the Sultan's son, Oronte. His mother tries in vain to dissuade him from declaring his love, as Giselda is of the Christian faith and is being held captive.

EXCERPT 3 Kal i pp. 162–76 7 1/2 min.

Two basses sing together in this excerpt—Hermit (Pagano) who has the main aria (C2–E♭3) and Pirro (G1–D3).

Pagano, exiled for having attempted to kill his brother, Arvino, and having killed their father by mistake, has now taken refuge as a hermit in the Holy Land. His former henchman, Pirro, also seeks refuge for the same reason; the Hermit, without revealing his identity, leads Pirro into his cave.

EXCERPT 4 Kal i pp. 227/1/2–240 8 min.

In this excerpt for Oronte, tenor, and Giselda, soprano (see earlier excerpts for descriptions), Giselda needs a pianissimo B♭4.

After some crusaders and some pilgrims have visited the Mount of Olives, Giselda and Oronte meet again to lament their respective fates—their love affair has caused their own people to cut them off. But Oronte has determined to embrace Giselda's Christian faith, and the two sing of the spiritual love that continues to bind them together.

EXCERPT 5 Kal i pp. 258–77 11 1/2 min.

This is an extremely beautiful trio for Giselda, Oronte, and the Hermit (Pagano), all previously described. It is preceded by a violin solo that has made this selection a favorite on orchestra concert programs. If the scene is performed with piano, it is suggested that, in addition, a violin obbligato be used throughout the excerpt.

Oronte has been wounded in battle and is found by Giselda. As the hermit (Giselda's uncle Pagano in disguise) approaches from having ministered to other wounded men, he arrives in time to baptize Oronte with holy water from the Jordan before he dies.

The Love for Three Oranges (L'amour des trois oranges)

Serge Prokofieff (1891–1953)

An imaginary kingdom, once upon a time

EXCERPT 1 B&H f, g 137–54/5/4 8 min.

Appearing in this excerpt are Celio, bass (B♭1–E3); Farfarello, a devil, bass (B♭1–F3); The Prince, tenor (C2–B3) who has florid, lyrical singing; and Truffaldino, tenor (C2–A♯3).

In the desert, Celio makes a vain attempt to restrain Farfarello from wafting the Prince and his companion to perdition with his bellows, but Farfarello tells him that his loss at cards has rendered his magic powers inoperative, and he proves as much by disobeying him. The Prince and Truffaldino appear, and the Magician, having discovered they are seeking the three oranges, advises them: the oranges are to be cut open only near water. He also warns them of Creonte, who takes the form of a gigantic cook. In case it may help, he gives Truffaldino a magic ribbon, hoping it may distract the cook's attention while they steal the oranges. Farfarello appears again with his bellows and like lightning the Prince and Truffaldino are transported toward their destination.

EXCERPT 2 B&H f, g 158–72/2/7 7 min.

The Prince and Truffaldino (see excerpt 1 for description) and the Cook, bass, sing in this scene.

The Prince and Truffaldino stand in front of a castle and are about to go into the kitchen, when from it emerges the colossal Cook. Both hide, but Truffaldino is quickly discovered and then saved by the Cook's interest in the ribbon around his neck. The Prince sneaks into the kitchen and emerges with the three oranges, and he and Truffaldino make their escape.

EXCERPT 3 B&H f, g pp. 176–207/3/1 17 1/2 min.

(Note: In order to eliminate the chorus parts for a workshop presentation, it is suggested that the accompaniment continue on p. 197 without the chorus and that the action be continued. Also, Ninetta should sing to p. 202/3/2 without the chorus and the accompaniment should continue to p. 203/1/2, just before the glissando, and then cut to p. 204/2/2.)

The Prince and Truffaldino (see other excerpts) sing with the three oranges in this scene. Linetta and Nicoletta are mezzo-sopranos, while Ninetta is a soprano. Four silent soldiers who appear in this scene could be used to get the bucket of water usually brought to the stage by the chorus.

The Prince has discovered that each stolen orange contains a lovely princess. Two immediately die of thirst, but the third, Ninetta, is saved by a bucket of water brought to the stage. Then she and the Prince rejoice in having found each other, but when the Prince says they must return to his father's palace, she says he must find a suitable dress for her before she can meet his father.

Lucrezia Borgia

Gaetano Donizetti (1798–1848)

Venice and Ferrara, early sixteenthth century

EXCERPT 1 Ric/Br i pp. 32–51 18 min.

The prologue of the opera features Lucrezia Borgia, soprano (B♭2–B♭4) who needs great flexibility for difficult coloratura passages; Gennaro, tenor who has a high tessitura to A3; and lesser roles for Rustighello, tenor; Gubetta, baritone; and the Duke, bass.

Lucrezia Borgia, who has done away with three husbands, is now married to Don Alfonso, Duke of Ferrara. When she sees Gennaro, her illegitimate son, asleep on the stone bench of the terrace, she is deeply moved. When she kisses his hand, he awakens and is attracted to her. But he swears devotion to his mother, whom he has never seen. Lucrezia, without revealing her identity, urges him always to love his mother, and they pray together that the two may someday be united.

EXCERPT 2 Ric/Br i pp. 71–78/2/2; 80/1/4–80/6/5 6 min.

This scene is between the Duke of Ferrara, bass (A♭1–E♭3), and Rustighello, lesser tenor. There is also an offstage men's chorus.

Alfonso, the Duke of Ferrara, is jealous of Gennaro and is persuaded that he is Lucrezia's paramour. He instructs Rustighello to kidnap Gennaro and bring him to the palace.

EXCERPT 3 Ric/Br i pp. 102/3/3–134; 138–39 18 min.

Lucrezia, soprano; the Duke, bass; and Gennaro, tenor (all previously described), are in this excerpt.

Lucrezia, not knowing it was Gennaro who, seeing the letters BORGIA under the escutcheon of the palace, has hacked off the first letter with his sword and has left visible the Italian word for ORGY, demands the perpetrator be put to death. Then Gennaro, who has been arrested, is led in. Lucrezia asks to be alone with her husband, and she implores him to be more lenient with Gennaro, which arouses the Duke's suspicions even more.

EXCERPT 3a Ric/Br i pp. 105/1/3–119 7 min.

From Excerpt 3, the duet of Lucrezia and the Duke.

EXCERPT 4 Ric/Br i pp. 151–66 8 min.

Orsini, a mezzo-soprano trouser role (C3–F4), requires flexibility. Gennaro, tenor (see excerpt 1), and Rustighello, tenor, with little singing, and a men's chorus complete the scene.

Orsini persuades his friend Gennaro to join the five young men from Venice in a party at the Negroni Palace that evening. Rustighello and his men overhear the arrangement and make plans to enter Gennaro's house to avenge the Duke.

EXCERPT 5 Ric/Br i pp. 172–227 28 min.

This excerpt includes Lucrezia, soprano; Orsini, mezzo-soprano; Gennaro, tenor; and the Duke, bass (see previous excerpts). Also included are Liverotto and Vitellozzo, tenors; Gubetta, baritone; Petrucci and Gazella, basses; a chorus; and an offstage baritone.

There is a party going well at the Negroni Palace, where Orsini sings a drinking song. Suddenly from a neighboring room comes the sound of monks' voices chanting a dirge. A door opens and the penitents, still chanting, enter, and the lights go out one by one. Then Lucrezia enters. The banqueters are her enemies, and she has poisoned the wine they have just quaffed to Orsini's song. When she finds that Gennaro, her illegitimate son whom she dearly loves, is with them, she offers him an antidote. He will not save himself while his friends die even after she discloses the fact that she is his mother. Lucrezia herself then drains the poisoned cup from which he has drunk, and sinks, dying, upon his prostrate form.

EXCERPT 5a Ric/Br i pp. 172–200 10 min.

This is the opening of excerpt 5 and does not include Lucrezia, the Duke, or the mixed chorus, but does include the offstage voice and men's chorus.

EXCERPT 5b Ric/Br i pp. 172–206; 228–41 21 1/2 min.

Substituting a different finale from the original one, this eliminates the Duke and chorus from the final scene, requiring only an offstage male chorus in the earlier segment of the scene.

EXCERPT 5c Ric/Br i pp. 228–41 8 1/2 min.

From the finale of 5b, this is the final duet for Lucrezia and Gennaro only.

Luisa Miller

Giuseppe Verdi (1813–1901)

A village in the Tyrol, early eighteenth century

EXCERPT 1 Kal i pp. 47–71 6 1/2 min.
(trad. 67/2/3–70/1/1)

This scene calls for Miller, father of Luisa, baritone (D♯2–G♭3, opt. A♭3) with the vocal weight usually required of baritone roles in Verdi's operas; and Wurm, bass (B♭1–E♭3) with a strong voice and acting ability.

Luisa is in love with a young huntsman known only to her as "Carlo." Wurm, a henchman of Count Walter and the villain of this opera, is in love with Luisa and pleads with her father for her hand in marriage. Responding in an aria, "Sacra la scelta," Miller declares that he cannot force such a marriage upon his daughter. Wurm then tells Miller that "Carlo" is really Rodolfo, son of Count Walter, and implies that he cannot possibly have honorable intentions. In the cabaletta that follows, Miller expresses his confirmed suspicions of the young man his daughter loves, and prays to heaven for her purity.

EXCERPT 2 Kal i pp. 72–106 15 min.

The characters in this scene are Federica, mezzo-soprano or contralto (G2–G4); Rodolfo, tenor (E2–A3), with medium tessitura but requiring vocal weight bordering on dramatic; and Walter, basso cantante (B♭1–G♭3), who sings the demanding aria "Il mio sangue" in this scene. A chorus appears briefly.

In a room of his castle, Count Walter awaits his son, Rodolfo, as he sings an aria expressing his ambitions for his son and also hints at remorse for some past misdeed. When Rodolfo enters, his father tells him that Federica, the widowed Duchess of Ostheim, a childhood friend, is about to arrive, and that he must propose marriage. Before Rodolfo has a chance to protest such an arranged marriage, the Duchess arrives with her retinue. In the duet that follows, Rodolfo tells

Federica that he loves her only as a friend and begs her pardon; she insists that a woman scorned cannot be expected to forgive.

EXCERPT 2a Kal i pp. 72–85/6/2; 90/3/1–106 13 1/2 min.

Same as excerpt 2, eliminating the chorus.

EXCERPT 2b Kal i pp. 91/4/3–106 6 1/2 min.

The portion of excerpt 2 with only Federica and Rodolfo.

EXCERPT 3 Kal i pp. 157–85 11 1/2 min.
(trad. 179/3/1–182/4/2)

The role of Luisa calls for a soprano of the lyric-spinto variety, but she should be able to portray the vulnerability and tenderness of a young girl (D3–B4); some florid singing is required in her aria. Wurm, bass (B♭1–E♭3), is described in excerpt 1. Laura, soprano or mezzo, sings with a mixed chorus in the opening of the scene.

Laura and a group of villagers bring Luisa the news that her father has been dragged to prison in chains. Wurm orders everyone but Luisa to leave; left alone with her, he tells her that her father has insulted the Count and will be executed unless she writes a letter required by the Count to save Miller. She yields to Wurm's demand, writing a letter that says she only loved Rodolfo for his money and intends to marry Wurm. The form of this scene, the dialogue between the two leading characters, Luisa's aria of which the cabaletta becomes a powerful duet, and the villain expressing his joy and the heroine her anguish, makes this one of the most dramatically intense excerpts from the lesser-known repertory.

EXCERPT 3a Kal i pp. 167–85 8 1/2 min.

Same as excerpt 3, eliminating Laura and chorus.

EXCERPT 4 Kal i pp. 186–218 12 1/2 min.

This contains a duet for two basses, Walter and Wurm. Both require a strong F3, but Walter has a wider range extending downward to F1 and takes the lower line in the a cappella quartet that follows in which they are joined by Luisa, soprano, and Federica, mezzo-soprano. Neither of the women's parts poses any great vocal difficulty, but all four characters must possess a secure enough sense of pitch to sing without accompaniment for an extended passage.

Wurm reports to Walter the success of his visit to Luisa (excerpt 3) and plans to have Luisa's letter delivered to Rodolfo. In the duet, the two men concern themselves with a dark secret from their past; Walter had murdered the old Count in order to inherit his title, and the murder had been attributed to bandits. Now Walter learns from Wurm that Rodolfo knows the truth and threatens to reveal it. Federica arrives; Walter tells her that Rodolfo never loved Luisa; to prove the fact, Luisa is summoned and, in order to save her father's life, tearfully tells Federica what she wants to hear. In the quartet, each of the characters expresses his or her thoughts about the situation.

EXCERPT 4a Kal i pp. 186–200 6 1/2 min.

The duet portion only from excerpt 4.

EXCERPT 4b Kal i pp. 201–18 6 min.

Same as excerpt 4, eliminating the opening duet.

EXCERPT 5 Kal i pp. 244–309 32 1/2 min.

Act 3 complete is demanding for the three leading characters: Luisa, soprano (B♭2–D♭5); Rodolfo, tenor (E♭2–B♭3); and Miller, baritone (C2–F3). Laura, soprano or lyric mezzo (E♭3–G4), has an important solo accompanied by women's chorus. Walter (bass), a servant, and Wurm (both silent in this scene) appear briefly at the end of the act; a mixed chorus sings offstage and can appear onstage if desired.

Miller, now released from prison, demands to see the contents of a letter Luisa is writing. Luisa is telling Rodolfo she has been betrayed and will now take her own life, and hopes Rodolfo will come to her house at midnight. Deeply moved, her father encourages her to live, telling her how much he needs her. She finally agrees, tears up the letter, and the two resolve to wander the rest of their lives as beggars.

Rodolfo steals into Luisa's room ordering a servant to ask his father to call for him when his wedding to Duchess Federica is ready to begin. After extracting a confession from Luisa that she indeed wrote the letter to Wurm, he asks for a drink and bids Luisa drink also. He then tells her they have both taken poison; only in the face of death does Luisa reveal the truth about the letter (excerpt 3). Rodolfo's curses of anguish are interrupted by the arrival of Miller, to whom Luisa bids a final farewell. Walter and Wurm arrive, the former in time to witness his son's death, the latter to receive a fatal blow from Rodolfo's sword as he expires.

EXCERPT 5a Kal i pp. 252–309 28 min.

This omits the opening chorus and solo for Laura.

EXCERPT 5b Kal i pp. 252–72 11 min.

The duet for Luisa and Miller from excerpt 5.

EXCERPT 5c Kal i pp. 273–97/1/6 12 1/2 min.

Luisa and Rodolfo only.

Les Mamelles de Tirésias (The Breasts of Tirésias)

Francis Poulenc (1899–1963)

French Riviera, 1910

EXCERPT 1 Heu f, e pp. 1–11 6 1/2 min.

This is the prologue sung by the Director, who is a baritone (A1–G3) singing in a rather high tessitura. It could be used as a solo but might better be used to introduce other excerpts.

EXCERPT 2 Heu f, e pp. 12–26 6 1/2 min.

This excerpt includes Thérèse, soprano (D3–C5), and her Husband, baritone (B♭1–A♭3), with optional notes to keep the role in the high baritone register.

When the scene begins, the eccentric, young, and pretty Thérèse enters with a broom in hand. She claims she is for women's rights and through with being a slave to her Husband, so she changes herself from a woman to a man, getting rid of her breasts (balloons that she takes from her dress and bursts) and donning a beard. When the Husband enters, he thinks there is a murderer there dressed in his wife's clothes, but she explains that she is now going to be a young man named Tirésas.

EXCERPT 2a Heu f, e pp. 12–23 5 min.

This portion of excerpt 1 could be done with or without the occasional offstage interjections by the Husband.

EXCERPT 3 Heu f, e pp. 27–33/1/1 2 min.

A short scene for Presto, a baritone (E♭2–E3), and Lacouf, a tenor (F2–G3). One should be a short, fat man and the other a tall, skinny one. They are typical, classic French card-player types and should be good actors.

Presto and Lacouf leave the café in Zanzibar, dancing a polka and visibly drunk. They continue with conversation and intermittent dancing, arguing which one lost to the other in roulette. Because they cannot settle the argument, they decide they must fight a duel, so they go gravely to the rear of the scene and from their pockets take two huge revolvers. Both aim, fire, and fall dead.

EXCERPT 4 Heu f, e pp. 40/4/2–53 7 min.

The Gendarme, baritone (B♭1–F3), has this scene with the Husband, baritone (C2–A♭3) with a very high tessitura. Both have a little singing in falsetto. The four-part chorus could be offstage, but a few people of Zanzibar need to be onstage.

The Husband is sitting in the café, dressed as a woman with his hands tied, when the Gendarme enters and approaches and courts the Husband. Disgusted, the Husband rips off his feminine attire, which shocks the Gendarme, and then he proceeds to announce that if the wives refuse to have babies, it will be up to the husbands to do it, and he will start.

EXCERPT 5 Heu f, e pp. 103/3/1–139 10 min.

An excerpt for the Gendarme, the Husband, and the Fortune-teller who is Thérèse in disguise. (All have been described previously.) With the final four-part chorus, there are also a Newspaper Woman (mezzo-soprano) and two Spectators, a large woman (soprano) and a bearded man (baritone).

While the Gendarme and the Husband are talking, Thérèse enters as the card-reading Fortune-teller. As the scene progresses, she takes off the Fortune-teller's garb and is seen in an elegant evening gown, while her Husband takes off his gown and appears in evening clothes.

They are reunited, and all of the participants urge the audience to go and have children.

Maria Golovin

Gian-Carlo Menotti (1911–)

A villa in a European country, 1919

EXCERPT 1 Bel e, i pp. 26/2/2–51/3/2 11 min.

This is a scene for the two leading characters of the opera, Maria Golovin, soprano (D3–B♭4), and Donato, bass-baritone (G1–F3). A chorus of prisoners (men) sing briefly offstage. The role of Donato has a rather high tessitura for a bass and could be sung by a baritone. A young man, Donato, is blind, which makes for a useful acting exercise.

Donato, a blind war victim, lives with his mother and their servant, Agata, near the frontier of an unspecified European country. Maria Golovin and her son, Trottolò, have rented the upper floor of the house for the summer months. This is the first of several exchanges between Maria and Donato in which Maria promises to keep Donato company and read to him sometimes, as she is also lonely, her husband being a prisoner of war. Donato offers her a birdcage, the only thing he can make since losing his sight.

EXCERPT 2 Bel e, i pp. 73/4/1–108 13 1/2 min.

Maria and Donato, described in excerpt 1, the chorus of prisoners offstage, and Trottolò, a young boy with a few spoken words, are in this scene.

Donato and Maria are seated by the fire, where Donato is teaching Maria to read Braille. They become increasingly attracted to each other, and when they kiss, Donato asks her if she has ever been unfaithful to her husband before. She hesitates and tells him that there was a young man, Aldo, who during the previous summer had fallen in love with her and on occasion had kissed her. He has written to Maria but she has not answered. They are interrupted by the arrival of Trottolò; Maria hides, fearful that he may have seen them. Donato tells the boy that his mother is upstairs, and Maria follows after him. Left alone, Donato becomes obsessed with jealousy for everyone whose existence threatens to separate him from Maria.

EXCERPT 3 Bel e, i pp. 109–62 17 1/2 min.

The first scene of act 2 calls for the six principals of the opera. In addition to Maria and Donato, there are Agata, mezzo-soprano (B2–A♭4), and the Mother, contralto (A2–F♯3). Dr. Zuckertanz, tenor (D2–A3), and a Prisoner, baritone (D2–F3), play smaller but important roles. Trottolò, eight years old, appears briefly.

On a terrace in front of the house, Agata tells Donato that a prisoner has escaped from a nearby camp and that a letter from Aldo has arrived for Maria. The prisoner arrives, asking for refuge; Donato offers his own room until nightfall. The mother, Maria, Trottolò, and his tutor, Dr. Zuckertanz, return from a picnic. When the boy is persuaded to go to bed, Donato's mother criticizes Maria for being too lenient with Trottolò, and at the same time is concerned about Donato's increasing love for Maria. Maria returns, and Donato scolds her for not having come to him the night before; her excuse is that Trottolò spies on her all of the time. Donato then hands her a letter, which she claims is from an old schoolmate. The other two women return and sing a trio with Maria as they sew together.

EXCERPT 3a Bel e, i pp. 131/2/1–162 11 min.

This is excerpt 3 without Dr. Zuckertanz, the Prisoner, and Trottolò.

EXCERPT 4 Bel e, i pp. 166/1/2–187/2/2 8 1/2 min.

This is another major scene for Maria and Donato (see previous descriptions). Agata, mezzo-soprano, appears briefly.

EXCERPT 5 Bel e, i pp. 220/3/2–253 13 min.

Maria, Mother, and Donato, all previously described, and a silent male servant are in this excerpt.

Maria has received word that her husband is soon to be released from prison and is planning a party for some of his relatives and friends. Worried about Donato's anguish, his Mother urges Maria to leave the house as soon as possible; Maria, too, realizes she must give up Donato. But when left alone with Donato, she does not have the courage to tell him of her decision; instead, she promises to leave her guests in order to meet him at midnight.

EXCERPT 5a Bel e, i pp. 233–53 8 1/2 min.

This is the portion of excerpt 5 for Maria and Donato only.

EXCERPT 6 Bel e, i pp. 258–75 8 min.

A scene for Maria, Mother, and Donato, all previously described, and the voice of Dr. Zuckertanz (tenor) heard briefly from offstage.

It is two o'clock in the morning and Maria has still not kept her midnight rendezvous with Donato. His mother wishes to stay with him, but he sends her impatiently away. When Maria finally arrives, she apologizes for being late saying she could not get away earlier from her guests. But Donato's grief is so intense that he takes the revolver left to him by the prisoner and calls for his mother to aim it at Maria. The mother motions Maria out of the way in order to save her life and then guides Donato's hand to fire into space, knowing that the only way he can be at peace is to destroy his own image of the woman for whom he had such obsessive love.

Maria Stuarda (Mary Stuart)

Gaetano Donizetti (1797–1848)

Elizabethan England

EXCERPT 1 Br i pp. 15–77 8 1/2 min.

The opening cavatina of the opera is sung by Elizabeth, who may be either a soprano or a mezzo-soprano (C3–B4) but needs flexibility and a trill. She is joined by Leicester, tenor (F♯2–B3) who also needs flexibility and a trill and must sustain a high tessitura, and by Talbot, a bass (F1–F3). An SATTB chorus is needed and Cecil, baritone, has a limited amount of singing.

Queen Elizabeth enters, revealing that she is secretly in love with someone else but nevertheless thinks of marrying the King of France. She discusses Mary Stuart with Talbot, who asks her to be merciful, and with Cecil, who reminds her of Mary's breach of faith. Leicester enters; it is soon apparent that he is Elizabeth's love. She orders him to be ambassador to France. Talbot gives him a letter from Mary, which impresses him deeply. When Elizabeth demands to see the letter, she realizes that Mary covets both her throne and her love, but nevertheless she consents to visit the imprisoned Queen.

EXCERPT 1a Br i pp. 37/3/4–56 8 min.

Leicester and Talbot's duet following Elizabeth's opening aria.

EXCERPT 1b Br i pp. 57–77 8 1/2 min.

The duet of Elizabeth and Leicester.

EXCERPT 2 Br i pp. 78–95 8 1/2 min.

Act 2 opens in Fortheringay Park, where Maria, soprano (A♭2–B4) is with her companion, Anna, contralto (C♯3–A4). Maria has an aria in this scene, and there is a small amount of singing for the offstage chorus.

Mary, with her companion Anna, is in the garden enjoying the beauties of nature when she hears the signal for the royal hunt and hears people calling, "The Queen." Mary contemplates fleeing, but when she sees someone appoaching, she stops, gesturing to Anna to go on without her.

EXCERPT 3 Br i pp. 96–113 7 1/2 min.

Leicester, tenor (F♯2–B3), has a high tessitura and some fioritura. Maria (see excerpt 2) is the other character in this scene.

Leicester announces Elizabeth's arrival, and he and Mary have an extended duet.

EXCERPT 4 Br i pp. 114–51; 163/1/4–169/1/4; 170/1/3–171 12 1/2 min.

This excerpt is primarily a sextet with Maria, Elizabeth, Anna, Leicester, Cecil, and Talbot (all previously described). A men's chorus is included.

When Elizabeth enters, the meeting of the two Queens is electric with suppressed emotions. Mary is at first submissive, but when Elizabeth accuses her of having connived the death of her husband, Darnley, she furiously calls Elizabeth the bastard of Anne Boleyn. Elizabeth, angry, calls to the guards to lead Mary toward her prison, while Elizabeth, followed by her courtiers, sweeps out in the opposite direction.

EXCERPT 5 Br i pp. 172–200/2/2; 201/3/2–202 13 1/2 min.

A scene for Elizabeth, Leicester, and Cecil (all described above).

When act 3 of the opera opens, Elizabeth is seated at a desk in the Palace of Westminster, and Cecil stands near by. She is uncertain about signing the manuscript that is before her, and she hesitates when Leicester enters. The three continue in a trio after Elizabeth has signed Mary Stuart's death warrant.

EXCERPT 6 Br i pp. 203–29 16 min.

Maria, Cecil, and Talbot are included in this excerpt, which ends with a duet for Maria and Talbot.

Mary is alone in her private chamber in the Castle of Fotheringay when Cecil enters to deliver the death warrant, followed by Talbot. In the famous confession scene, Mary thinks she sees Darnley's ghost, and tells Talbot that Darnley died because Elizabeth was jealous of him. Talbot, a Catholic priest, absolves Mary, and as she goes off, supported by Talbot, to another room within the castle, she holds up the crucifix before them as they go.

EXCERPT 6a Br i pp. 208–29 12 1/2 min.

This is the section of excerpt 5 that excludes Cecil.

Markheim

Carlisle Floyd (1926–)

London, 1880

EXCERPT 1 B&H e pp. 2/3/1–40 16 min.

This is the opening scene of the opera for tenor Josiah Creach (D2–G3); Markheim, bass-baritone (A1–F3); and Tess, soprano (E♭3–C5); and an offstage chorus singing a Christmas hymn. Creach is a portly, middle-aged man and Markheim is in his late thirties, so these voices should be mature. The maid Tess, who has a small part in this scene, is a teenager.

In the interior of a musty, dark pawnshop lighted by two lamps, Josiah Creach sits on a tall stool at the counter, absorbed in his accounts. Disgusted with the carolers, he flings open the door when the doorbell is insistent and is surprised to find Markheim standing there. He invites him in and they convey their thoughts of Christmas. Tess, the maid, enters and exchanges greetings with the men as she leaves for her Christmas holiday. Then, before Markheim can state his business, Creach displays his anger toward Markheim for his ability to charm women and thus create many problems in the neighborhood.

EXCERPT 1a B&H e pp. 2/3/1–24/2/4 9 1/2 min.

This scene begins just as excerpt 1 but ends with Markheim's aria about Christmas.

EXCERPT 1b B&H e pp. 10–40 14 min.

The doorbell could ring insistently and then the singing could begin on p. 10 without the carolers.

EXCERPT 1c B&H e pp. 10–24/2/4 7 1/2 min.

This scene is similar to excerpt 1b but ends with Markheim's aria and includes neither Tess nor the chorus.

EXCERPT 1d B&H e pp. 10–29 10 min.

This is the same scene as 1c but includes Tess until she exits with her "Merry Christmas to all!"

EXCERPT 1e B&H e pp. 2/3/1–29 12 min.

This excerpt opens with the carolers and ends when Tess exits.

EXCERPT 2 B&H e pp. 41/2/3–80/1/3 18 1/2 min.

A very dramatic scene for Creach, tenor (C2–A3), and Markheim, bass-baritone (G1–F#3).

Creach pretends not to notice that Markheim is still in the pawnshop, begging for a loan before his creditors catch up with him. Markheim tries to pawn a stolen statue and Creach refuses to take it, pointing out all of the treasures of the Markheim fortune that have been pawned and never reclaimed. Then he thrusts a hand mirror in Markheim's face and asks him what he sees—a liar, a thief, a lecher. Markheim, stunned, looks at Creach and suddenly lunges at him, taking him by the throat and shaking him back and forth until he crumples to the floor dead. When the clocks in the room begin to chime the hour, Markheim runs from one clock to another, pounding on the cases and shouting. He then covers the mirrors in the room and stares at Creach's body while he wonders why Creach pretends to be dead. At last Markheim realizes that he has murdered Creach.

EXCERPT 2a B&H e pp. 41/2/3–72/2/2 13 min.

This is the same as excerpt 2 except that it ends on the first chord of p. 72/2/3 with Markheim standing over the body of Creach and staring fiercely into his face.

EXCERPT 3 B&H e pp. 85/1/2–113/4/5 14 min.

This excerpt is primarily for the Stranger, tenor (D♭2–B3), who appears while Markheim (G♯1–C♯3) is looking for the money that Creach must have hidden in the cabinet in his pawnshop.

The Stranger is a man of Markheim's age but looking more youthful. He is elegantly dressed, like Markheim, but where Markheim's clothes are faded and worn, the Stranger's should be new and spotless. When Markheim cannot understand why the Stranger has come, the Stranger reminds Markheim of his longing for "pleasure, the crown of life." Then the Stranger offers to tell Markheim where he can find the money he needs to escape without being suspected of the murder he has committed.

I Masnadieri (The Brigands)

Giuseppe Verdi (1813–1901)

Germany, eighteenth century

EXCERPT 1 Kal, Ric i pp. 24–35/2/2; 38/1/1–38/5/6 8 1/2 min

Francesco Moor, baritone (D2–F3, opt. A♭3), opens this scene with a recitative and forceful aria with many dynamic changes. He then calls Arminio, tenor (G2–E♭3), who has little singing in the scene. When Arminio exits, Francesco again sings of his plans for the future.

Francesco, younger son of the reigning Count of Moor, is in a room in the castle, expressing his disappointment that he is the younger son and cannot reign when his father dies. Then he seizes upon an idea that will aid him in becoming master. He tells Arminio, steward to the Count's family, to disguise himself and tell the Count that his elder son, Carlo, has died in battle. Then Francesco, as the surviving son, can reign.

EXCERPT 2 Kal, Ric i pp. 39–65 17 min.

This scene includes Francesco and Arminio, tenor to A3 (described in excerpt 1), Massimiliano Moor, bass (A1–E3), and Amalia, soprano (G♯3–C5) who needs a very high, flexible voice for this role written by Verdi for Jenny Lind. There is quartet singing in this scene. Excerpts 1 and 2 could be combined for a longer scene.

In a bedroom in the castle, Count Massimiliano Moor is asleep in a chair and Amalia, an orphan and niece of the Count, quietly enters and stands looking at him while she sings her opening aria. Massimiliano is still dreaming when he first sings, and when he awakens, he bemoans the fact that he is old and that his son, Carlo, is far away. Amalia, too, feels she cannot live if Carlo is not there. When Francesco and Arminio arrive, disguised, they tell Massimiliano that Carlo has been killed in battle; the Count swoons in grief. Amalia cries out and then leaves, while Francesco in jubilation declares he is master.

EXCERPT 3 Kal, Ric i pp. 66–82/1/2; 84/2/1–97 16 min.

Arminio, Amalia, and Francesco (described in preceding excerpts) sing in this scene, which ends in a duet with Amalia and Francesco. An offstage chorus is included.

Amalia, in the chapel of the castle, is standing by the tomb of Massimiliano Moor when she sings her aria. Arminio enters to reveal to Amalia that Carlo lives and that her uncle, also, is still alive. He quickly leaves and soon Francesco enters and attempts to woo Amalia. She pretends to embrace him but instead snatches his dagger and threatens him. He leaves, vowing to seek vengeance.

EXCERPT 3a Kal, Ric i pp. 66–67/3/2; 74–82/1/2; 84/2/1–97 14 1/2 min.

This is the same as excerpt 3 but without the chorus.

EXCERPT 4 Kal, Ric i pp. 124–41 9 min.

A scene for Amalia (see excerpt 1) and Carlo, tenor (E♭2–A3), with a short offstage chorus for men.

Amalia, to escape from Francesco, has run into the forest, where the brigands with their captain, Carlo, are staying. When she hears their voices she is frightened, until Carlo appears and identifies himself.

EXCERPT 5 Kal, Ric i pp. 152/4/2–164/4/1 8 min.

Carlo, Arminio, and Massimiliano (see excerpts 1, 2, and 4) are in this excerpt.

Carlo regrets that he has joined the robbers and has deceived Amalia, when Arminio enters and Carlo hears him talking to someone. It is Massimiliano, who was buried alive by Francesco and later, when he revived, was hurled into a dungeon to die. Carlo hears Massimiliano tell of the horror and kneels as his father falls into a faint.

EXCERPT 6 Kal, Ric i pp. 175–84 7 min.

This is primarily a powerful aria for Francesco, baritone (C2–F3), preceded by some conversation with Arminio. A few mute servants are needed.

Francesco has had a dream in which he has come to the Day of Judgment and has been accused of his sins.

Miss Julie

Ned Rorem (1923-)

Sweden, 1880

EXCERPT 1 B&H e pp. 6/2/1–21/1/4 7 min.

This scene is primarily an aria for the twenty-eight-year-old cook, Christine, mezzo-soprano (B♭2–F4), but includes three children, a boy and two girls disguised as wildcats, and an offstage mixed chorus. The Wildcat Boy (F3–F4), who could be a soprano or boy soprano, has solo singing. The girls can be silent or sing with the offstage chorus toward the end of the excerpt. The scene should end in the key of C major.

Christine, the cook, is sitting at the kitchen table fussing with her hair before a small mirror and singing a sensuous, sinuous, but furtive aria. In the distance revelers are heard singing a folk song and Christine continues her reverie. Soon three children, all disguised as wildcats, race across the garden, and the Wildcat Boy bursts into the kitchen while the girls stand in the doorway observing until Christine chases all of them back into the garden.

EXCERPT 1a B&H e pp. 6/2/1–9; 15–21/1/4 5 1/2 min.

The portions of excerpt 1 that include Christine and the children only. The two girls could sing the treble chorus.

EXCERPT 2 B&H e pp. 72/2/1–86/3/5 8 1/2 min.

This scene contains an aria for Miss Julie, soprano (G2–B♭4), and a duet for Miss Julie and John, the valet, who is a bass-baritone (G1–G♭3).

Miss Julie, daughter of the Count, has insulted her fiancé, Niels, and now she has flirted with John, the valet, and he has taken her into the garden, where they express their fantasies.

EXCERPT 3 B&H e pp. 140/2/1–180/2/4 20 min.

Another excerpt for Miss Julie, soprano (C♯3–A4), and John, bass-baritone (B1–F3). They are making plans for the future, which would take them far away from Julie's father, the Count.

EXCERPT 4 B&H e pp. 180/2/5–212/1/4 (G-major chord) 13 1/2 min.

The three main characters, Christine, mezzo-soprano (G2–G♯4); John, bass-baritone (G1–D3); and Miss Julie, soprano (B2–B♭4), are included in this excerpt, which has a range of emotions.

Christine is getting ready to go to church and is expecting John to go with her, but John is waiting for Miss Julie to come so they can leave forever. When Miss Julie does come, she has her canary and John will not allow her to take it with her, so he kills it. This incites Julie, and when Christine returns, Julie tells her of the trip she and John are planning and asks Christine to come with them. Christine insists that she and John must stay with the Count, and as the excerpt ends with a touching hymnlike tune, Christine leaves for church.

Nabucco

Giuseppe Verdi (1813–1901)

Jerusalem and Babylon, 586 B.C.

EXCERPT 1 Kal i pp. 40–48 6 1/2 min.

Abigaille is a dramatic soprano (B2–C5) who has many florid passages as well as sustained, emotional lines. In this scene she is joined by Fenena, mezzo-soprano (E3–G4), and Ismaele, tenor (G2–A3).

Ismaele, nephew of the King, tells the captive Fenena, daughter of Nabucco (Nebuchadnezzar), that he will protect her. Ismaele loves Fenena who rescued him when, as Jewish envoy in Babylon, he was thrown in prison. They are interrupted by Abigaille, reputedly Fenena's elder sister, also in love with Ismaele. Abigaille tells Ismaele that if he will love her, she can save both him and his people, the Hebrews.

EXCERPT 2 Kal i pp. 172/4/3–191 10 min.

Abigaille, soprano (see excerpt 1), and Nabucco, baritone (B1–F3), are in this scene with silent guards.

Abigaille has been installed as Regent, with the support of the priests, who demand the death of the captive Jews, amongst them Fenena. Nabucco is led into Abigaille's presence, and there is an extended duet between the King and his supposed daughter.

Nightingale

Charles Strouse (1928–)

Ancient China

EXCERPT 1 GS e pp. 17/1/2–42/2/2 11 min.

The Storyteller, baritone, begins this scene with the Nightingale, soprano, singing offstage. Children may be used in the scene, but they may be omitted. Later the Emperor, baritone, and his two Aides (simple solo and two-part singing) are heard. There is also a Maid, soprano, and optional parts for additional Maids, if desired. The music, designed to be sung either by adults for children or by children for adults has easy ranges and would be appropriate for workshops training singers for musicals.

Adapted from the Hans Christian Andersen story, the Storyteller tells of an Emperor who is reading about the Nightingale in a book. The Emperor bemoans the fact that he has not heard the Nightingale sing when all the people of China love the bird. Then the Maid is seen beginning her day of drudgery in the castle and telling that she is happy because she often hears the Nightingale reminding her that life is worthwhile. The Emperor's Aides, hearing what the Maid says, ask her to show them where they can find the Nightingale to take to the Emperor who is demanding to see it.

EXCERPT 2 GS e pp. 81/3/1–89/2/3; 100/4/3–101; 111/3/2–117 8 1/2 min.

The Emperor, the Maid, and the Nightingale have the major speaking, singing, and acting in this scene. The Aides could be used in all other parts or characters could be added. (See excerpt 1 for vocal descriptions.) At the cut, the Emperor should collapse and appear to be dying (use any of the music within the cut to accompany this mime) in order that the Nightingale may restore him to life.

The opening conversation includes the Emperor, the Maid, and the Aides, all of whom are making ready for the Nightingale's appearance. When the Nightingale sings, the Emperor is moved, but soon he collapses, and everyone is sure he is dying until the Nightingale sings again, and he recovers.

EXCERPT 3 GS e pp. 126/2/2–135/1/1 5 min.

A scene for the Emperor, baritone, and the Nightingale, who has a two-octave range, G2–G4.

The Emperor is happy to have the Nightingale singing to him, but the Nightingale protests that an artist must be free.

Oberon

Carl Maria von Weber (1786–1826)

Oberon's kingdom, Baghdad, France, Tunis, early ninth century

(Note: English is the original language of this opera, but because Weber was German, the opera is often performed in German. Timings are for the G. Schirmer version in which dialogue is replaced with recitatives by Artur Bodanzky. The English dialogue is not easily available.)

EXCERPT 1 GS e, g pp. 18–25 (E-major cadence) 5 1/2 min.
Kal g pp. 18–21

The first scene begins with dialogue by Puck and Droll and continues with an aria by Oberon, tenor (C2–G3), and ends after Oberon's speaking line, "Der dir's befahl." In the G. Schirmer version, there is only a recitative for Puck.

Oberon and Titania, fairy king and queen, have quarreled and will not be reunited until they find a pair of unquestionably faithful lovers. Puck suggests Huon de Bordeaux, who is being punished by Charlemagne and required to kidnap the Caliph of Baghdad's daughter, Rezia.

EXCERPT 2 GS e, g pp. 35/3/2–44 7 min.
Kal g pp. 30/3/3–35

Huon of Bordeaux, Count of Guyenne, is a dramatic tenor (D2–B♭3) who sings in a high tessitura and needs flexibility and a trill. For such a tenor, this scene including the dialogue with Sherasmin, would be short but very impressive. In some performances, there is more explanation written into the dialogue and this could be done by the director. Sherasmin is a baritone in the recitative version.

This is the beginning of the adventures of Huon and his squire Sherasmin.

EXCERPT 3 GS e, g pp. 45–61 10 min.
Kal g pp. 36–48

Rezia is a soprano (B♭2–B4) who has a difficult role that requires a dramatic voice for both flexible and sustained passages. Fatime, mezzo-soprano (A2–F4) who also needs flexibility and a trill, has solo singing as well as a duet with Rezia. A chorus could be used, as shown in the score, but it is not necessary because the solo can be sung without the chorus under it.

In a splendid hall in the palace of Harun al Raschid in Baghdad, Rezia is waiting to be rescued. Soon Fatime, her servant, rushes in to tell her that the knight has come to claim her as she so desires.

EXCERPT 3a GS e, g pp. 45–56/2/1 7 min.
Kal g pp. 36–44/3/1

This excerpt is the same as excerpt 3, ending before the entrance of the chorus.

EXCERPT 4 GS e, g pp. 71–83 6 min.
Kal g pp. 52–61 (dialogue)

Huon, Rezia, and Fatime (described in previous excepts), and Scherasmin, baritone, are together in this scene. Fatime has an ariette that is missing from the G. Schirmer score but could be inserted at p. 72/1/3;

this is followed by a quartet for the two couples. If dialogue is used, cuts could be made on p. 55 of the Kalmus score.

In a garden behind the Caliph's palace, the two couples are making their escape. All are joyous as they head for the ship that will take them to Huon's homeland, Askalon.

EXCERPT 5 GS e, g pp. 96–107 10 min.
(plus four E♭-major chords)
Kal g pp. 71–79/2/5

Huon and Rezia are in this scene, but Huon has only a short prayer. Rezia has her aria, the famous "Ocean, Thou Mighty Monster!"

Puck has had the ship washed onto a deserted shore during a storm at sea, and now Huon, who has lost the magic horn given him to summon Oberon, prays that Rezia be saved. When he finds that she is alive, he goes for help while she sings about the sea.

EXCERPT 6 GS e, g pp. 128–48 12 min.
Kal g pp. 92–104

This excerpt includes Fatime, Sherasmin, and Huon (see excerpts 2 and 3) with a short dialogue by Puck, who could be lyric tenor or mezzo-soprano in the recitative version.

Fatime and Sherasmin have been sold as slaves to the Emir of Tunis, and they open the scene with arias and a duet. Puck then brings Huon in, and he learns that Rezia, whom the pirates captured, is also in the palace. The three rejoice in a trio, which ends the scene.

EXCERPT 6a GS e, g pp. 128–41/3/6 8 min.
Kal g pp. 92–101/4/6

The portion of excerpt 6 for Fatima and Sherasmin only.

L'Oca del Cairo (The Goose from Cairo)

Wolfgang Amadeus Mozart (1756–1791)

Ripasecca, capital of Marchesato

EXCERPT 1 Car i pp. 8–57/2/5 23 1/2 min.

This unfinished opera has seven characters, all of whom appear in this scene. Auretta, soprano (E3–A4), would be the lightest of the three sopranos; Lavina (E♭3–B♭4) has a lower line in the ensembles; and Celidora, lyric-spinto with flexibility (C3–A♭4), must carry the top line in the quartet. Biondello is a lyric tenor (E♭2–G3), while Calandrino (B♭1–F♯3) is a character tenor (in spite of the range, the tessitura is definitely too high for a baritone). Don Pippo, bass-baritone (A1–F♯3), and Chichibio, baritone (C2–D3), complete the cast. The excerpt ends with a quartet for two sopranos and two tenors.

Don Pippo, absolute ruler of the seaport of Ripasecca, has exiled his wife and wants to marry Lavina, who is really in love with Calandrino. Biondello is in love with Don Pippo's daughter, Celidora, who has been promised in marriage to someone else; however, Don Pippo makes a bet with Biondello that he may marry Celidora if he can penetrate the fortress in which the girls are imprisoned. As the opera opens, Don Pippo is giving orders to his chambermaid, Auretta. She is then joined by her lover, Chichibio, the Majordomo, and explains how the other two pairs of lovers plan to catch Don Pippo in his own trap. Celidora appears in the garden; Biondello comes to meet her; they are later joined by Lavina and Calandrino; the four plot their escape in a lively quartet.

EXCERPT 1a Car i pp. 8–27 9 min.

Auretta, Chichibio, and Don Pippo, as described in excerpt 1, are in this scene.

EXCERPT 1b Car i pp. 19–27 4 min.

A short scene from excerpt 1 for Auretta and Chichibio.

EXCERPT 1c Car i pp. 30–57/2/5 13 1/2 min.

Celidora and Biondello have individual arias in this portion of excerpt 1, ending with a quartet when they are joined by Lavina and Calandrino.

EXCERPT 1d Car i pp. 30–41 7 1/2 min.

Celidora and Biondello have individual arias, but the scene ends before the quartet with Lavina and Calandrino.

EXCERPT 2 Car i pp. 58/1/2–82 11 1/2 min.

The already described Auretta, Calandrino, and Chichibio are in this excerpt.

Calandrino bribes Auretta into helping him and Biondello build a mechanical toy goose in which Biondello can hide. As they are singing the duet, Chichibio appears and becomes extremely suspicious. After confronting Auretta, Chichibio leaves the stage and Calandrino ends the scene with a very fast aria about the fickleness of women.

EXCERPT 2a Car i pp. 71/2/1–82 5 1/2 min.

Auretta and Chichibio sing in this portion of excerpt 2.

EXCERPT 3 Car i pp. 83–97/2/4 7 min.

Don Pippo and Lavina sing a duet in this scene; Auretta, Calandrino, and the Goose (tenor) sing only in the recitatives.

Don Pippo, determined to marry Lavina, calls in his servants. Auretta announces that the Sultan of Cairo has sent a special present of a large goose who can predict the future. The goose announces that if Don Pippo marries Lavina, disaster will strike, and that if Celidora is allowed to marry the man she loves, all will be well. Don Pippo immediately begins plotting to change the course of events, and Lavina pretends to be on his side even though she has no intention of marrying him.

EXCERPT 3a Car i pp. 91/3/1–97/2/4 3 min.

This is the short duet of Don Pippo and Lavina from excerpt 3.

Of Mice and Men

Carlisle Floyd (1926-)

A ranch in California, 1930s

EXCERPT 1 Bel e pp. 1–36 20 1/2 min.

Act 1, scene 1, calls for two physically strong young men with rather dramatic voices. Lennie, tenor (C2–B♭3), should be able to project childlike innocence as well as physical strength, and should be able to sing high pianissimo. George, baritone (F♯1–F♯3), requires authority and strength throughout range but has legato singing as well. (Lower and higher options are found throughout his role.)

George and his slow-witted traveling companion, Lennie, who has the strength of a giant and the mind of a child, are in constant difficulty with their employers and the law. As part of their almost daily routine, George expresses his exasperation at Lennie in an aria, "I must be crazy trav'lin' with you," followed by a reconciliation. Lennie is carrying a dead mouse that he has killed by petting it. When George forces him to throw it away, Lennie protests in the aria "It was something I could stroke," telling of his love for soft things he can pet. To humor Lennie, George recounts their dream of a small house and farm of their own, with many pets for Lennie. As Lennie becomes more excited, this develops into a rapturous duet.

EXCERPT 2 Bel e pp. 41–53 6 1/2 min.

Curley's wife is a lyric-spinto soprano (A2–C5) and should be an attractive, flirtatious young woman. Curley, tenor (D2–A3), needs to be young and handsome but temperamental. Candy, an old ranch hand (bass), sings only a few lines.

Curley's wife comes to the bunkhouse against Curley's wishes, while Curley is there waiting for his new ranchhands. This triggers a violent argument as she accuses him of neglect and indifference, threatening to seek attention elsewhere.

EXCERPT 3 Bel e pp. 91/2/1–138 21 1/2 min.

In addition to Curley's wife, Curley, Lennie, and George, the scene calls for Slim, lyric baritone (B1–G3), and Candy, bass (A♭1–D3). There is an optional Ab3 for George in his aria, "I ain't gonna buck grain." Carlson, a ranch hand, is silent in this scene.

Perusing a newspaper, George discovers a want ad for a small house and farm. Reading the want ad to Lennie, George is overheard by Candy, who asks to join them in their venture. As the three men sing of their excitement and dance exuberantly, Curley's wife enters and the merriment abruptly stops. George urges her to leave before her husband finds her, but she insists on staying until Curley arrives. Suspicious and threatened, Curley provokes a fight with Lennie, who, when George shouts to him to defend himself, crushes Curley's hand. After extracting a promise from Curley that George and Lennie won't be fired, Slim and Carlson exit with Curley and his wife. George reads the want ad again as the curtain falls.

EXCERPT 3a Bel e pp. 91/2/1–103/1/4 7 min.

The opening of excerpt 3—Slim and George only.

EXCERPT 3b Bel e pp. 91/2/1–117/3/3 12 min.

The opening of excerpt 3 through the trio—Slim, George, Lennie, and Candy are included.

EXCERPT 4 Bel e pp. 139–64/4/1 13 1/2 min.

Curley's wife (soprano) and Lennie (tenor).

Lennie enters the barn holding his puppy that he has inadvertently killed. He hides the puppy quickly when Curley's wife enters. In a melodic duet, she tells how she is leaving the ranch to go to Hollywood to become a movie star, while he dreams of his own farm with lots of pets. He tells her of his love for stroking soft things, and she invites him to stroke her hair. As he continues to stroke her hair, she becomes first annoyed and then terrified, screaming at him to let go. Lennie, frightened that he might be discovered with her, first tries to smother her screams, and then, shaking her violently, breaks her neck. He leaves the barn quietly, hoping not to be discovered near her dead body.

EXCERPT 5 Bel e pp. 183/3/1–206 13 1/2 min.

Lennie and George, as described in excerpt 1, with Slim and Curley who have a few lines offstage, and a chorus of ranch hands. At the end, a Ballad Singer sings, whistles, or plays a few bars of music on a harmonica, as the ranch hands appear onstage without singing.

Lennie, shivering with dread and filled with remorse, waits for George in the same clearing where they were seen in excerpt 1. When Slim and Curley are heard offstage, George assures Lennie that they are not the target of the search and, to Lennie's delight, recounts their dream once again. At the moment Lennie ecstatically imagines their house in the distance, George takes his pistol and shoots Lennie. When the ranch hands and Curley converge on the two men, they realize what has happened. They exit, indifferent to the tragedy, and only Slim stays behind as the ballad is heard before the curtain falls.

L'Ormindo

Francesco Cavalli (1602–1676), realized by Raymond Leppard

North Africa: The city of Fez

EXCERPT 1 Fab f, e, g pp. 1–41 22 min.

The opening scenes of the opera begin with a solo by Ormindo, tenor (D2–G3), who is in love with Erisbe, and this is followed by a declaration by Amida, baritone (C♯2–E3), also in love with Erisbe. They continue with a duet and then Amida's page, Nerillo, mezzo-soprano (D3–F4), left alone onstage, sings humorously of a young page's observation. Sicle, mezzo-soprano (E3–G4), Melide, mezzo-soprano (C3–C4), and Erice, tenor (E2–G3), enter to find the page and indulge in conversation. After Nerillo leaves, Sicle has a solo, and Erice, who remains onstage, concludes the scene with an aria. None of the music is difficult except for learning the style of this early baroque period, and the possibility of singing all the optional ornamentations.

Ormindo, Prince of Tunis, and Amida, Prince of Tremisene, discover that they are in love with the same woman, Erisbe, Queen of Morocco and Fez. Because they are friends, they decide not to fight but to let Queen Erisbe decide between them. Nerillo then has a comic interlude, and Sicle, Princess of Susio, enters with her waiting woman, Melide, and her old nurse, Erice. They are disguised as Egyptians. In a fortune-telling sequence, Nerillo admits that Erisbe is loved by both Amida and Ormindo, and Sicle swears revenge because Amida has abandoned her for Erisbe. Erice comments cynically in an aria at the end of the scene.

EXCERPT 1a Fab i, e, g pp. 1–22/2/4 11 1/2 min.

The scene with Ormindo, Amida, and Nerillo, ending with Nerillo's comic commentary.

EXCERPT 1b Fab i, e, g pp. 22/3/1–41 10 1/2 min.

The portion of excerpt 1 beginning with the entrance of Melide, Sicle, and Erice and their encounter with Nerillo.

EXCERPT 1c Fab i, e, g pp. 22/3/1–37 8 min.

This excerpt omits the aria by Erice.

EXCERPT 2 Fab i, e, g pp. 42–82 23 min.

Erisbe, soprano, and Mirinda, mezzo-soprano, are the principal characters in this scene. Both have singing demanding some flexibility. Ormindo, tenor, and Amida, baritone, also have extended declarations of love for Erisbe (see excerpt 1 for ranges). King Ariadeno, bass (A1–C3), has a short expression of love for his young Queen.

Erisbe, Queen of Morocco and Fez, enters the royal gardens with her waiting woman, Mirinda. Erisbe tells Mirinda that being married to such an old man as King Ariadeno makes her enjoy arousing desire in young admirers. When Ormindo and Amida arrive, each hides while the other pours out his love to Erisbe. When Mirinda announces that the old King is arriving, Ormindo and Amida must leave, and now the King expresses his love for his young wife, and she returns his affection as well. They exit from the garden, and Mirinda sings of the disaster that accompanies a young woman married to an old, old man.

EXCERPT 2a Fab i, e, g pp. 42–70/2/1 14 1/2 min.

The portion of excerpt 2, concluding before the entrance of King Ariadeno.

EXCERPT 2b Fab i, e, g pp. 42–76 19 min.

The scene without Mirinda's solo at the conclusion.

EXCERPT 3 Fab i, e, g pp. 83–109/2/7 14 1/2 min.

This excerpt opens with a duet by Erisbe, soprano, and Mirinda, mezzo-soprano. It also includes Amida, baritone; Sicle, mezzo-soprano; Melide, mezzo soprano; and Erice, tenor (see excerpt 1 for ranges).

Queen Erisbe and Mirinda are in the palace when Amida enters. They begin to converse, but very shortly Sicle enters with Melide and Erice, still disguised as Egyptians. Having acquired some knowledge earlier from Nerillo, Sicle reads Amida's palm and reveals to Erisbe Amida's faithlessness to her. Erisbe turns her affections to Ormindo. The scene again ends with a ritornello by a servant, this time Melide.

EXCERPT 3a Fab i, e, g pp. 83–104 11 min.

The same as excerpt 3 without the final solo by Melide.

EXCERPT 4 Fab i, e, g pp. 109/3/1–121 7 min.

Scene 7 of the opera is a short scene between Queen Erisbe, soprano, and Ormindo, tenor, ending in a duet.

The frivolous young Queen has been gradually replaced by a more mature, ardent woman who has chosen Ormindo over Amida. Erisbe maintains that she will go with Ormindo when he leaves with his troops, regardless of the consequences.

EXCERPT 5 Fab i, e, g pp. 122–53 19 min.

Nerillo, mezzo-soprano, could open this scene with the aria that begins act 2. Others include Erice, the old nurse, tenor; Sicle, mezzo-soprano; and Amida, baritone. Melide appears but does not sing in this excerpt.

The page, Nerillo, sings about the city of Fez as he and Amida journey toward a cavern outside the walls, where Amida has been told he should go. When Sicle and her servants arrive at the cave, they dispense with the Egyptian disguises, and when Amida appears, he is told that Sicle has killed herself because Amida has been unfaithful. Amida, believing she is dead when she appears as a ghost, is restored to his love for her when she reveals that she lives. They conclude with a love duet.

EXCERPT 5a Fab i, e, g pp. 128–53 15 1/2 min.

The same as excerpt 5 except the aria for Nerillo is not included.

EXCERPT 6 Fab i, e, g pp. 154–212 29 min.

Mirinda, mezzo-soprano, opens this excerpt with a ritornello. The sinfonia that precedes King Ariadeno's aria could be cut if the scene is being done without the proper instruments. Captain Osmano of King Ariandeno's forces, baritone (D2a–E3), Ormindo, Erisbe, Sicle, and Amida (see earlier excerpts for description) are included in this final scene. The repetition of an earlier duet for Ormindo and Erisbe has been added after the final quintet.

Mirinda wonders what the King will do when he finds that Ormindo and Erisbe have eloped but have been blown back to Fez by an unfavorable wind and cast in prison. Soon we find that the King asks Osmano to go to the prison and give them poison. Osmano substitutes a sleeping potion. The lovers wake to be greeted by the King, who abdicates the throne and the Queen to his younger rival.

EXCERPT 6a Fab i, e, g pp. 159–212 26 min.

This could begin with the sinfonia on p. 159 or could start with King Ariadeno on p. 160, eliminating only Mirinda's ritornello from excerpt 6.

EXCERPT 6b Fab i, e, g pp. 154–200; 213–15 27 1/2 min.

Excerpt 6, omitting the entrance of Sicle and Amida; ending with the original duet in place of the quintet.

EXCERPT 6c Fab i, e, g pp. 159–200; 213–15 24 1/2 min.

A shorter version of excerpt 6b could omit Mirinda's ritornello.

EXCERPT 6d Fab i, e, g pp. 159–64; 172–200; 213–15 21 min.

An even shorter version of 6b, eliminating the character of Mirinda altogether.

Owen Wingrave

Benjamin Britten (1913–1976)

London, late nineteenth century

EXCERPT 1 Fab e, g pp. 1–26 14 1/2 min.
3/3/5–26 11 1/2 min.

Owen Wingrave, the last of the Wingraves, is a baritone (G♯1–G3), who with Spencer Coyle, bass-baritone (A1–F♯3), has most of the singing in this scene. Lechmere, tenor with a high B♭, is a young student at Coyle's military cramming establishment and is also included in this excerpt.

If the ten portraits of the Wingrave men are shown at the beginning of the excerpt, the prelude is needed. If not, the excerpt could begin with p. 3/4/1. It takes place in the study at Mr. Coyle's military establishment.

Lechmere is an ardent student in Mr. Coyle's school, but Owen Wingrave, also a student, tells Coyle that he cannot bring himself to follow in the footsteps of all the preceding generations of Wingrave men who have been in the military. Coyle cannot believe that his most gifted, heroic student refuses to become a soldier.

EXCERPT 2 B&H e, g pp. 40/5/2–58/4/1 9 min.

Again, Owen, Lechmere, and Coyle are present (see descriptions in excerpt 1), and Mrs. Coyle, a soprano (C3–B♭4), is included.

In a room at the Coyle's, Mr. and Mrs. Coyle are drinking sherry poured for them by Lechmere. Mrs. Coyle is the only one sympathetic to Owen's plight. When Owen enters, he asks if Coyle has spoken to his aunt, Miss Wingrave, and Coyle tells Owen he has, and that she has asked that he return to Paramore where they will "straighten you out."

EXCERPT 3 B&H e, g pp. 59/2/2–79/3/2 10 1/2 min.

A scene for three women: Mrs. Julian, soprano (E♭3–A4), a widow and dependent at Paramore; Kate, mezzo-soprano (B♭2–G♯4), Mrs. Julian's daughter; and Miss Wingrave, dramatic soprano (B♭2–A♭4), Owen's aunt. Each woman has solo lines and a short trio portion before Owen (previously described) enters.

Each of the women has been looking out a window of the house, waiting for Owen to arrive. (It would be possible to place them in other circumstances as long as their reflective speeches were not said to each other.) When Owen arrives he remains resolute. He will not be a soldier.

EXCERPT 3a B&H e, g pp. 59/2/2–68/3/1 5 min.

The portion for the three women before Owen enters.

EXCERPT 4 B&H e, g pp. 79/3/2–92 4 min.

Another scene for the three women described in excerpt 3, and General Sir Philip Wingrave, tenor (D2–B♭3). Owen has no singing but he must be there. There is quartet singing in this scene.

For a week, Owen has been under constant attack from these members of the Wingrave household who cannot understand his attitude. Again they are upbraiding him for insulting the family with his behavior.

EXCERPT 5 B&H e, g pp. 155/1/2–180/2/2 12 min.

This excerpt features Owen with Mrs. Julian, Kate, Lechmere, Mr. and Mrs. Coyle, and Miss Wingrave (all described in previous scenes). It includes an aria for Owen. If the ten portraits are not used, there could be a cut from p. 173/2/5 to p. 175/3/1.

Owen has been disinherited by Sir Philip Wingrave, which causes Mrs. Julian to feel that all her dreams of Kate marrying Owen and becoming the next mistress of Paramore have been lost. Kate even seems to accept the flirtatious suit of Lechmere. Only Mrs. Coyle has sincere sympathy for Owen. Left alone, Owen rejoices in his freedom and, addressing the portraits of his ancestors, extols the virtues of peace.

EXCERPT 6 B&H e, g pp. 173/3/1–197/1/1 13 min.

This scene begins with the aria of Owen (excerpt 5) and concludes with the duet of Owen and Kate (see descriptions in excerpts 1 and 3). The apparitions of an old man and a boy appear.

Kate makes one final plea with Owen to become a soldier; he steadfastly refuses, begging her not to leave him but to share his life. Defiantly, he offers to prove his bravery by sleeping in the haunted room. He enters, and she turns her key to lock him in.

The Pilgrim's Progress

Ralph Vaughan Williams (1872–1958)

Bedford, England, about 1675

EXCERPT 1 Ox e, g pp. 1–19/3/4 (E-major cadence) 12 min.

This combination of the prologue and act 1, scene 1, uses John Bunyan, bass-baritone (E2–E3); the Pilgrim, baritone (D2–F♭3); and the Evangelist, bass (D2–D3). In lesser roles are the four neighbors, who are two tenors, a baritone, and a bass. None of the voice ranges in this opera are extreme.

The scene opens with Bunyan who is writing the last words of *The Pilgrim's Progress.* Then he stands and, turning to his hearers, reads from the beginning. As he reads, there appears a vision of the Pilgrim with a burden on his back, and this leads directly into the scene where the Evangelist appears and directs the Pilgrim to the Wicket Gate. As the Pilgrim is about to leave, the four neighbors warn him of the dangers to come.

EXCERPT 2 Ox e, g pp. 85–93 6 min.

A very short excerpt requiring the Pilgrim and the Evangelist (see excerpt 1) and Two Heavenly Beings, soprano and mezzo-soprano.

The Pilgrim, exhausted from fighting Apollyon who has barred his way, collapses. The Two Heavenly Beings restore him with leaves and the water of life, and the Evangelist appears once more to give the Pilgrim the Staff of Salvation, the Roll of the Word, and the Key of Promise, and to warn him of further dangers at the town of Vanity.

EXCERPT 3 Ox e, g pp. 155–68 11 min.

This is a solo scene for the Pilgrim and could be combined with other scenes from this opera.

The Pilgrim, who has been thrown into prison, cries out that God has forsaken him. Suddenly, he remembers the Key of Promise, and as if by magic, the prison gates fly open, and the Pilgrim once more goes on his journey.

EXCERPT 4 Ox e, g pp. 169–87 11 min.

In the first scene of act 4, the part of the Woodcutter's Boy can be taken by a soprano or boy treble (E♭3–F4). Also included are the Pilgrim, baritone, and Mr. and Mrs. By-Ends, buffo tenor and mezzo-soprano.

At the edge of a wood, a boy sings cheerfully at his work. The Pilgrim interrupts his song to ask how far it is to the Celestial City, and he says it is not far. Mr. and Mrs. By-Ends enter and would like to join the Pilgrim but do not care for his stern views. The Pilgrim refuses to accept such companions who will not desert their old principles, and he goes on his way.

EXCERPT 5 Ox e, g pp. 190–212/6/2 20 min.

The cast of this excerpt includes the Pilgrim (previously described); Three Shepherds—tenor, baritone, and bass; the Voice of a Bird, soprano; and the Celestial Messenger, tenor.

As his journey continues, the Pilgrim meets Three Shepherds, who welcome him and ask him to rest in the Delectable Mountains, where flowers appear in the land and birds sing the praises of God. A Messenger enters to warn the Pilgrim that he must make ready to cross the river.

EXCERPT 5a Ox e, g pp. 190–206/1/4 9 1/2 min.

The same as 4c except ending before the Celestial Messenger sings.

Porgy and Bess

George Gershwin (1898–1937)

Charleston, South Carolina, 1930s

EXCERPT 1 Chap e pp. 14/4/1–41/1/2 (end on G-minor chord) 11 1/2 min.

The excerpt opens with the famous solo "Summertime" sung by Clara, soprano (F♯3–F♯4), while other black women have a three-part chorus with the second verse. Clara's husband, Jake, baritone (D2–F3); Mingo, tenor; Sporting Life, tenor; Jim, baritone; and Robbins, tenor, are shooting craps with a group of black men who have a short three-part chorus. Jake sings "Yes, a woman is a sometime thing" and is joined by the other men and women.

Clara is sitting in a chair, holding her baby, and surrounded by friends while singing the well-known lullaby. Then she moves to the area where her husband, Jake, is shooting craps with his friends, and he takes the child and attempts to sing him to sleep. When Jake hands the crying child back to Clara, his friends urge him to return to the crap game.

EXCERPT 1a Chap e pp. 14/4/1–17/2/4 2 1/2 min.

Clara's "Summertime," sung either with or without the women's chorus, is a very short excerpt.

EXCERPT 1b Chap e pp. 14/4/1–17/2/3; 32/2/2–41/1/2 (end on G-minor chord) 6 min.

This excerpt eliminates the solo lines of Jim as well as much of the music between the two well-known selections mentioned in excerpt 1.

EXCERPT 2 Chap e pp. 150/1/2–161/1/4 5 1/2 min.

After Porgy, baritone (C♯2–D3), ponders what has happened to his friends since Crown killed Robbins, Serena, soprano (E3–B4), sings the familiar "My man's gone now," supported by a mixed chorus.

Porgy, a crippled beggar, must play his role on knees on a little cart. He opens this scene explaining how Crown has killed Serena's husband, Robbins, but now Crown has gone his way, while Peter has been jailed. Then Serena, surrounded by her friends, sings of the death of her husband.

EXCERPT 2a Chap e pp. 154–61/1/4 4 min.

This is Serena's aria only.

EXCERPT 3 Chap e pp. 196/1/2–207/2/2 3 min.

A short conversation between Clara and Jake leads into Porgy's famous "I got plenty o' nuttin'" (C2–D3), which he sings as a solo and then with mixed chorus. Serena, soprano, and Maria, mezzo-soprano, each have one solo line.

A crowd is gathered at Catfish Row, talking about getting the nets ready for fishing, when Porgy appears at his window and sings his aria. The crowd joins him on the reprise.

EXCERPT 3a Chap e pp. 197/2/2–207/2/2 2 1/2 min.

The scene could begin without Clara and Jake's conversation, but start directly with "I got plenty o' nuttin'."

EXCERPT 4 Chap e pp. 244–60; 270/1/5–276 10 min.

Bess, soprano; Sporting Life, tenor (F2–A3); and Jake, baritone, have opening lines in this excerpt. The major singing is done by Porgy (B♭1–D3, opt. E♭3) and Bess (C♯3–A♯4) in their duet of "Bess, you is my woman now." Both should have strong voices capable of sustained singing. Then, at the cut, Maria, contralto, also has a few lines.

All of those on Catfish Row are planning a picnic on Kittiwah Island and they urge Bess to go with them. Bess insists she is going to stay with Porgy, but after Porgy and Bess have expressed their affection for each other in a duet, Maria enters and convinces Bess she should go. Porgy gives his permission and ends the scene with a short reprise of "I got plenty o' nuttin'."

EXCERPT 4a Chap e pp. 244–60 7 1/2 min.

The portion of excerpt 4 that concludes with "Bess, you is my woman now."

EXCERPT 4b Chap e pp. 252–60; 270/1/5–276 7 min.

This begins with Porgy and Bess singing their duet and continues with Maria convincing Bess to go to the picnic.

EXCERPT 5 Chap e pp. 277–95 6 1/2 min.

This excerpt requires a crowd, some dancing, some playing mouth organs, combs, bones. Some are playing African drums, a washboard, and a washtub. They are also the chorus for Sporting Life, tenor (D2–G♭3), when he sings "It ain't necessarily so."

At the picnic on Kittiwah Island, everyone is full of gaiety. All participate in the singing and dancing, which feature Sporting Life, who should be excellent in stage movement as well as an exciting singer.

EXCERPT 6 Chap e pp. 302/4/2–322 7 min.

Crown, baritone (C2–F3, opt. G♭3), and Bess, soprano (E♭3–B4), have considerable action and singing in this scene, including a duet portion.

Crown, responsible for Robbins' death, has been hiding on Kittiwah Island for some time and misses Bess, with whom he lived for five years. He stops Bess as she starts to leave with the crowd and speaks with her. He urges her to stay with him and she refuses, but he insists and she finally weakens.

EXCERPT 7 Chap e pp. 524/2/1–559 11 min.

Porgy, offstage, calls for Bess, and as he enters, he asks Maria where Bess is. Maria, mezzo-soprano, and Serena, soprano, try to tell him that he is better off without Bess. A mixed chorus is necessary for the finale of the opera, and those singers can take the small solo lines in this scene, including Lily (mezzo-soprano) and Mingo (tenor). Scipio, a small boy, completes the scene.

During the time that Porgy has been in jail for contempt of court, Bess has gone to New York with Sporting Life. When Porgy learns that she is in New York, he calls for his goat cart and claims that he will go the thousand miles to find her.

Postcard from Morocco

Dominick Argento (1927–)

A railway station, about 1914 (can be very abstract)

EXCERPT 1 B&H e 1–46 8 min.

The opera calls for seven singers of contrasting vocal types, each playing more than one character in a very surrealistic manner. They are: Coloratura Soprano (D♭3–E5, opt. G5), with much sustained singing in an extremely high tessitura; Soprano, lyric or spinto (B♭2–C5, opt. C♯5), capable of sustaining a line in the middle range; Mezzo-Soprano (G♭2–G♯4, opt. A4); Lyric Tenor (C♯2–B3, opt. B1) with some flexibility, has a high tessitura; Tenor (C2–B♭3) of a heavier timbre and control of pianissimo; Baritone (F1–G3), preferably a dramatic baritone; and Bass (F1–F3, opt. D1 and B♭3) with the same wide range but lower timbre than the Baritone. All specific characters listed for future scenes will refer to the capitalized voice types specified by the composer and listed above.

This excerpt features a Lady with a Hand Mirror (Coloratura Soprano) supported by the remainder of the ensemble.

The seven principals, along with several cardboard figures, are presumably waiting in a railway station. The Bass approaches one of the cardboard figures and carries on a conversation about the person for whom he is waiting. The Lady with a Hand Mirror sings about her mirror, and eventually the other seven singers join in with thoughts about themselves and occasional questions to the other real or imaginary people.

EXCERPT 2 B&H e pp. 47–81 7 min.

Time suddenly shifts ahead to a puppet show in which the Lyric Tenor and the Baritone actually play puppets. Soon the remainder of the ensemble join in their dialogue.

EXCERPT 3 B&H e pp. 82–107/2/6 10 1/2 min.

The Foreign Singer (Mezzo-Soprano) sings a cabaretlike exotic song in an unidentifiable language (gibberish), and the Lyric Tenor sings an amusing aria about his old suitcase, joined by the rest of the ensemble. The Foreign Singer should also be able to do some sort of exotic dance.

EXCERPT 4 B&H e pp. 117/2/1–141 5 1/2 min.

A trio for the three women's voices described in excerpt 1.

The Mezzo-Soprano is now a Lady with a Hatbox; the scenario becomes quite amusing as the other two women question her incessantly about her profession.

EXCERPT 5 B&H e pp. 177–205 12 min.

The featured singers in this scene are Coloratura Soprano, Soprano, Lyric Tenor, and Tenor (see excerpt 1), with supporting parts from Mezzo-Soprano, Baritone, and Bass.

Two Operetta Singers (Coloratura Soprano and Lyric Tenor) sing a romantic operetta duet (in German!), while the Lady with a Cake Box (Soprano) watches attentively. When questioned about the box she is carrying, she sings an aria, while all others are quiet. The Tenor speaks up, saying that he may have seen her with her lover, and the scene ends with the Operetta Singers and the Soprano and Tenor singing two duets simultaneously.

EXCERPT 5a B&H e pp. 185–205 10 min.

Because of the surrealistic nature of this opera, the three supporting parts in the above scene could be eliminated in this shortened version. The Baritone line on p. 186 could be sung by the Tenor, while the word "Where?" on p. 192 could be sung by the three remaining principals rather than all six.

Le Prophète (The Prophet)

Giacomo Meyerbeer (1791–1864)

EXCERPT 1 Kal f pp. 39–46 5 1/2 min.

An excerpt for the two leading ladies of the opera: Berthe, soprano (E3–C5), and Fidès, mezzo-soprano (A2–A4), both requiring flexibility.

The Count Oberthal's permission is needed in order for Berthe to marry Jean (John of Leyden); because the Count himself has fallen in love with Berthe, he denies it and orders Berthe to his castle; she insists on being accompanied by Jean's mother, Fidès. In this duet, Berthe is pleading her case to her beloved's mother, who is sympathetic.

EXCERPT 2 Kal f pp. 62/3/4–109 27 1/2 min.

This excerpt features seven principals of the opera—Berthe, Fidès (opt. F♯2 at end of aria); Jean, dramatic tenor (C♯2–B♭3, opt. D4); Oberthal, bass (B♭1–E♭3); and the three Anabaptists—Jonas, tenor; Mathisen, baritone; and Zacharie, bass.

Jean is visited by the leader of the Anabaptists who tries to enlist him in their religious movement. Jean, being very much in love, declines their offer. Just then Berthe arrives, having escaped from the castle and Count Oberthal's unwanted attentions; she begs Jean to hide her. No sooner has he hidden his beloved in a safe place than Count Oberthal himself shows up. He drags forth Fidès, declaring he will kill her in front of her son if Jean refuses to give up Berthe. Unable to sacrifice his mother's life, Jean permits Berthe to be taken captive and agrees to join the religious movement.

EXCERPT 2a Kal f pp. 62/3/4–76/3/3 8 1/2 min.

Jean, who has an aria, is joined by Jonas, Mathisen, and Zacharie in this portion of excerpt 2.

EXCERPT 2b Kal f pp. 76/3/3–82 4 min.

This is the portion of the scene with Berthe, Jean, and Oberthal.

EXCERPT 2c Kal f pp. 87–109 11 min.

Jean, Jonas, Mathisen and Zacharie sing in this scene.

EXCERPT 3 Kal f pp. 171/1/3–195 10 min.

A rather difficult buffo trio for Jonas, Oberthal, and Zacharie (see decription above), with Mathisen singing only briefly in a recitative.

Count Oberthal has now been taken prisoner by the Anabaptists. Knowing he cannot escape, he joins them in their merriment in order to find out just what they are planning.

EXCERPT 4 Kal f pp. 231–61 16 1/2 min.

This excerpt contains an aria for Fidès and a duet for Fidès and Berthe. The scene also requires four burghers (tenor and bass).

Fidès is now wandering as a beggar in the streets of the captured city of Munster. Much to her joy, she meets Berthe, who has conceived a secret plan to destroy the "prophet," not knowing he is her own beloved Jean, Fidès' son, believed to have been killed in the revolt.

EXCERPT 4a Kal f pp. 245–61 9 1/2 min.

This is only the duet for Berthe and Fidès.

EXCERPT 5 Kal f pp. 319–64 27 min.

This excerpt contains a bravura aria for Fidès (with coloratura passages to C5), the duet of Fidès and Jean, after which they are joined by Berthe in a trio. Soldiers (silent) and an Officer (tenor) complete the scene.

Fidès, after many sad reproaches, finally forgives her son, Jean, and he agrees to give up his position as false prophet. Berthe enters, having just carried out her plan to destroy the prophet, and discovers to her horror that the prophet and her beloved Jean, thought to be dead, are the same person. Knowing that she is responsible for his demise, she stabs herself.

EXCERPT 5a Kal f pp. 319–46 16 1/2 min.

The portion of excerpt 5 with Fidès, Jean, and the Officer only.

Regina

Marc Blitzstein (1905–1964)

Bowden, Alabama, spring 1900

EXCERPT 1 Chap e pp. 11–32/3/2 12 1/2 min.

This excerpt begins with Birdie's aria, "Music, music, music," and continues through a large ensemble known as "Small Talk." Birdie (C3–D♭5) should be a lyric soprano with some coloratura flexibility; Regina (C3–F4) has a part that lies rather low in this scene—should be dramatic or spinto soprano; and her daughter, Alexandra, is sung by a lyric soprano (F3–B♭4). Of the two tenors, William Marshall has the higher tessitura (D2–B♭3); the other is Leo Hubbard (G2–A♭3). Oscar and Ben are both baritones; Oscar (C2–D3) has no particular range problems, while Ben is definitely the larger of the two baritone parts (B♭1–E♭3). Addie has only a small speaking part in the beginning of the scene, and Cal is silent.

As the scene opens, we hear Birdie Hubbard singing to Addie about her love for music. Her husband, Oscar, interrupts her to tell her that Mr. Marshall, honored guest from Chicago, and the rest of the family are retiring from the dining room. Ben Hubbard and Mr. Marshall have just closed a business deal, and everyone is celebrating.

EXCERPT 2 Chap e pp. 56 (dialogue)–69 7 min

The story is based on *The Little Foxes,* by Lillian Hellman, and in this scene we have Regina, soprano (C3–A4), who has most of the singing. Her daughter, Alexandra, reacts in this scene with speaking lines only.

Regina should begin with her speech on p. 56, "I have great news for you, Alexandra. You are going to Baltimore in the morning to bring your father home." To this Alexandra replies, "Papa said I should come?" and then Regina begins her singing on p, 57 and continues through p. 69. The last speech on p. 64 should be omitted, making it a scene for only two characters.

Regina Giddens' husband, Horace, president of the local bank, is under treatment for a heart ailment in a Baltimore hospital. After letters to Horace fail to bring the necessary money for Regina and her two brothers to establish a cotton mill in their small Southern town, Regina sends Alexandra to bring her father home.

EXCERPT 3 Chap e pp. 71–78 4 1/2 min.

An excerpt for Oscar's wife, Birdie Hubbard, soprano (E3–B4), and her niece, Alexandra Giddens, soprano (E3–G4), often called Zan. Birdie should have the stronger, more mature voice of the two lyric-coloratura sopranos.

Birdie is afraid that Alexandra will be forced to marry Birdie's son, Leo, and she urges her not to let this happen.

EXCERPT 4 Chap e pp. 98–115/4/1 10 1/2 min.

This scene is Horace's return from Baltimore. Horace is a bass (F1–D3), and the other singers in the excerpt are Regina, soprano (C3–G4); Oscar Hubbard, baritone (D2–D3); Benjamin Hubbard, baritone (E♭2–E♭3); Leo Hubbard, tenor (E2–G2); and Birdie Hubbard, soprano (F3–A4). Alexandra and Addie, the black maid, have speaking parts.

Alexandra has brought Horace, her father, home from Baltimore, and he is greeted by Addie as he enters the house. Then his wife, Regina, and her brothers, Oscar and Ben, enter. Finally Oscar's wife, Birdie, and their son, Leo, greet Horace. The balance of the excerpt is between Horace and his wife, Regina, and should end on the pianissimo chord at p. 115/4/1.

EXCERPT 4a Chap e pp. 108–15/4/1 5 min.

This is the portion of excerpt 4 using Regina and Horace only.

EXCERPT 5 Chap e pp. 179–93/2/1; 197/1/5–211 13 min.

The rain quartet requires Birdie, soprano (D3–G4); Alexandra, soprano (E3–B♭4); Addie, mezzo-soprano (G2–B♭3); and Horace, bass (G1–E♭3).

This rain quartet scene has no required action, and Birdie's aria that follows is reminiscent in quality. However, the characterizations should be well executed, and the director's creative ideas should make this an outstanding excerpt.

EXCERPT 5a Chap e pp. 179–93/2/1; 197–99 6 1/2 min.

This is the rain quartet only.

EXCERPT 5b Chap e pp. 200–211 6 1/2 min.

Birdie's solo could be staged with only Alexandra there as a companion.

Riders to the Sea

Ralph Vaughan Williams (1872–1958)

Ireland, nineteenth century

EXCERPT 1 Ox e pp. 2/4/1–24/4/1 11 min.

There is no problem with range for the major characters of this short opera: Maurya, contralto; Bartley, baritone; Cathleen and Nora, both sopranos.

Bartley is the youngest of Maurya's six sons, four of whom have been lost at sea, and the fifth, Michael, is presumed to have drowned recently as well. Bartley is planning to go to a horse fair when this scene begins. Maurya, mother of the boys and of two daughters, Cathleen and Nora, is distraught and pessimistic. She predicts, as Bartley leaves, that they will never see him again.

EXCERPT 2 Ox e pp. 31/2/3–60 16 min.

A scene for Maurya, contralto, her two daughters, Cathleen and Nora, and a mezzo-soprano who has a small amount of singing. There is also a four-part chorus of women, with some solo lines, singing offstage and later onstage. A few men are needed but they have no singing.

Maurya, who has been outside, enters and sits by the fire, while Cathleen asks questions over Maurya's laments. Again Maurya says that her youngest son will not return, and as the scene continues, Bartley's body is brought in and placed on the table. He has been thrown off the gray pony and into the sea. Now that her sons are all gone, Maurya is desolate and alone, while her two daughters are powerless to comfort her.

EXCERPT 2a Ox e pp. 48/3/2–60 7 min.

EXCERPT 2 might open with the body of Bartley already on the table, and Maurya, Nora, Cathleen, and the women's chorus in the room. Nora and Cathleen could serve as two of the voices in the wordless lament of the chorus. Maurya, contralto, has most of the solo singing.

Il Ritorno d'Ulisse in Patria (The Return of Ulysses to His Country)

Claudio Monteverdi (1567–1643)

2d millenium B.C., soon after the fall of Troy

EXCERPT 1 UE i pp. 13–239 1/2 min.

Penelope, mezzo-soprano (B♭2–D4), should be an actress capable of portraying nobility and chastity. The role contains mostly sustained, lyric singing. Ericlea, her nurse, has little singing in this scene; she is also a mezzo (E3–C4). (The Dallapiccola realization lists Penelope as a contralto, Melanto as a mezzo, Telemaco as a mezzo [in lieu of a male alto], and Eurimaco as a tenor. In d'Indy's version, Ulysses, Eurimaco, and Anfinomo were baritones, Telemaco a tenor, and Penelope a soprano.)

The opening scene takes place in a room of the royal palace. Penelope, Ulysses' wife, is attended by her nurse, Ericlea, as she bemoans her state of loneliness in a magnificent lament. Ulysses still has not returned from the war and she is desolate.

EXCERPT 2 UE i pp. 24–36 9 min.

Melanto is a soprano role with a low tessitura, typical of the early baroque era, and requiring agility; the role could be performed by a mezzo-soprano accustomed to doing coloratura (B2–G4). Eurimaco, tenor (C2–G3), also needs agility, sometimes in a low-to-middle tessitura.

A love scene for Melanto, Penelope's attendant, and Eurimaco.

EXCERPT 3 UE i pp. 48–70/2/4 17 1/2 min.

Ulysses, tenor (C♯2–G3), should be able to portray an aging character. The role, occasionally sung by a lyric baritone, calls for a great deal of strength in the lower range, yet requires agility throughout the range. Minerva is a light lyric soprano (C3–G4).

Ulysses awakens on the shore of Ithaca, where he has been abandoned by the Phaecians. He thinks he has been deposited in an unknown land and laments the fate that seems always to keep him from his native country. Minerva, disguised as a shepherd, appears to Ulysses, to comfort him and to spur him on to return home to his wife and the throne. Ulysses eventually recognizes Minerva, who tells him she will disguise him and he can return home to rout the suitors who have taken possession of his palace. Ulysses rejoices at his turn of fortune.

EXCERPT 4 UE i pp. 70/3/1–79/2/4 7 1/2 min.

Penelope, mezzo, and Melanto, soprano or mezzo, both sing in the same general range (B2–E4); however, the voice of Melanto should be somewhat the brighter of the two. Melanto's singing in this scene is less difficult than in excerpt 2.

Penelope, saddened by the absence of her husband, believed to be dead, refuses to follow Melanto's advice to find amusement in a new love.

EXCERPT 5 UE i pp. 84–102 13 min.

Ulysses, tenor, and Minerva, soprano, are described in excerpt 3. The new characters introduced in this scene are Telemaco, tenor (C2–G3) or mezzo-soprano (C3–G4), and Eumete, tenor (E2–G3). Telemaco should give the appearance of a young man and be able to sing a florid vocal line, while Eumete is considered more of a "character" part.

Telemaco, son of Ulysses, rejoices over his voyage, but Minerva advises him to be cautious now that he has arrived in his own country. Eumete, Ulysses' old herdsman, recognizes and greets Telemaco, saying that the old man he has with him (in reality Telemaco's father, but not known to either of them) has encouraged him to think Ulysses may be on his way to Ithaca. There is a short duet for Ulysses and Eumete on the subject of hope, and Telemaco bids Eumete go to the Queen and warn her that her son has come home to her and that she should not give up hope of seeing Ulysses himself. As soon as he has gone, Ulysses changes into his own form and reveals his identity to his son. There is a rapturous duet of rejoicing for father and son, and the scene ends with Ulysses telling Telemaco to go and warn his mother of Ulysses' imminent return.

EXCERPT 5a UE i pp. 94/4/1–102 6 1/4 min.

The portion of excerpt 5 with Telemaco and Ulysses only.

EXCERPT 6 UE i pp. 177–86/1/4 7 1/2 min.

Melanto, Penelope, Eumete, and Telemaco have been described; however, here we find Eumete indicated as a soprano in the score.

Penelope, grieving for her beloved Ulysses, refuses to believe Eumete and Telemaco when they try to tell her Ulysses is still alive and within the palace.

EXCERPT 7 UE i pp. 197–218 13 min.

Penelope, Ericlea, Eumete, Ulysses, and Telemaco are all described in previous excerpts.

Penelope is not convinced that the old man before her is Ulysses until Ericlea affirms that she has recognized him by the scar on his shoulder. Penelope allows caution to be replaced by love and the opera ends as she and Ulysses join in a final duet to celebrate their reunion.

Roberto Devereux (Robert Devereux)

Gaetano Donizetti (1797–1848)

Elizabethan England, 1601

EXCERPT 1 Br i pp. 1–20/2/5 15 1/2 min.

This excerpt features Elizabeth, dramatic coloratura soprano (C3–C5) who must possess fine vocal and acting potential, including strength and flexibility throughout the range. It also includes Sara, mezzo-soprano (B2–A4) who must be able to sing both dramatic sustained lines and flexible high ones. Lesser characters in the scene are Cecil, tenor; Gualtiero and the Page, both basses; and a chorus.

Queen Elizabeth confides in Sara, Duchess of Nottingham, that her love for Robert Devereux, Earl of Essex, transcends even her suspicion that he loves another. Sara is the object of this love, but this is not known by her aging husband, the Duke of Nottingham, and of course not to the Queen. Lord Cecil and the Royal Council demand Devereux's execution for treason in the recent campaign in Ireland, but she refuses saying she requires more proof. The Page's announcement of the Earl of Essex's arrival causes different reactions in the angry Lords, the worried Queen, and the distraught Sara.

EXCERPT 2 Br i pp. 20/3/1–28/3/7; 33/4/1–38 9 min.

Queen Elizabeth (see description in excerpt 1) and Roberto, tenor (F2–A3), requiring strength and flexibility, are featured in this scene.

Devereux enters and kneels before Elizabeth. He denies that he has plotted against her and asks why she has ordered him executed. She reminisces about the happy past when Devereux's love made each day seem like a dream. Thinking the Queen has discovered his and Sara's secret, he traps himself in answering further questions, and the Queen departs vowing to destroy both Devereux and her unknown rival.

EXCERPT 3 Br i pp. 50–65; 66/3/3–66/5/7 12 1/2 min.

Sara and Roberto (both described in earlier excerpts) have this scene together. Sara has a C5 and Roberto a B♭3 in this excerpt.

Sara is thinking of the danger facing Devereux, when he suddenly appears. She begs Devereux to save himself even though she still loves him but has been forced by the Queen to marry Nottingham. He tears off the ring Elizabeth has given him as a token that she will always come to his aid if it is presented to her, and leaves it with Sara. She in turn gives him a blue scarf as a remembrance of love.

EXCERPT 4 Br i pp. 75/3/1–107 19 min.

There are five leading roles in this scene—Elizabeth, Roberto, Cecil and Gualtiero (described in previous excerpts), and Nottingham, baritone (C2–F3), who needs power and flexibility throughout his range. A men's chorus is included.

Lord Cecil enters to announce to Queen Elizabeth and her Court that the Royal Council has ordered Roberto's execution. Nottingham pleads with the Queen not to sign the order but to pardon Devereux. Elizabeth refuses to listen to him, and at the sight of the blue sash she holds, Devereux realizes he is doomed. Elizabeth, believing it is her dishonor he is avenging, prevents Nottingham from drawing his sword against Devereux, declaring that he is already condemned. When Devereux refuses to name Elizabeth's rival, the Queen signs the order for his beheading.

EXCERPT 4a Br i pp. 75/3/1–84 8 min.

The portion of excerpt 4 with Elizabeth and Nottingham. Lesser roles for Cecil and Gualtiero are included.

EXCERPT 4b Br i pp. 85–91 5 min.

Elizabeth, Nottingham, and Roberto are heard in this scene from excerpt 4.

EXCERPT 5 Br i pp. 108–23 11 min.

Act 3, scene 1, of the opera is between Sara and Nottingham (both previously described).

Nottingham returns home to find Sara with a letter that Devereux has sent, urging her to rush to the Queen with the ring. Ignoring Sara's tearful protestations of innocence, the revengeful Nottingham orders her kept a prisoner until Devereux's death.

EXCERPT 6 Br i pp. 134/3/1–149 13 min.

The final scene of the opera is sung by Elizabeth, Sara, and Cecil (see earlier excerpts for description). Nottingham has one line and there is a chorus.

Surrounded by her Court, Queen Elizabeth awaits the hour of Devereux's execution. Although prepared, even at this late moment, to pardon Devereux if he should send her the ring, the Queen is told by Lord Cecil that Devereux had no message for her. Sara rushes in with Devereux's ring and begs that Devereux's life be spared. The Queen orders the Lords to being Devereux to her, but it is too late. In her grief, Elizabeth turns her vengeance upon Sara, who took Devereux's love, and Nottingham, who allowed him to die.

Romeo und Julia (Romeo and Juliet)

Boris Blacher (1903–1975)

EXCERPT 1 UE g, e pp. 13–21 3 1/2 min.

This is another setting of the famous Shakespearean text and the scenes might be used in a workshop program featuring the many versions. The first excerpt includes Capulet, bass (B1–D3); Romeo, tenor (E2–A3); Tybalt, tenor (C♯2–G3); and Juliet, soprano (B2–B4). Other women could be used to simulate the selecting of dance partners at a ball.

Capulet greets his guests and Romeo meets Juliet.

EXCERPT 2 UE g, e pp. 36–41; 49/2/1–52; 61–66/2/6 12 1/2 min.

This excerpt, a combination of the balcony and bedroom scenes, is for Romeo and Juliet (described above) with a lesser amount of singing by Juliet's Nurse, mezzo-soprano or contralto (B2–E♭4).

The well-known balcony scene begins with Romeo appearing near Juliet's house hoping to see her once again, while she likewise waits for an opportunity to be with him, continues with Juliet's conversation with her Nurse, and concludes with Romeo and Juliet's farewell at dawn.

EXCERPT 3 UE g, e pp. 89–91/4/4; 95/2/1–103/3/1; 105–6 10 1/2 min.

Romeo and Juliet (described in excerpt 1) are heard in the famous death scene in this excerpt.

Romeo und Julia auf dem Dorfe (A Village Romeo and Juliet)

Frederick Delius (1862–1934)

Seldwyla, Switzerland, middle of nineteenth century

EXCERPT 1 B&H g, e pp. 5–40 16 min.

All of the principal characters in this opera are included in this excerpt, which is scene 1 of the opera. Manz, baritone (C2–G3), and Marti, baritone (B♭1–F3), are two wealthy farmers. In general, Manz has the higher tessitura. The two children are Sali, tenor (F2–G3), son of Manz; and Vrenchen, soprano (B2–A♭4), daughter of Marti. The Dark Fiddler, baritone (G♯1–F♯3), completes the cast in this scene. If performed with piano (or two-piano) accompaniment, a solo violin is suggested in any of the scenes involving the Dark Fiddler.

This takes place in September on a piece of land luxuriantly overgrown on a hill, with the broad fields of Manz and Marti lying on either side. The men are plowing their fields, and each is contemplating adding to his land by plowing another strip off the wild land. The children, Sali and Vrenchen, enter with the midday meal of their fathers. After they have spread it out, they go to the woods to play and soon hear a strange sound, which is the Dark Fiddler in the distance. He enters and is recognized by Marti as the heir to the land between the two fields. Marti and Manz argue about the land that they slowly have been usurping, and finally each angrily takes his child and strides away.

EXCERPT 1a B&H g, e pp. 17/1/3–40 11 1/2 min.

The scene excluding the opening portion for Marti and Manz.

EXCERPT 2 B&H g, e pp. 41–54 (C-major cadence) 7 min.

A scene for Vrenchen (D♭3–A♭4) and Sali (D2–A3), six years after they have parted in excerpt 1.

This excerpt takes place in front of Marti's house that has run wild with neglect. Sali looks longingly toward the house, and Vrenchen presently comes to the door. The fight between their fathers over the land (see excerpt 1) has devastated both estates, and the young people vow to resume their friendship, feeling that if they hold together all may come out right again.

EXCERPT 3 B&H g, e pp. 60/4/1–82/1/3 8 1/2 min.

Another scene for Vrenchen and Sali, which includes an appearance of the Dark Fiddler, baritone (B1–F3).

Vrenchen and Sali, happy to be together once again, feel as if all their cares have vanished. The appearance of the Dark Fiddler frightens them because they recall the dreadful strife that took place after the first time they met him. Then they talk of their affection for each other, and the scene ends in a kiss.

EXCERPT 4 B&H g, e pp. 88/4/1–110 10 min.
(B♭-minor cadence)

Vrenchen and Sali are now alone—Sali has accidentally killed Vrenchen's father, and Sali's father has gone insane from the problems that overwhelmed them. The scene is a love scene with a considerable amount of duet singing. The voice ranges remain about the same as in the previous excerpts.

EXCERPT 5 B&H g, e pp. 192–229/2/1 12 min.

This excerpt requires the Dark Fiddler, baritone (B♭1–G3); Sali and Vrenchen (described in excerpt 2); and four Vagabonds: Slim Girl, soprano (D3–B♭4); Wild Girl, mezzo-soprano (B2–F3); Poor Horn Player, tenor (E2–A3); and Hunchbacked Bass Player, bass (G1–D3). In excerpt 4, Sali and Vrenchen have fallen asleep in the field and this excerpt is part of their dream.

On the veranda of a run-down country house, now used as an inn, the Dark Fiddler is seen addressing the four Vagabonds, telling the story of the land that was fought over by the fathers of Sali and Vrenchen. The young lovers then enter; the Fiddler fills all the glasses and proposes a toast; all join in a rollicking septet and dance. The Vagabonds wander off; Sali and Vrenchen are left alone; and the scene ends with a kiss.

Le Rossignol (The Nightingale)

Igor Stravinsky (1882–1971)

Ancient China

EXCERPT 1 B&H f, g, e pp. 3/3/2–37 12 1/2 min.

This opera is written to have the singers in the pit while some of the action is mimed onstage, an invitation to any stage director for innovative staging. This is a nocturnal scene by the seashore, near the edge of the forest. Singers include the Fisherman, tenor (E2–A3); the Nightingale, coloratura soprano (F3–B♭4); the Chamberlain, bass (G1–C♯3); the Bonze, bass (G1–B2); the Cook, soprano (F3–A4); and a four-part chorus of men who are Courtiers. Because of the difficulty of the Stravinsky score, two pianos should probably be used if an orchestra is not available.

The excerpt opens with a short aria by the Fisherman, followed by another short aria by the Nightingale. Then the Chamberlain, Bonze, Courtiers, and Cook enter and listen for the Nightingale because the Cook tells them she has heard the song and it is so beautiful. Finally the Nightingale appears and is invited to the palace to sing for the Emperor of China.

EXCERPT 2 B&H f, g, e pp. 59/2/3–77 10 min.

This excerpt begins with a portion of the Chinese March, which may be used for whatever type procession the director wishes. It may also be used for the Emperor's exit if the director prefers. The scene includes the Chamberlain, bass (A1–D♯3); the Emperor, baritone (B♭1–D♯3); the Nightingale, coloratura soprano (A3–F5) whose aria is very florid and difficult in a high tessitura; the Courtiers, a men's chorus; the Courtesans, a women's chorus; and three Japanese Envoys (2 tenors and a bass), and the Fisherman, tenor (A2–F3). A court lackey and other servants are needed for the action.

A Nightingale is perched on a staff held by the court lackey, and when the procession has entered, the Emperor gives the Nightingale a signal to start. The very difficult aria follows. While the court is praising the Nightingale, the Japanese Envoys approach with a golden box on which is perched a large mechanical nightingale. It is presented to the Emperor. During the scene, the real Nightingale disappears, unobserved, while the mechnical nightingale (a flute could be used here if piano is being used in lieu of an orchestra) performs until stopped by the Emperor. When he discovers the Chinese Nightingale has flown, he names the Japanese nightingale as "first singer." When the Emperor and his entourage have left, the voice of the Fisherman is heard in a short prediction.

EXCERPT 2a B&H f, g, e pp. 59/2/3–76 9 min.

Excerpt 2 without the voice of the Fisherman.

EXCERPT 3 B&H f, g, e pp. 78–97 12 min.

The Nightingale, coloratura soprano (E♭3–D♭5), again has the major portion of the singing in this excerpt. Also included are the Emperor, baritone; Death, mezzo-soprano (A♭2–B♭3); and a chorus of Specters (altos). The Fisherman (see excerpts 1 and 2) closes the opera with his song.

The sick Emperor is lying in his gigantic bed, while Death sits by his bedside wearing the imperial crown and holding the sword of state and the standard. The Nightingale sings and enchants not only the Emperor but also Death, who returns the crown, sword, and standard to the Emperor so he may live.

Rusalka (The Mermaid)

Antonin Dvořák (1841–1904)

A mythical kingdom

EXCERPT 1	Pr	cz, g	pp. 38/6/2–86/4/3	30 1/2 min.
	Pr	cz, g, e	pp. 29/5/2–82/4/3	

Rusalka is a dramatic or spinto soprano (B♭2–B4) who needs strength throughout the range, as she sings with the Watersprite, bass (G1–F♯3), and then with Ježibaba, mezzo-soprano (B♭2–B4).

The water nymph, Rusalka, has fallen in love with a mortal Prince and seeks advice from the Watersprite, who sends her to the witch, Ježibaba. The witch promises to help her on condition that she remain mute, and that if the Prince proves unfaithful, Rusalka must return to the depths of the lake.

EXCERPT 1a	Pr	cz, g	pp. 38/6/2–57/3/2	15 min.
	Pr	cz, g, e	pp. 29/5/2–51	

The portion of excerpt 1 for Rusalka and the Watersprite, ending with the well-known Song to the Moon.

EXCERPT 1b	Pr	cz, g	pp. 59/1/3–85/2/5	13 1/2 min.
	Pr	cz, g, e	pp. 53/3/2–81/1/5	

Ježibaba and Rusalka are heard in this portion of excerpt 1.

EXCERPT 2	Pr	cz, g	pp. 93/5/1–103	6 1/2 min.
	Pr	cz, g, e	pp. 90/5/5–102	

Rusalka is silent in this scene when the Prince, tenor (C2–B♭3), beholds her, now a woman. The Watersprite and the other water nymphs (three-part women's chorus) may sing from offstage where the score reads "under the water." The Prince, who has been hunting, dismisses the other hunters and sits down on the shore of the lake. When he looks up, he sees Rusalka standing before him. She is barefoot and clad in a gray garment of a destitute child with her beautiful golden hair streaming down along her body. He is enthralled, and Rusalka stretches out her hands and goes to him but heeds Ježibaba's warning and does not speak.

EXCERPT 3 Pr cz, g pp. 122/4/2–136/4/1 7 1/2 min.
Pr cz, g, e pp. 121/5/1–138/3/1

Again Rusalka must be present, but she is still mute. Singing is done by the Prince, who has nothing higher than an A3 in this scene, and the Foreign Princess, soprano (B♭2–C5).

Rusalka, beautifully attired, but always sad and pale, arrives with the Prince in a park surrounding the Prince's castle. He remarks that she has lived with him for a week but still flees from his passion. He hopes this will change when they are married, but Rusalka cannot answer for she must remain mute (see excerpt 1). When the Foreign Princess enters she reminds the Prince that he has been neglecting his guests recently, since he has been with Rusalka. He realizes she is right, and he and the Princess go off to dress for the ball. Rusalka stares after them as if she would like to restrain the Prince from going, but then, heartbroken, she departs through the gallery.

EXCERPT 4 Pr cz, g pp. 159/2/1–188 14 min.
Pr cz, g, e pp. 165–98

This scene begins with an aria for Rusalka and continues with the Prince and Princess (all previously described). The Watersprite, bass, is important to the scene but has little singing.

Rusalka has come from the ball, where the Prince has appeared among his guests, courting the Foreign Princess and neglecting Rusalka. The Watersprite appears and Rusalka suddenly regains her speech and talks with him. When the Prince and Princess appear, they have a passionate scene ending in a duet, before Rusalka, desperate, runs out of her hiding place and throws herself into the Prince's arms. A warning from the Watersprite perplexes the Prince as the excerpt ends.

EXCERPT 5 Pr cz, g pp. 190/6/6–218 15 min.
Pr cz, g, e pp. 201/3/1–235/1/2

This is another scene for Rusalka and the witch Ježibaba (both previously described).

Rusalka is sitting near the lake; she is white and pale, her hair has turned ashen, and her eyes are sad. Ježibaba arrives and they speak of Rusalka's fate. Ježibaba offers her another hope—if she will sacrifice her lover's blood, she may be free of the curse. But Rusalka still loves the Prince and refuses to do this.

EXCERPT 6 Pr cz, g pp. 257/4/3–278 15 1/2 min.
Pr cz, g, e pp. 282/4/3–307

The final scene of the opera with Rusalka and the Prince, who sings a C4 and a pianissimo A3. The Watersprite has a little offstage singing.

The Prince runs out to the lakeside where he had met Rusalka. He is deeply burdened with guilt. She appears and warns him of the danger of her kiss, but he gladly atones by embracing her. Rusalka is freed at last from the curse and can go back to her life as a water nymph.

Salome

Richard Strauss (1864–1949)

The terrace of the Palace of Herod in Galilee, about 30 A.D.

EXCERPT 1 B&H g, e pp. 35/2/1–73/1/6 18 1/2 min.
(orchestral interlude could be extended to any suitable stopping point)

Salome, dramatic soprano (A2–B4), needs great stamina and intensity in her singing and her acting. Jokanaan, baritone (G♯1–F♯3), needs a very dark, prophetic quality. Neither role should be attempted by a young student. Narraboth, a young Syrian, a tenor (E♭2–A3) with a limited amount of singing in this scene, kills himself in despair at Salome's wantonness.

Salome, daughter of the evil Herodias and stepdaughter of Herod, is fascinated by a prisoner her father has confined in a cistern. She persuades Narraboth, who loves her, to let her speak to Jokanaan, who is the prophet John the Baptist. Even though this is strictly forbidden, Narraboth lets Jokanaan come forward, and the sight of him stirs Salome's morbid desires. He turns on her and rages at her as the daughter of an iniquitous mother, and Salome tells him in music of rising intensity of her desire for his body, his hair, and finally his mouth. The prophet spurns and curses her and returns to his dungeon.

EXCERPT 2 B&H g, e pp. 111/2/1–148 15 1/2 min.

This is the scene for Salome that includes her Dance of the Seven Veils. (If this scene is performed as a staged excerpt, it is suggested that the singer performing the title role work out detailed choreography for the dance. With the help of an expert choreographer, such a soprano could be provided with an excellent learning experience in preparation for adding the complete role to her repertoire.)

The excerpt begins with Jokannan, previously described baritone, singing from his dungeon. Two Nazarenes, bass-baritone (G1–F♯3) and tenor or baritone (G2–E3), sing briefly. Onstage Herod, powerful dramatic tenor (D2–G♯3), sits with his wife, Herodias, mezzo-soprano (F3–A4) whose voice can be harsh and dark. Salome, described in earlier excerpts, has some singing and then the sensual dance. Slaves are needed to bring in the veils and take off Salome's sandals.

Herod and Herodias, his wife, are on the terrace where Jokanaan is confined to his cistern. His voice is heard in prophecy while two Nazarenes try to convince Herod of the truth. Herodias hates what she is hearing, both from Jokanaan and the Nazarenes, and even more so from her lecherous husband as he begs Salome to dance for him. Finally, Salome agrees to dance if Herod will then give her whatever she shall ask, which is, of course, the head of Jokanaan.

The Scarf

Lee Hoiby (1926–)

An isolated farmhouse, late nineteenth century

EXCERPT 1 GS e pp. 3/2/3–27/4/1 10 1/2 min.
(overture could be included)

There are two characters in this scene of the chamber opera: Miriam, soprano (D3–B♭4), a tall and beautiful young woman with dark hair, who can project strength and intensity; and Reuel, tenor (D♯2–A3), her husband, who is old, small, skinny and gray-haired.

Based on a story by Chekhov, the action takes place in the kitchen, serving in winter also as the bedroom, of an isolated farmhouse. It is a blizzardly February night. As the scene opens, Miriam sits at a spinning wheel, a long scarf of scarlet wool in her lap, while her husband Reuel sits on the bed watching her. He asks Miriam to come to bed, but as she continues to knit, he accuses her of weaving a spell to attract strange young men to their home; this time he thinks he hears the postman outside their house, lost in the blizzard, which proves what he has been saying.

EXCERPT 2 GS e pp. 41/4/3–44/2/2; 45/3/1–56/2/2 (downbeat) 8 min.

The portion of the opera in which Reuel speaks occasionally from his bed has been cut, and the scene remains one between Miriam (C♯3–A4) and the Postman, baritone (C♯2–E3), with most of the singing for the soprano.

The Postman, lost in the storm, has found his way to the farmhouse, and Reuel reluctantly has helped him bring in his mailbags and take care of his horse. Now Miriam has made hot tea for the Postman and is telling him about the lonely life she leads.

EXCERPT 3 GS e pp. 61/3/1–79/4/2 10 1/2 min.

This is another very emotional scene for Miriam (B♭2–A4) with the Postman (B♭1–E3) and Reuel (E♭2–A♭4).

Reuel, enraged, insists that the weather has improved and that the Postman must leave the farmhouse. As this scene opens, Reuel is going out to get the Postman's horse. The Postman and Miriam have a short time together, and then they kiss and slowly separate. Miriam puts the scarlet scarf around the Postman's neck as he leaves and then has a very dramatic scene in which she exerts all of her magic powers in the hope that the red scarf will bring the Postman back to her.

School for Wives

Rolf Liebermann (1910–)

Provincial French town, seventeenth century

EXCERPT 1 UE e pp. 8/1/4–45/2/3 14 min.

This excerpt features Poquelin, baritone (C♯2–E♭3); Arnolphe, baritone (B1–G♭3); Horace, lyric tenor (C2–C4); and Georgette, mezzo-soprano (A2–E♭4).

Poquelin, representing Molière, introduces the play and explains the character of Arnolphe, who has taken in the young girl, Agnès, and hopes to marry her. Horace, son of Arnolphe's friend, Oronte, arrives and tells of having won the affections of a young girl, who turns out to be Agnès herself. Arnolphe does not admit to Horace that he knows it is Agnès. He calls for his servants, Georgette and Alain; Poquelin obliges by taking on the role of Alain himself. Arnolphe warns the servants to watch out for any meeting of Agnès and a young man; left alone, the two servants comment on their having allowed the young man into the house to begin with.

EXCERPT 1a UE e pp. 8/1/4–31/2/1 9 min.

This is the opening portion of excerpt 1 with Poquelin, Arnolphe, and Horace.

EXCERPT 1b UE e pp. 29/2/2–45/2/3 5 1/2 min.

Arnolphe, Georgette, and Poquelin (Alain) are in this scene from excerpt 1.

EXCERPT 2 UE e pp. 45/2/4–81/3/4 14 min.

This is a scene for Agnès, lyric soprano (E♭3–A4), and Arnolphe and Poquelin (described in excerpt 1). Poquelin sings in both his normal voice and in falsetto (to F4).

Arnolphe chides Agnès for having fallen in love with a young man; she says an Old Woman begged her to receive the young man, saying he would die without her love. When the Old Woman appears and Arnolphe reprimands him, Poquelin throws off his disguise. He (Molière) begs Arnolphe to have some respect for him and agrees to continue the play. Agnès continues to describe what has happened, and Arnolphe insists that he will marry her himself, but warns her to behave and do everything he commands.

EXCERPT 3 UE e pp. 83/3/6–138/4/3 17 min.

Agnès, Georgette, Arnolphe, Horace, and Poquelin as Alain, all previously described, sing in this excerpt.

Horace claps his hands outside Agnès' window; she throws a stone and closes the window. A letter is attached to the stone. As Horace is reading the letter, Arnolphe confronts him. Poquelin assures Horace that Agnès awaits him and then steps once more into the role of Alain.

A quartet ensues before Arnolphe reenters and scolds the young girl for disobeying his orders.

EXCERPT 3a UE e pp. 83/3/6–96 5 1/2 min.

The portion of excerpt 3 for Arnolphe and Horace only.

EXCERPT 4 UE e pp. 139/4/2–154/2/3 6 1/2 min.

Arnolphe, Horace, and Agnès (to C♭5) (see earlier excerpts) are included in this scene.

Horace has been beaten unconscious by the servants. Arnolphe takes stock of the situation, then exits; Agnès enters, sobbing; Horace revives and they sing of their love. Arnolphe seizes Agnès and drags her into the house.

EXCERPT 5 UE e pp. 154/3/1–190 10 min.

A scene for Oronte, bass (G1–D3), with Agnès, Georgette, Horace, Arnolphe, and Poquelin, all described in earlier excerpts. This time Poquelin is in the role of Monsieur Henry.

Oronte arrives in time to greet his son, Horace, and his dear friend Arnolphe, with the news that a marriage has been arranged for Horace with the daughter of Monsieur Henry. Arnolphe is relieved; Horace and Agnès are distressed. When M. Henry arrives, it turns out that Agnès is his long-lost daughter. Arnolphe must now accept the inevitable, and the opera ends with an ensemble quoting (in French) the words of Beaumarchais "Voulez-vous donner de l'esprit à une sotte, enfermez-là."

Semiramide

Gioacchino Rossini (1792–1868)

Ancient Babylon

EXCERPT 1 Kal i, e pp. 74–109 26 min.

The vocal lines of this opera are very difficult with pervasive bel canto and demanding ornamentation. They should not be attempted by singers unable to handle this style well.

In this excerpt Arsace, low mezzo-soprano or contralto (G2–G♯4) with a very low tessitura has a recitative and florid aria before being joined by Oroe, bass (B♭1–E♭3), and later by Assur, bass-baritone (A1–F3), who needs vocal flexibility in his duet with Arsace. Two Ministers (silent) complete the scene.

Queen Semiramide has had her husband, Nino, murdered and has taken Assur as her lover. Semiramide's son, Ninia, whom she has not seen since he was a boy, has taken the name Arsace and opens this scene by telling that he has been called back to Babylon by Semiramide. In the aria, Arsace also sings of his love for the Princess Azema to whom he is pledged. When the high priest, Oroe, enters, Arsace gives him the caskets containing sacred relics preserved by his father and asks how his father died. Before Oroe can answer, footsteps are heard and Oroe exits as Assur enters. Assur and Arsace discuss Arsace's return to Babylon and his love for Azema in the duet that follows.

EXCERPT 1a Kal i, e pp. 91/3/3–109 13 1/2 min.

The final portion of excerpt 1, which is the duet of Assur and Arsace.

EXCERPT 2 Kal i, e pp. 120–53 21 min.

A women's chorus introduces Semiramide's famous aria, "Bel raggio lusinghier," but it can be sung without the chorus. It is a brilliant soprano aria (D3-B♭4) with a great deal of fioritura. This is followed by a recitative for Mitrane, tenor, captain of the guard; and Semiramide and Arsace, contralto, who then join in a glorious, florid duet.

Semiramide, not knowing that Arsace is her son, has fallen in love with him and has called him to Babylon expecting to marry him and make him king. In this scene Mitrane announces that Arsace has arrived; they meet, and she promises him that she will rid herself of Assur and make Arsace her new love and king.

EXCERPT 2a Kal i, e pp. 133–53 12 min.

Excerpt 2 without the women's chorus.

EXCERPT 2b Kal i, e pp. 136/5/4–153 9 1/2 min.

The duet only from excerpt 2, eliminating Mitrane and the chorus.

EXCERPT 3 Kal i, e pp. 237–65 19 min.

The opening of act 2 begins with a short recitative by Mitrane, tenor, accompanied by guards (silent), and continues with Semiramide and Assur, again with difficult, florid singing (see excerpts 1 and 2).

Mitrane enters with his guards and announces that Assur will not accept the fact that he has been ordered to leave Semiramide's palace. When Assur enters, Semiramide tells him he must accept Arsace as his king, but Assur reminds her of the events surrounding Nino's death, and she expresses regret that she also lost her son to whom she would gladly have relinquished her power. When the band is heard playing in the royal palace, Semiramide feels she has triumphed, for her soldier husband will now be the king.

EXCERPT 3a Kal i, e pp. 239–65 17 min.

Same as excerpt 3, without Mitrane and guards.

EXCERPT 4 Kal i, e pp. 313–41 17 min.

In this scene Semiramide and Arsace (described in excerpts above) have a recitative followed by a duet.

Semiramide finds Arsace, and he shows her a letter written by his dying father, Nino, which reveals everything. Arsace now knows that Semiramide and Assur killed Nino and that he himself is Semiramide's son. When she reads the letter, she admits her guilt, but Arsace finds himself unable to take revenge on his mother.

EXCERPT 5 Kal i, e pp. 381/4/1–402 12 1/2 min.

The three principal characters, Semiramide, Arsace, and Assur (see descriptions above), are brought together in the final scene and have solo lines as well as a trio. A mixed chorus is needed for the finale. Oroe, bass, has important singing in the recitative.

Arsace must go to the vaults of the royal sepulcher, where Nino is buried, and there, with the sword of the departed monarch, slay a victim in revenge. Semiramide, anticipating Assur's murderous intents toward Arsace, visits the tomb of Nino in order to shield her son. Arsace makes what would be a fatal thrust at Assur, and as Semiramide interposes herself between the two men, she is killed with the avenging sword of her own husband. Divine justice being satisfied, Arsace ascends the throne and shares it with Azema, his faithful love.

Signor Deluso

Thomas Pasatieri (1945–)

Small town outside of Paris, about 1650

EXCERPT 1 Bel e pp. 1–21 9 1/2 min.

Célie, soprano (E3–B4); her father, Gorgibus, bass-baritone (C♯2–E♭3); her maid, Rosine, mezzo-soprano (B2–F4); a neighbor, Signor Deluso, baritone (C♯2–F3); and his wife Clara, soprano (D♭3–G♯4), are included in this excerpt. None of the roles are too difficult.

Célie comes out of Gorgibus' house followed by her father and Rosine, her maid. She refuses to marry anyone until her Léon returns from Paris. Rosine, quite plump, tries to cheer up Célie by describing her own life without a man. When Célie faints and drops the locket with Léon's picture in it, Deluso comes to carry her into her house. His wife, Clara, sees him with Célie in his arms and rushes outside only to find him gone and Célie's locket there. When Deluso returns and sees his wife looking at the picture in the locket, he presumes she has a young lover, and now both of them are disillusioned.

EXCERPT 1a Bel e pp. 1–12/1/1 5 min.

This very short section ends when Signor Deluso carries Célie into the house. It uses all the characters except Clara.

EXCERPT 2 Bel e pp. 22/1/2–39/3/4 8 min.

We are now introduced to Léon, tenor (E2–A♭3), and the Town Magistrate, bass-baritone. Others included have been previously described: Célie, Deluso, and Clara, who has very little in this excerpt.

Léon has returned from Paris and hopes his Célie has not married while he was gone. When he meets Deluso carrying the locket he has retrieved and Deluso says it is his wife's, Léon is devastated. He assumes that Deluso has married Célie. While he is bemoaning the fact, Clara sees him and invites him in for a glass of wine. Deluso and the Magistrate enter, and when Léon leaves Clara's, both Deluso and Célie feel they have been jilted and must get revenge in one way or another.

EXCERPT 3 Bel e pp. 39/4/1–57 7 1/2 min.

The final scene of the opera for Célie, Léon, Rosine, Clara, Deluso (all previously described), and Gorgibus, who has a very small part. This excerpt has ensemble singing by the principal characters.

In this excerpt, the solution to all the problems is worked out, and everyone lives "happily ever after."

Simon Boccanegra

Giuseppe Verdi (1813–1901)

Genoa, fourteenth century

EXCERPT 1 Kal i pp. 22 (with upbeat)–38 11 min.

This scene from the prologue of the opera has Simon Boccanegra, baritone (B1–F3), and Fiesco, bass (F1–F3), with an offstage chorus. Boccanegra has a dramatic role in the opera, while Fiesco has a dignified role demanding a rich vocal quality.

Fiesco, who is the Doge when the story begins, bids farewell to his palace and laments the loss of his daughter Maria from whose deathbed he has just come. His noble, restrained cry of grief is his aria "Il lacerato spirito." He sees Simon Boccanegra enter the square and confronts him; Boccanegra, a Genoese corsair, has been the lover of Maria, and she has borne him a daughter. Fiesco does not tell Simon that Maria is dead but states that only the sight of his granddaughter, who supposedly is living in Pisa, can bring peace between them.

EXCERPT 2 Kal i pp. 48–79/2/1 16 min.

Amelia Grimaldi (Maria Boccanegra), lyric-spinto soprano (D♭3–B4), sings with Gabriele, tenor (D2–A3), and Fiesco, bass (F1–C♯3), in this excerpt. Lesser characters are the Maid, soprano or mezzo-soprano, and Pietro, baritone.

Twenty-five years have passed. Amelia, Boccanegra's daughter, is standing in the garden of the Grimaldi palace. She sings of the beauty of the scene and memories of her childhood in "Come in quest'ora bruna." She hears the voice of Gabriele, her lover, and, when he appears, tells him of her fears for his safety and that of Andrea (in reality, Fiesco in disguise), whom she knows is plotting against the Doge. When Pietro announces that the Doge wishes to see Amelia, she knows he will be asking for her hand in marriage to his henchman, Paolo. Gabriele resolves immediately to ask the blessing of Andrea, Amelia's guardian, on their marriage. Fiesco, not knowing that Amelia is really his granddaughter, blesses Gabriele in his affection for Amelia.

EXCERPT 2a Kal i pp. 48–72/1/5 (G-major cadence) 10 min.

The portion of excerpt 2 with Amelia and Gabriele only.

EXCERPT 3 Kal i pp. 79/3/1–98/3/2 9 min.

Simon Boccanegra, baritone, and Amelia, soprano (see earlier scenes for descriptions).

When the Doge, Simon Boccanegra, arrives at the Grimaldi palace, he asks if she is content with her life of seclusion. She answers that she has a lover and is pursued by one she hates—Paolo. She confides to the Doge that she is not Grimaldi's daughter but an orphan, whose only clue to her identity is a locket containing the portrait of her mother. With great emotion, Boccanegra recognizes it as that of Maria and knows he has found his daughter at last.

EXCERPT 4 Kal i pp. 151–94 23 1/2 min.

Previously described characters, Amelia, soprano; Gabriele, tenor; Boccanegra, baritone; and Fiesco, bass, are in this excerpt with Paolo, a dramatic baritone (C2–G3).

Paolo Albiani, a plebian, is alone. He sees himself as rejected by all, patricians and plebeians alike, but is determined to threaten the absent Doge with the most terrible and most secretive vengeance at his command—poison. Fiesco and Gabriele Adorno are brought in, and he offers the former his liberty if he will kill the Doge. Fiesco refuses, and as Adorno prepares to leave with Fiesco, he asks him if he knows that Amelia is here in the palace as Boccanegra's mistress. Adorno prays that his fears may be groundless, and when Amelia enters, he confronts her with the accusation, which she denies. Adorno hides as Boccanegra enters, and Boccanegra realizes that Amelia is in love with Adorno, who is a traitor and a plotter against the state. She entreats her father to pardon Gabriele Adorno with whom she would rather die than live on alone. He tells her to leave, and he drinks water from the jug that Paolo has poisoned.

EXCERPT 4a Kal i pp. 159/3/2–194 19 min.

The portion of excerpt 4 for Amelia, Gabriele, and Boccanegra.

EXCERPT 4b Kal i pp. 159/3/2–175 8 1/2 min.

Amelia and Gabriele Adorno's scene from excerpt 4.

EXCERPT 5 Kal i pp. 213–46 16 min.

Amelia, Gabriele, Boccanegra, and Fiesco (all previously described) are in this excerpt, which has some chorus singing.

In the hall of the Doge's palace, the Doge enters, already affected by the poison he has taken. He sings of memories of the life he once led as a free man. He wonders why he did not find death at this early, happy stage of his career. Fiesco reveals himself, and Boccanegra announces that there can be peace between them now that in Amelia he has found the daughter he had lost. Fiesco's hate turns to pity for the man he knows has only a short time to live. Boccanegra then summons up strength to tell Amelia of her descent and to appoint Adorno as his successor before he dies. Fiesco announces to the assembled crowd that Gabriele Adorno is their new Doge; when they shout for Boccanegra, they are told that he is dead.

EXCERPT 5a Kal i pp. 213–28 8 1/2 min.

The portion of excerpt 5 between Fiesco and Boccanegra, including a stirring duet for the two.

Sir John in Love

Ralph Vaughan Williams (1872–1935)

Windsor, England, fifteenth century

EXCERPT 1 Ox e, g pp. 25/4/1–36/1/1 6 min.

This is an aria for Anne, soprano (D3–A4), and a love duet for her with Fenton, tenor (E♭2–A♭3). Page calls to his daughter Anne from offstage.

Anne is unhappy because her father has chosen Slender as a husband for her, while she prefers Fenton, who suddenly appears and sings of his love for her.

EXCEPT 2 Ox e, g pp. 38/2/1–54/4/3 4 1/2 min.

A quartet for Mrs. Quickly, mezzo-soprano (D♭3–F♯4); Caius, tenor who must sing in French and heavily accented English (C2–E3); Simple, tenor or baritone (E2–E3); and Rugby, bass (B♭1–B2).

Dr. Caius, a French physician, is determined to marry Anne Page and is quite upset when Simple, Slender's servant, delivers a letter to

Mrs. Quickly, the housekeeper of Parson Hugh Evans, because Slender is a rival for Anne's love and is her father's choice.

EXCERPT 3 Ox e, g pp. 58/2/1–79/4/4 5 1/2 min.

A men's quintet for Bardolph, tenor (C2–A3); Nym, baritone (B♭1–F3); Falstaff, baritone (B♭1–E3); the Host of the Garter Inn, baritone (A♭1–E3); and Pistol, bass (D1–D3). There are no range problems except for a few low notes for Pistol. Robin, a page, is silent.

The scene begins with a drinking song; Falstaff interrupts to tell the others that he means to make love to both Mrs. Ford and Mrs. Page and has written letters to both of them. When Nym and Pistol refuse to deliver the letters, Falstaff gives them to the page, Robin, and dismisses the others defiantly.

EXCERPT 4 Ox e, g pp. 79/4/5–94 6 min.

A scene for Nym and Pistol (see excerpt 3); Ford, bass (C2–E3); Mrs. Page, soprano (E3–G4); and Mrs. Ford, mezzo-soprano (B2–E4).

Nym and Pistol inform Mr. Ford that Falstaff loves his wife, whereupon Ford sings a soliloquy about cuckolded husbands and his own jealousy. Mrs. Page and Mrs. Ford are heard singing the ballad "When daisies pied," further reminding Ford of the shame of being branded a cuckold.

EXCERPT 4a Ox e, g pp. 79/4/5–90/4/2 4 1/2 min.

Nym, Pistol, and Ford only.

EXCERPT 5 Ox e, g pp. 95–115/3/2 8 1/2 min.

This is a scene for Mrs Page, soprano (D3–A4); Mrs. Ford, mezzo-soprano (C3–E4); and Mrs. Quickly (B2–F♯4).

Mrs. Page and Mrs. Ford have received identical love letters from Sir John Falstaff. While they are comparing the letters, they become greatly agitated. Mrs. Quickly enters and tries to calm them down with the ballad "Sigh no more, ladies," which the others then join.

EXCERPT 6 Ox e, g pp. 118/5/5–149/1/4 15 min.

Mrs. Quickly, Bardolph, Falstaff and Ford, all previously described, are in this excerpt.

Mrs. Quickly arrives at the Garter Inn to inform Falstaff that Mrs. Ford has received his letter and will be glad to receive him at her home between ten and eleven; Mrs. Page, too, has received his letter but has a husband who is seldom away from home. Ecstatic, Falstaff begins to compose a lovesong but is interrupted by Bardolph, who explains that a Mr. Brook (Ford in disguise) wishes to see Falstaff. "Brook" encourages Falstaff to pursue the affections of Mrs. Ford and offers money to the knight in a plot, of course, to trap Falstaff at Ford's home.

EXCERPT 6a Ox e, g pp. 120/2/1–133/3/3 5 min.

The portion of excerpt 6 with Falstaff and Mrs. Quickly only.

EXCERPT 6b Ox e, g pp. 134/1/5–149/1/4 7 1/2 min.

Falstaff and Ford only from excerpt 6.

EXCERPT 7 Ox e, g pp. 187/2/1–208/4/4 6 1/2 min.

Mrs. Page, Mrs. Ford, Mrs. Quickly, and Falstaff sing in this scene. Servants Robert and John and Falstaff's page, Robin, are all silent.

Mrs. Ford is preparing to receive Falstaff in her home, instructing the servants to prepare a laundry basket in which Falstaff will hide when Mr. Ford returns home. She instructs the other ladies in their parts in the plot. Falstaff arrives, and just as Mrs. Ford pretends to yield to his embraces, she signals Mrs. Quickly, who warns them of Mr. Ford's return. The basket is ready; Falstaff is confronted by Mrs. Page as well. The ladies succeed in getting the fat knight into the basket, and this excerpt ends with the three ladies sitting on the lid of the basket to keep it from opening.

EXCERPT 8 Ox e, g pp. 224–34 5 1/2 min.
(resolve in B♭-major)

A scene for Mrs. Page, Mrs. Ford, Mr. Ford (see previous excerpts), Mr. Page, baritone, and Sir Hugh Evans, high baritone.

Ford apologizes for his jealousy and begs his wife's forgiveness. The others explain all that has happened, and the husbands agree to join the plot to further make a fool of the fat knight. Mrs. Page tells the story of Herne the hunter, and they all devise a way to entice Falstaff to the haunted oak in order to disgrace him in public.

The Sojourner and Mollie Sinclair

Carlisle Floyd (1926–)

Colonial North Carolina, mid-eighteenth century

EXCERPT 1 B&H e pp. 3/2/2–43/3/3 18 min.

A scene for Jenny MacDougald, soprano (D3–B♭4), a girl in her late teens; and a young man, Lachlin Sinclair, tenor (D2–A3), who is in his early twenties. The voices may be youthful but must be able to project the subtleties of the text. Dougald MacDougald, the sixty-year-old father of Jenny, is a mature bass-baritone (G1–E3) who has considerable vitality and personal magnetism.

When the scene opens, Lachlin has just caught Jenny, who was playfully trying to run away from him, and has put his arms tightly around her waist. The scene includes a rather humorous duet and an aria for each of them as they try to explain their feelings for each other. It is Dougald MacDougald's sixtieth birthday, and he is expecting his kinsmen to come to celebrate with him. Although he left Scotland twenty years before, he is still homesick for his native land. When he appears from the house, he is wearing the full regalia of a Highlander chieftan— kilts, tartan, and Tam O'Shanter—and his aria is about his homeland.

EXCERPT 1a B&H e pp. 3/2/2–23/2/1 10 min.

The opening of excerpt 1 featuring only Jenny and Lachlin.

EXCERPT 1b B&H e pp. 24/2/2–43/3/3 7 1/2 min.

A shorter version of excerpt 1, which begins with Dougald MacDougald singing from inside the house.

EXCERPT 2 B&H e pp. 67/4/1–90/2/2; 104/2/1–115/1/2 16 min.

Mollie Sinclair, mezzo-soprano and dramatic at times (A♭2–A4), is Lachlin's mother, and she has the major portion of this scene with Dougald MacDougald, baritone (A1–E3). Supers could be included, but the scene has been cut so that it is a confrontation between Mollie and Dougald and needs no chorus, only a Spokesman for the clan (baritone).

Dougald asks Mollie to state her business and leave, but she is persistent in her effort to change his way of thinking. There are arias for both characters, which reveal their feelings about their homeland, Scotland, and their newly adopted land, North Carolina.

EXCERPT 2a B&H e pp. 70/3/1–80/1/2 4 min.

The opening of excerpt 3 with Mollie Sinclair, mezzo-soprano, and Dougald MacDougald, bass-baritone (B♭1–E3). This includes some conversation between the two and ends with Dougald's aria.

EXCERPT 2b B&H e pp. 104–15/1/2 5 1/2 min.

This is an aria for Mollie Sinclair, mezzo-soprano (A♭1–A3), but it is directed to Dougald, who has no singing in this excerpt.

The Sweet Bye and Bye

Jack Beeson (1921–)

United States in the twenties

EXCERPT 1 B&H e pp. 38–45 5 min.

Sister Gladys, coloratura soprano (D3–A♭4), and Mother Rainey, mezzo-soprano (B2–G4), sing in this excerpt.

At the beach at Atlantic City, an evangelical sect known as the Lifeshine Flock, mourn the passing of their leader. When the service is over, Sister Gladys, a close friend of the deceased, lingers and is questioned by Mother Rainey.

EXCERPT 2 B&H e pp. 47/2/4–75/1/5 14 min.

This is a scene for Rose Ora Easter, spinto soprano (C3–B♭4), the former leader of the Flock, and Billy, a handsome, young tenor (D2–B♭3), with whom she has spent the night.

Rose, who is usually very confident when "leading the flock," is less self-assured as she appears in the hotel room in a long, flowing negligee, her hair still down. Her people believe she has drowned, but Billy warmly and patiently encourages her to forget the evangelism and think only of the two of them together.

EXCERPT 3 B&H e pp. 76–88 5 1/2 min.

See excerpts 1 and 2 for the descriptions of Sister Gladys, Mother Rainey, and Rose Ora, who are again in this scene.

Mother Rainey and Sister Gladys come to Rose Ora's New York City hotel room. Billy is not there at the moment, and Mother Rainey reminds Ora of her duty to her flock. With repressed anger, Ora tells of her plans to stay with Billy.

EXCERPT 4 B&H e pp. 198/5/1–213/1/2 8 min.

Billy and Rose Ora, previously described, sing again in this excerpt.

In the Miracle Room, decorated with cast-off canes, crutches, and a picture of Sister Rose Ora Easter as healer, Billy waits for Ora. He is convinced that she has gone back to the Flock. She enters and tells him she has broken with the Lifeshine Flock for good, and they can again look forward to their life together.

A Tale of Two Cities

Arthur Benjamin (1893–1960)

Paris and London, 1783–1790

EXCERPT 1 B&H e pp. 55–105 37 min.

Scene 2 of the opera uses Lucie Manette, lyric soprano (E♭3–B4) who has a great deal of singing in this scene; Miss Pross, character contralto (A2–E♭4), Charles Darnay, tenor (E♭2–A♭3); Dr. Manette, tenor (E♭2–G♭3); and three baritones, Sydney Carton (B1–F3) who needs dramatic power, and Lorry and the Hurdy Gurdy Man whose parts are small.

The action takes place in Dr. Manette's garden in Soho in 1789, where Sydney Carton is delivering a package for Lucie's birthday party, and Miss Pross is bemoaning the fact that there are to be guests cluttering up the place. Lucie and Dr. Manette, her father, enter the garden. Lucie is happy because Charles Darnay, a French nobleman who has left his country to teach in England, is in love with her. Sydney Carton, attending the party, is also in love with Lucie, and when the others have gone into the house, he stays in the garden and sings of his wasted life. The two men, Charles and Sydney, look a great deal alike.

EXCERPT 1a B&H e pp. 55–69/2/3 9 min.

This portion of excerpt 1 includes Sydney Carton and Miss Pross at the opening and then Dr. Manette and Lucie. Only Lucie has an appreciable amount of singing.

EXCERPT 1b B&H e pp. 55–95/3/3 21 1/2min.

This is excerpt 1 ending with the toast to Lucie and Charles and omitting the final aria of Sydney Carton.

EXCERPT 2 B&H e pp. 210/1/4–238/4/1 14 1/2min.

This excerpt uses Charles Darnay, tenor, and Sydney Carton, baritone, who must look alike (see excerpt 1), and three comprimario singers: the Young Countess, lyric soprano; the Spy, tenor; and the Old Marquis, bass. The Captain of the Guard has one spoken line. A flute player, a guitar player. and a few dancers are also used in this scene. Other silent men and women may be used, but the cut marked from p. 237/1/5 through p. 238/2/5, makes it unnecessary.

Mme Defarge has plotted the downfall of her aristocratic enemies, and Charles Darnay, who is really the son of the Marquis de St. Evremonde, has been imprisoned in the Bastille. He sings of his misfortune, and then he writes a letter to his dear Lucie. Sydney and a Spy enter, and Sydney, exchanging clothes with Charles, stays in the cell while Charles is released with the Spy. The Old Marquis introduces Sydney to his daughter who is also to be guillotined, and as the excerpt ends, Sydney, thought to be Charles Darnay, and the Young Countess are called by the Captain of the Guard.

Thaïs

Jules Massenet (1842–1912)

Egypt, fourth century

EXCERPT 1 Kal f, e 26–58/1/2 13 1/2 min.

Athanaël, baritone (B2–F♯4), needs vocal weight and stamina for his aria, "Voilà donc la terrible cité." The role of Nicias, tenor (E2–A3), is not particularly difficult. The cast is completed by Crobyle, light soprano (D3–A4); Myrtale, lyric mezzo (B2–F♯4); and a Servant, baritone, who appears only briefly.

Athanaël, a Cenobite monk, has returned to his native Alexandria in an effort to convert the courtesan Thaïs. He seeks out his old friend, Nicias, a love of Thaïs, who laughs at the monk's resolve. Nicias commands his slaves, Crobyle and Myrtale, to dress Athanaël in rich robes, concealing his monk's habit, for the occasion of his meeting with the beautiful Thaïs.

EXCERPT 1a Kal f, e pp. 30/3/1–58/1/2 11 min.

Same as above without Servant.

EXCERPT 2 Kal f, e pp. 83–113/1/1 17 1/2 min.

Thaïs, conceived for a lyric soprano with a strong top (C3–B4, opt. D5), nonetheless contains many passages requiring strength in the middle voice, making the role appealing for lyric-spinto voices as well. Appearance and acting ability are important prerequisites for this role. Athanaël, baritone, is described in excerpt 1. Nicias, tenor, sings briefly offstage and needs a strong A3.

Thaïs, alone in her home, wearies of her world of luxury and contemplates herself in the mirror, invoking the goddess Venus to preserve her beauty eternally. Athanaël appears, speaking to her of life everlasting and spiritual beauty. She first tries to triumph over him, then gives in to fear. Awaiting her decision, Athanaël agrees to meet her again at dawn.

EXCERPT 2a Kal f, e pp. 83–108/1/3 15 min.

Same as above without Nicias.

EXCERPT 3 Kal f, e pp. 118–31/2/4 8 min.

Thaïs and Athanaël (see excerpts 1 and 2 for vocal descriptions).

Athanaël comes to meet Thaïs outside her home as promised. Repentant, she is now ready to follow this holy man into the wilderness. She begs to take with her only a small statue of Eros, to which Athanaël agrees until he learns that it was a gift from Nicias, his former friend and her lover. He then seizes the statue, throws it to the ground, and demands that she destroy her palace and all the worldly treasures therein, a sacrifice that she accepts.

EXCERPT 4 Kal f, e pp. 203–20 12 min.

See earlier excerpts for vocal descriptions of Thaïs and Athanaël. Albine, mezzo-soprano, has only a few lines, accompanied by a chorus of nuns.

On their pilgrimage, Thaïs and Athanaël, reach an oasis in the desert, whereupon Thaïs becomes very weak. He pleads with her to walk on in penitence to mortify the flesh. Finally, he does allow her to rest while he bathes her feet and gives her fruit and water. She then rejoices when the Abbess Albine and the White Sisters come to lead her to the convent. It is now Athanaël's soul that is troubled, as he cries out in despair that he will never see her again.

EXCERPT 5 Kal f, e pp. 256–70 8 1/2 min.

Thaïs (B2–D5 in this scene) is described in excerpt 2. Athanaël (D2–E3, opt. F♯3) has a less demanding part in this final duet. Albine, mezzo-soprano (C3–E4), has a short but important solo accompanied by a chorus of nuns.

Having saved Thaïs at the expense of his own soul, Athanaël has dreamed of her in her former life as a courtesan. No longer able to resist this vision, he returns to the convent where she has taken refuge. Worn by months of repentance, she is dying. He begs her to return to Alexandria with him, where they can live happily, admitting that his conversion of her was a mistake. But growing weaker, she completely ignores his words as she sees the gates of Heaven opening before her. When she expires, her soul at peace at last, Athanaël cries out in despair.

EXCERPT 5a Kal f, e pp. 262/2/3–270 4 min.

Same as above, omitting the opening portion with Albine and female chorus.

Tiefland (The Lowlands)

Eugen d'Albert (1864–1932)

The Pyrenees and Catalonian Lowlands, early twentieth century

EXCERPT 1 Pet g, e pp. 6/3/4–51 (A-major cadence) 22 min.

There are two tenors in this excerpt—Pedro (E2–A3), the more difficult role with two arias, and Nando (C2–A♭3). Marta, dramatic soprano, has the leading role in the opera but very little to sing in this scene. Others are Sebastiano, baritone (C♯2–F3), and Tommaso, bass (G1–C3).

Two shepherds, Pedro and Nando, are seen at dawn on the side of a mountain in the Pyrenees. Pedro speaks of his loneliness and his wish for a wife and tells Nando that while praying, he had a vision of the Virgin Mary telling him he would soon have a wife. Sebastiano, Marta, and Tommaso enter looking for Pedro. Sebastiano, the master, has picked Pedro as a husband for the servant Marta. He offers Pedro the position as head of his mill in the valley if he will take Marta as his wife. Nando is somewhat skeptical about Pedro's desire to live in the valley, but this does not deter him.

EXCERPT 2 Pet g, e pp. 56/3/1–94/3/2 20 1/2 min.

Marta, dramatic soprano (B2–A♭4), has a sustained aria in this scene with Pepa, light soprano; Nuri, lyric soprano; Antonia, mezzo-soprano; Rosalia, contralto or mezzo-soprano; and Moruccio, baritone.

Pepa, Antonia, and Rosalia enter the mill excitedly, begging Moruccio to tell them if the rumor is true that Marta is soon to become a bride. Nuri is the one who finally comes in and tells the other women the truth. Marta then enters, and furiously orders everyone out of the mill after they mock her. Only Nuri stays behind, rather hurt, and manages to calm Marta's anger somewhat. Left alone at the end of the scene, Marta falls on her knees in prayer.

EXCERPT 2a Pet g, e pp. 86/4/3–94/3/2 6 1/2 min.

This is the portion of excerpt 2 with Marta and Nuri only.

EXCERPT 3 Pet g, e 126/4/2–137/2/3 6 1/2 min.

Sebastiano, baritone to F♯3, has most of the singing in this scene with Marta, dramatic soprano (described in previous excerpts).

Marta begs her master Sebastiano not to force her to marry Pedro; Sebastiano insists she belongs to him and will do what he orders.

EXCERPT 4 Pet g, e pp. 143/2/4–152/3/4 (F♯-major cadence) 4 min.

The three men described in excerpt 1—Sebastiano and Moruccio, baritones, and Tommaso, bass—are the cast of this excerpt.

Moruccio is being upbraided by his master, Sebastiano, and Tommaso for being in love with Marta, who can never be his. After an argument, Sebastiano tells him to leave the mill; before he does so, Moruccio exposes his master's affair with Marta. The church bells begin ringing; it is now too late to stop the wedding of Marta and

Pedro, who knows nothing of her past. Shamefully, Tommaso leaves with Moruccio.

EXCERPT 5 Pet g, e pp. 152/4/1–179 17 min.

Marta, dramatic soprano, and Pedro, tenor (see earlier excerpts), are in this scene. There is also a Voice, bass, with little singing.

Left alone with Marta after their wedding, Pedro attempts to make love to her; she wants nothing to do with him. By pouring out his heart to her, Pedro almost forces Marta to tell him the truth about her past and her relationship with Sebastiano. Completely oblivious to her implications, Pedro eventually says a prayer, and both fall asleep, Marta in her chair and Pedro on the floor at her feet.

EXCERPT 5a Pet g, e pp. 154/4/2–179 15 1/2 min.

The same as excerpt 5 but without the bass voice.

EXCERPT 6 Pet g, e pp. 180–256 43 1/2 min.

Again, all of the characters have been described—Marta, dramatic soprano; Nuri and Pepa, sopranos; Antonia and Rosalia, mezzo-sopranos; Pedro, tenor; and Tommaso, bass.

At dawn, Pedro is seen sitting in the same position as at the end of the preceding scene. Nuri, behind the scenes, sings a little song, then comes onstage to waken Pedro. Pedro cannot help wondering who lighted the lamp in Marta's chamber. Marta enters, grows insanely jealous at seeing Nuri and Pedro together, and orders Nuri, once her best friend, away from the house. Pedro starts to go with her, which infuriates Marta all the more. As Marta runs to the gate, Tommaso appears. The two argue as to whose fault it is that Marta entered this unhappy marriage; Marta breaks down and tells Tommaso the story of her childhood, as the daughter of a beggar woman, saved from poverty by Sebastiano, who treated her cruelly. She cannot bear to tell Pedro of her own past. Tommaso is sympathetic to her plight. The women come in and beg Nuri to tell them the latest gossip, to which Nuri replies with a parable. The unhappy Pedro arrives, only to be laughed at by the women. When Marta comes, the women leave the couple alone. Pedro tells Marta he plans to leave her and return to his home in the mountains. She confesses her deception and begs him to kill her. He stabs her in the arm; when he realizes what he has done, and that he really does love her, she finally sinks into his arms, and for the first time, she yields to him. They vow to go to the mountains together as they sing a rapturous duet.

EXCERPT 6a Pet g, e pp. 180–191/4/2 8 1/2 min.

Marta, Nuri, and Pedro sing this portion of excerpt 6.

EXCERPT 6b Pet g, e pp. 191/4/3–215/1/4 14 1/2 min.

When Tommaso appears, Marta and Tommaso argue, and then Marta tells Tommaso the story of her childhood.

EXCERPT 6c Pet g, e pp. 233/2/2–256 13 min.

The last portion of excerpt 6 for Marta and Pedro.

EXCERPT 7 Pet g, e pp. 233/2/2–289 27 1/2 min.

This scene begins with the duet of Marta and Pedro (excerpt 6c). It includes Sebastiano's song accompanied by a mixed chorus of peasants, which could include the brief roles of Pepa (soprano) and Rosalia (mezzo-soprano). Tommaso has only a few, but important, lines. Marta needs B4 for this scene.

Marta and Pedro's love duet is interrupted by Sebastiano, with the news that he himself has arranged to take a wife and is awaiting her father. While waiting, Sebastiano sings a merry song and asks Marta to dance for him. When Marta demands that she be allowed to accompany Pedro to the mountains, Sebastiano protests, claiming Marta as his own. Pedro is dragged off by the peasants. At this point Tommaso arrives with the news that he has told the bride's father of Sebastiano's relationship with Marta, and the marriage has been called off. Sebastiano claims Marta as his own; Pedro returns to take Marta, and the two men fight. Sebastiano falls dead; the peasants enter and witness Pedro picking up Marta in his arms and carrying her off to the mountains.

EXCERPT 7a Pet g, e pp. 267/2/1–285/1/5 8 1/2 min.

Marta (to B4), Pedro, and Sebastiano (see excerpt 1 for descriptions) are in this scene, and Tommaso has a few lines.

This portion of excerpt 7 ends with the death of Sebastiano, before the peasants enter.

Die tote Stadt (The Dead City)

Erich Wolfgang Korngold (1897–1957)

Brugge, late nineteenth century

EXCERPT 1 Sch g pp. 1–40/4/2 34 min.

The four principals singing in this excerpt are Marietta, soprano (D♯3–B♭4); Brigitta, mezzo-soprano (C3–A4); Paul, tenor (D2–B♭3); and Frank, baritone (E2–F♯3). All singers need control of a high pianissimo.

Paul's friend Frank and the chambermaid Brigitte are awaiting Paul's return home. When he arrives, he tells the story of a woman he has seen who resembles his dead wife so thoroughly, even to her voice, that he is convinced his wife, Marie, is still alive. He invites the woman to his home and she turns out to be Marietta, a dancer. He offers her the shawl Marie is wearing in her portrait, and then Marietta picks up the lute that Marie is playing in the portrait and begins a song; Paul remembers it and sings a second verse. They end the scene singing together.

EXCERPT 1a Sch g pp. 8/1/4–24 14 1/2 min.

Paul and Frank are in this scene from excerpt 1.

EXCERPT 1b Sch g pp. 28–40/4/2 13 min.

This is the final portion of excerpt 1 with Marietta and Paul.

EXCERPT 2 Sch g pp. 41–64 15 min.
(suggested cuts indicated in score)

This ensemble calls for Marietta and Paul (described in excerpt 1), with Juliette, soprano, and Lucienne, mezzo-soprano, who sing only a few lines each. Gaston, tenor (E2–B♭3), has a major part. Marietta doubles as Marie, as the portrait of Marie comes to life.

Juliette, Lucienne, and Gaston, all members of Marietta's dance troupe, have listened outside the window to Marietta's singing, and now they interrupt her. Paul begs Marietta not to leave him, but she insists she must go to a rehearsal. After she has left, the portrait of Marie on the wall comes to life and sings to him.

EXCERPT 2a Sch g pp. 54/1/3–64 8 1/2 min.

The final portion of excerpt 2 with Paul and Marie only.

EXCERPT 3 Sch g pp. 87–121/1/1 14 min.

This scene calls for Marietta and her troupe: Juliette and Lucienne, previously described; Victorin, tenor (D2–B3); Count Albert, tenor (E2–A3); and Fritz, baritone with several pianissimo G♭3's. Chorus parts could be sung by any of the principal singers, making the excerpt easy to perform without a chorus.

The players arrive in a boat in the harbor of Brugge and perform their play. Fritz, in the role of Pierrot, sings an aria known as "Pierrot's Tanzlied."

EXCERPT 4 Sch g pp. 127–45 13 min.

Only Marietta and Paul (see excerpt 1 for description) are in this excerpt.

The members of the troupe have left after Paul has interrupted. He cannot believe that this woman he loves is really Marietta, the dancer, but still thinks of her as his wife, Marie. He cannot even love her as Marietta. She is very sympathetic toward him and finally convinces him to love her.

Troilus and Cressida

William Walton (1902–1983)

Troy, about the twelfth century, B.C.

EXCERPT 1 Ox e, g pp. 52–99 25 min.

Antenor, baritone (B♭1–C3), is the first to sing in this excerpt, followed by Troilus, romantic tenor (D2–B♭3), and Cressida, soprano (B2–A♭4) who needs a strong voice throughout the range. When Cressida exits, Pandarus, buffo tenor with high falsetto (D♯2–A3), enters, and Cressida's second entrance is with Evadne, mezzo-soprano, and Calkas, bass (A1–E♭3). The chorus of priests is offstage; two priests are visible.

Antenor, a young captain of spears and friend of Troilus, the Prince of Troy, has seen Troilus in front of the temple, and believes him to be interested in Cressida, a widow and the daughter of Calkas, high priest of Pallas. Troilus is taken aback by the thought that others know of his love, and when Antenor leaves, he sings an aria confirming his love for Cressida.

Cressida enters and Troilus speaks with her, but his pleas for her love are of no avail. When she reenters the temple, Pandarus, who has heard Troilus' pleas, tells him that he will speak to his devoted niece, the Lady Cressida, and try to woo her for Troilus. Troilus leaves, having been told to come back quickly.

Calkas, Cressida, and Evadne, servant of Cressida, enter with Calkas bidding them good-bye because he is deserting to the Greeks. They plead with him to stay but he will not relent, and Evadne and Pandarus follow him. Alone, Cressida has an aria.

EXCERPT 1a Ox e, g pp. 52–71 12 min.

This is excerpt 1 through the aria in which Troilus expresses his love for Cressida, who has spurned him. A final chord is necessary on the last beat of p. 71/4/2.

EXCERPT 1b Ox e, g pp. 52–81/3/1 16 min.

From the beginning of excerpt 1 to the point where Troilus leaves Pandarus who has promised to speak to Cressida.

EXCERPT 1c Ox e, g pp. 72–81/3/1 4 min.

The portion of excerpt 1 with Troilus and Pandarus only.

EXCERPT 1d Ox e, g pp. 81/1/5–99 9 min.

The scene beginning with the entrance of Cressida, Evadne, and Calkas, through Cressida's aria.

EXCERPT 2 Ox e, g pp. 126–203 27 1/2 min.

Cressida, leading soprano, and Horaste, baritone (D2–E3), are seated at a table, while Evadne, mezzo-soprano, and one of the other ladies in attendance, soprano, are at another. Four more ladies-in-waiting, two sopranos and two mezzo-sopranos, are needed. Pandarus, buffo tenor described previously, opens the scene, and later the young, handsome Troilus enters (see descriptions in excerpt 1).

While Cressida, Horaste, Evadne, and others are playing chess, Pandarus enters to tell them a storm is coming and to urge them to stay all night at his house rather than trying to go home through the rain. When Cressida is alone, ready to go to bed, she sings of her thoughts of Troilus. Soon Pandarus enters the room and tells her that Troilus has come. The excerpt ends with a love scene for Troilus and Cressida.

EXCERPT 2a Ox e, g pp. 126–61/1/4 11 1/2 min.

This is the portion of excerpt 2 that has the women's quartet, with Cressida, Evadne, Pandarus, and Horaste. It ends with Cressida's aria when, unable to sleep, she thinks only of Troilus.

EXCERPT 2b Ox e, g pp. 154–203 20 min.

A scene beginning with Cressida's aria, continuing through the scene with Pandarus to the end of excerpt 2 with Troilus and Cressida's duet.

EXCERPT 2c Ox e, g pp. 181/3/2–203 10 min.

The love scene of Troilus and Cressida only.

EXCERPT 3 Ox e, g pp. 217/3/3–245 11 min.

Diomede, baritone (C♯2–G♭3), and Pandarus, buffo tenor, open the scene with Cressida, soprano, and Troilus, tenor (see excerpt 1), joining them. There are also Evadne, mezzo-soprano, who has one short singing line, and two silent Greek soldiers, who could be omitted.

Diomede, Prince of Argos, enters to tell Pandarus of the battle between the Trojans and the Greeks. In the exchange of prisoners, he has come to take Cressida to her father and return Antenor. Cressida and Troilus find no way to disobey the King's orders, so Cressida leaves with the Greeks.

EXCERPT 3a Ox e, g pp. 231/1/3–245 6 min.

At the end of excerpt 3, Troilus and Cressida's duet, with Pandarus and Evadne in supporting roles.

EXCERPT 4 Ox e, g pp. 246–314/1/2 31 min.

Evadne, mezzo-soprano, has more to sing in this scene than she has in the other excerpts. Also included are Diomede, baritone; Troilus and Pandarus, tenors; Calkas, bass; and Cressida, soprano (all described in earlier excerpts). The offstage watchmen have a few lines.

Cressida waits for word from Troilus and worries that he has been killed in battle. Her father, Calkas, enters and reproaches her for her coldness toward Diomede, the Prince of Argos. When Diomede intrudes, Cressida is reminded of her father's warnings, and she yields. Diomede bids her make ready to be acclaimed that very night as Queen of Argos. Evadne, who has overheard this, secretly destroys the last several messages from Troilus that she has withheld from Cressida. Then Troilus and Pandarus come upon Evadne and urge her to bring Cressida whose ransom is being arranged. Cressida then tries to convince Troilus that he has come too late, for she is promised to Diomede.

EXCERPT 4a Ox e, g pp. 248–64/2/4 8 1/2 min.

This excerpt is the opening of Excerpt 4 and uses only Cressida and Evadne. The offstage watchmen's lines can be omitted if necessary.

EXCERPT 4b Ox e, g pp. 246–77/3/1 17 min.

Calkas has a long aria in this scene, which uses Cressida and Evadne and also needs the watchmen for a few lines offstage.

EXCERPT 4c Ox e, g pp. 246–97 25 min.

An excerpt for Cressida, Evadne, Calkas, and Diomede, with the offstage watchmen.

EXCERPT 4d Ox e, g pp. 264/3/1–277/3/1 6 1/2 min.

From the entrance of Calkas in Excerpt 4 and continuing through to the end of Cressida's aria, which expresses her reaction to her father's words.

EXCERPT 4e Ox e, g pp. 264/3/1–297 12 1/2 min.

This scene begins with the entrance of Calkas and continues until Diomede has expressed his thoughts and Evadne has burned the messages. The watchmen, behind scenes, end this excerpt. It is possible to cut at Diomede's exit in order to eliminate Evadne and the watchmen.

EXCERPT 4f Ox e, g pp. 264/3/1–314/1/2 20 1/2 min.

Another excerpt using Cressida, Calkas, Diomede, Evadne, the watchmen, Pandarus, and Troilus.

EXCERPT 4g Ox e, g pp. 273/1/2–297 10 1/2 min.

This excerpt begins with Cressida's aria, following the exit of her father, and continues with the scene with Diomede. Evadne and the watchmen are again required briefly.

EXCERPT 4h Ox e, g pp. 273/1/2–314/1/2 16 1/2 min.

Beginning with Cressida's response to her father's warnings, the excerpt also includes Diomede, Evadne, the watchmen, Troilus, and Pandarus.

EXCERPT 4i Ox e, g pp. 298–314/1/2 6 min.

When Troilus and Pandarus enter to return Cressida to Troy, she must tell them, in grief, that she cannot go. Evadne has only a little singing in this scene.

Il Turco in Italia (The Turk in Italy)

Gioacchino Rossini (1792–1868)

Naples, 1814

EXCERPT 1 Kal i pp. 32–47 10 1/2 min.

This excerpt calls for Fiorilla, lyric-coloratura soprano (D3–B4, opt D5), and Selim, bass with agility (B1–E3). A men's chorus sings briefly, and Fiorilla's handmaidens are silent.

Prosdocimo, a poet, has been searching for a plot for a new comedy he is writing and has found the goings-on in a gypsy camp much more interesting than the usual plot of a wayward wife and her jealous elderly husband, such as the couple Geronio and Fiorilla who live near him. In this excerpt, Fiorilla strolls by the seaside declaiming her ideas on love, and how it is impossible for her to love only one man, a fact that her husband refuses to recognize. A boat carrying Prince Selim arrives; actually he is seeking his runaway favorite from the harem, Zaide, who has taken refuge in the gypsy camp. The Prince and Fiorilla are immediately attracted to each other.

EXCERPT 2 Kal i pp. 48–60 5 min.

This scene is a trio for Narciso, tenor (G2–A3); Poet, baritone (C2–G3); and Geronio, bass (C2–E3), all requiring flexibility.

The Poet is delighted with the turn of events in excerpt 1 and is determined to use the unexpected material for his new comedy. Narciso is also an admirer of Fiorilla's and therefore is in a similar position to that of Geronio; Fiorilla has cast off both of them for the handsome Selim. The three discuss how the plot is to proceed.

EXCERPT 3 Kal i pp. 61–80 9 minutes

This is a quartet for Fiorilla, Narciso, Geronio, and Selim, all previously described.

Geronio returns to his home with Narciso, to find Fiorilla entertaining Selim. Fiorilla manages to allay Geronio's suspicions and encourages him to become friendly with the Turkish prince. Narciso, however, tries to arouse Geronio's jealousy, while Fiorilla and Selim try to arrange a rendezvous in a quartet that later became the same music used in Rossini's *La Cenerentola*.

EXCERPT 4 Kal i pp. 81–90 6 min.

This excerpt is a duet for Geronio and Fiorilla (described in excerpts 1 and 2).

After Selim and Narciso leave the couple's home, Geronio attempts to reason with his wife, but she is even more obstinate than usual. She declares that she would take a thousand lovers if she wishes, and laughs when her husband threatens to beat her. She soothes him by saying she still loves him, and the two are happy once more.

EXCERPT 5 Kal i pp. 93/1/6–98 4 1/2 min.

A trio for Zaida, mezzo-soprano (F3–B♭4), the Poet, and Selim.

Selim visits the gypsy camp to have his fortune told and immediately recognizes his runaway favorite, Zaida. He is so overjoyed to see her that he cannot possibly be angry at her for running away. The Poet watches this scene with great interest.

EXCERPT 6 Kal i pp. 142–155 7 1/2 min.

This excerpt is a duet for Selim and Geronio, previously described.

Selim tries to talk Geronio into selling Fiorilla to him; outraged, Geronio insists that such a custom would never be allowed in Italy, and that despite her flirtations he still loves her and would never give her up.

The Turn of the Screw

Benjamin Britten (1913–1976)

A country house in the East of England, mid-nineteenth century

EXCERPT 1 B&H e pp. 1–5/1/3; 10–22/3/2 7 min.

Because this opera uses two children in major roles, this opening scene has been chosen, but other scenes with the children have been omitted. This is the prologue sung by a tenor (E♭2–G3) and followed by the meeting of the new Governess, soprano (B2–A4), with the two children, Flora (B3–G4) and Miles who is a boy soprano (B3–G4); and Mrs. Grose, soprano or mezzo-soprano (B2–G4), the elderly housekeeper.

The opening prologue, sung in the opera by the tenor playing Peter Quint, tells that this is the story of a Governess being hired and given complete charge of two children. She is forewarned by the guardian not to bother him with any problems.

When the Governess arrives on the porch of Bly, she is greeted by Mrs. Grose and the two lively children.

EXCERPT 1a B&H e pp. 1–5/1/3 3 min.

The opening prologue could precede other scenes, telling the story of the hiring of the Governess.

EXCERPT 1b B&H e pp. 10–22/3/2 4 min.

The greeting of the Governess by Mrs. Grose and the children.

EXCERPT 2 B&H e pp. 34/1/2–40; 48/1/4–60/2/3 (downbeat) 13 1/2 min.

This excerpt includes the Governess, soprano (C♯3–B♭4), in a rather dramatic aria and then the conversation between Mrs. Grose, soprano or mezzo-soprano (B♭2–G4), and the Governess.

The Governess is out strolling on a sweet summer evening and remarking how her first fears have now vanished, how each day seems more beautiful, and how enchanted she is with the children. Suddenly, she looks up and sees Peter Quint, former caretaker, visible in the tower. She does not know whom she is seeing but she is frightened. When she tells Mrs. Grose what has frightened her, the housekeeper says she is describing Peter Quint, the master's valet who, with the former governess, was close to the children before he died. The Governess resolves to protect the children from the influence of these two.

EXCERPT 2a B&H e pp. 34/1/2–40 3 1/2 min.

This is the aria the Governess sings while out for an evening stroll.

EXCERPT 2b B&H e pp. 48/1/4–60/2/3 (downbeat) 10 min.

The portion of excerpt 2 beginning with the Governess telling Mrs. Grose of her experience while walking.

EXCERPT 3 B&H e pp. 105/2/2–118/1/1 5 1/2 min.

An excerpt for Miss Jessel, soprano (C♯3–C♭5), the previous governess; Peter Quint, tenor (E2–A3), the former valet; and finally for the Governess, soprano (C♯3–G♯4). Jessel and Quint have some duet passages, but much of their singing together is in unison.

The ghosts of Miss Jessel and Peter Quint express their need and desire to exercise control over the boy and girl until they possess their souls. The Governess, who knows nothing of evil, is apprehensive.

L'Ultimo Selvaggio (The Last Savage)

Gian-Carlo Menotti (1911-)

India and Chicago, late twentieth century

EXCERPT 1 Bel i, e pp. 8/5/3–66/1/1 16 min.

Singers in this scene are Kitty, coloratura soprano (C3–D5); Sardula, lyric soprano (C3–B♭4); Maharani, mezzo-soprano (A2–G4); Kodanda, tenor (D2–A3); Mr. Scattergood, bass-baritone (G1–F3); and Maharajah, bass (F1–E3). The servants are silent.

The American millionaire Scattergood and his daughter, Kitty, are guests of the Maharajah of Rajaputana in his palace. Kitty, a student of anthropology, is attempting to capture a wild man, while her father is eager to marry her off to the Maharajah's son, Kodanda, the hereditary prince. The two men are discussing the terms of the marriage contract when the Maharani enters, so fat she can hardly walk, supported by her lady-in-waiting, Sardula. Quickly, a wall is put up by some masons; the Indians converse on one side, Mr. Scattergood and

Kitty on the other. Kodanda enters and immediately objects to this marriage, being in love with Sardula, who spurns him and tries to convince him that his parents have the right idea. On the other side, Kitty refuses to consider marriage until she has completed her studies and found her wild man. The Indians then wonder if they should not help Kitty find this wild man to speed the process along; each expresses his or her feelings in an amusing sextet.

EXCERPT 2 Bel i, e pp. 66/3/1–103 12 1/2 min.

This is an excerpt for Sardula, soprano; Maharani, mezzo-soprano; Scattergood, bass-baritone; Maharajah, bass (all previously described); and Abdul, baritone (B1–G3).

The wall erected in excerpt 1 has been removed. The Maharani suggests that if a wild man cannot be found immediately, one must be invented. Sardula has found the perfect solution in Abdul, a servant with whom she is in love; he will be paid a large sum of money for acting the part, and then he and Sardula can live in comfort. At first he hesitates, but Sardula employs her feminine charms to persuade him; all sing a happy quintet.

EXCERPT 3 Bel i, e pp. 175–204/1/3 10 min.

Kitty and Abdul (described in excerpts 1 and 2) are joined by an English tailor, tenor, and two American tailors, tenor and baritone, for this excerpt.

Kitty has captured her "wild man" and has brought him back to her penthouse in Chicago, where Abdul is being measured by three tailors while Kitty talks to a friend on the telephone. The three tailors argue about the way the wild man is to be dressed for his presentation to society while Kitty continues chatting on the phone; suddenly Abdul rebels wildly. Kitty wards off Abdul with a whip; the three tailors take their leave. Continuing to "civilize" Abdul, Kitty, left alone with him, attempts to teach him the refined art of lovemaking. Not immune to her charms, he becomes an obedient and dangerously affectionate pupil.

EXCERPT 3a Bel i, e pp. 188/3/3–204/1/3 6 1/2 min.

The portion of excerpt 3 with Kitty and Abdul only.

EXCERPT 4 Bel i, e pp. 214–226/2/1 4 min.

Abdul and Mr. Scattergood (both previously described) are in this scene.

Mr. Scattergood, increasingly alarmed at the length of the lessons Kitty has given Abdul in her boudoir, warns Abdul that immediately after the reception a Mercedes will be waiting to take him to the airport, and that he will be given the money owed him before boarding a plane to India.

EXCERPT 5 Bel i, e pp. 326/2/1–338/2/1 4 1/2 min.

Maharani, mezzo-soprano or contralto, and Mr. Scattergood, bass-baritone, sing in this excerpt.

When they first met in act 1, the Maharani insisted to Mr. Scattergood that they had met before. Again, in their search for the "wild man" who has fled to the jungle, this conversation is resumed. To their horror, it seems that in their youth (when the Maharani was still slim) they did meet in Egypt and had a brief love affair. The Maharani then reveals her secret—the result of that affair was her only son, Kodanda, heir to the throne! Of course, this changes the plot completely—Kitty can no longer marry Kodanda, but as the Maharajah has always believed the prince to be his son, he must never know the reason for the cancellation of the marriage.

I Vespri Siciliani (Les Vêpres Siciliennes) (The Sicilian Vespers)

Giuseppe Verdi (1813–1901)

Palermo, 1282

EXCERPT 1 Kal i pp. 59/2/1–83 12 min.

The cast of this scene includes Duchess Elena, soprano with no extremes of range in this scene; Arrigo, dramatic tenor (D♭2–B♭3); Guido di Monforte, baritone (A♭1–G♭3); Ninetta, mezzo-soprano; and Daniele, lyric tenor.

An abortive rising has been quelled by the appearance of Monforte, alone and unarmed, at the door of his palace. As the square clears, Elena, supported by her attendants, Ninetta and Daniele, is left alone with Monforte. Their quartet is mostly unaccompanied, and at its end Arrigo, who has been imprisoned, rushes up to Elena with news of his release. He does not see Monforte but, in spite of his openly expressed patriotic sentiments, is ordered by him to remain behind. The scene ends with a duet between the two.

EXCERPT 1a Kal i pp. 59/2/1–66 3 1/2 min.

This is the quartet only from excerpt 1, featuring Elena, Ninetta, Daniele, and Monforte.

EXCERPT 1b Kal i pp. 70/3/1–83 6 1/2 min.

The duet between Monforte and Arrigo that ends excerpt 1.

EXCERPT 2 Kal i pp. 84–108 19 1/2 min.

Giovanni da Procida, bass (F1–F3); Elena, soprano (B♭2–C5); and Arrigo, tenor (D2–A♭3), are involved in this excerpt.

In a valley outside the city, Procida, who has been the leader of the Sicilian patriots, has secretly returned to stir up resistance. He sings of his beloved native land in "O tu Palermo," and urges the patriots to prepare with him the deliverance of Sicily. Elena and Arrigo have arranged to meet the exiled patriot, and before Procida leaves them, he enrolls Arrigo as one of the leaders of the projected revolt. Arrigo declares his love to Elena and swears to avenge the death of her beloved brother.

EXCERPT 2a Kal i pp. 102/3/3–108 5 1/2 min.

This is the portion of excerpt 2 for Elena and Arrigo alone.

EXCERPT 3 Kal i pp. 158–83 21 min.

Arrigo, tenor, and Monforte, baritone, have been described in excerpt 1. This scene also uses the bass Bethune, a French official, in a lesser role.

Monforte is alone in his palace. He reflects on the injustice he did to the woman who became the mother of his son, and how she took the child away and reared him to hate his father as oppressor of the Sicilians. Now she has written him that his son is none other than Arrigo, his sworn enemy. The scene ends with Arrigo singing of his mother; then, when the time comes, he does accompany his father to the great hall to watch the ballet.

EXCERPT 3a Kal i pp. 161/4/4–183 18 min.

This is excerpt 3 without Bethune.

EXCERPT 4 Kal i pp. 276–302 20 1/2 min.

A scene with Elena, soprano (opt. F♯2 in cadenza), and Arrigo, tenor (to B3).

Arrigo has come to the courtyard of the fortress, with a pass from Monforte to see the prisoners. He knows that Elena hates him because he protected his father when the conspirators at the ball attempted to assassinate Monforte. When Elena appears from her cell, she greets Arrigo as a traitor, but he admits to her that their enemy is his own father. Her tone changes to one of pity as she sings her aria. Their music then takes on the character of a love duet.

EXCERPT 5 Kal i pp. 303–316 7 1/2 min.

Elena, soprano; Arrigo, tenor; Monforte, baritone; and Procida, bass, are the principal characters in this scene (see earlier excerpts for description). There is also a small role for Bethune, bass.

Monforte arrives at the prison and orders preparations for the execution of Elena and Procida. Arrigo pleads with him and demands to die with them. Monforte tells Arrigo to pay no attention to his companions but to remember that he is his son. When Procida hears this, he bids farewell to the country for whose ideals he has fought. A stirring quartet follows, and at last, as the victims are about to be beheaded, Arrigo consents to acknowledge Monforte as his father. Pardon is granted and the approaching marriage of Elena and Arrigo is announced.

EXCERPT 6 Kal i pp. 365–74; 381–409 18 min.

This is another scene for Elena, soprano (A2–C♯5); Arrigo, tenor; Monforte, baritone; Procida, bass; and a chorus.

In the garden of the Monforte palace, the wedding of Elena and Arrigo is about to be celebrated. After a chorus, Elena sings her Bolero, a lively display piece. Procida, still planning revenge, tells Elena that the Sicilians will attack the French at the sound of the wedding bells. Because Elena cannot persuade Procida to cancel his plans, Elena can only refuse to go through with the wedding, much to Arrigo's consternation. Monforte enters and sweeps aside all objections, pronounces the betrothal, and orders the bells to ring out. The Sicilians rush from their hiding places and Procida's revenge is complete.

EXCERPT 6a Kal i pp. 381–404/4/5 12 min.

Excerpt 6 beginning after Elena's aria and continuing until just before the massacre uses only Elena, Arrigo, and Procida.

La Vida Breve (A Short Life)

Manuel de Falla

Granada, beginning of the nineteenth century

EXCERPT 1 Esch sp, f pp. 14/3/1–44/1/1 19 1/2 min.

An excerpt using Salud, soprano (B2–B4) who must have dramatic force as well as a lyrical line; her Grandmother, mezzo-soprano (A2–F4); Paco, tenor (D2–A♯3); Uncle Sarvaor, bass (B1–A2); an offstage tenor voice and men's chorus.

Salud enters, looking unhappy. Her Grandmother tries to reassure her; of course Paco will come. Salud is fearful that she may lose one of the two things she most values: Paco's or her Grandmother's love. Then her Grandmother comes to tell her that Paco is coming. Her joy is complete, and in her duet with Paco, her innocence contrasts with his more conventional utterances. When Paco enters, Salud's Grandmother and Uncle Sarvaor observe the scene, and Sarvaor mutters that he would gladly take revenge on Paco, whom he knows to be planning to marry another girl the very next day.

EXCERPT 1a Esch sp, f pp. 14/3/1–20/1/4; 18 min.
22/2/1–26/3/4;
27/2/2 (piano only)–44/1/1

The same excerpt, but with these cuts and by continuing the accompaniment on pp. 38/2/4 through 39/1/2 without voices, one might eliminate the chorus completely.

EXCERPT 1b Esch sp, f pp. 14/3/1–20/1/4 4 min.

This is the very short opening scene for Salud, soprano, and her Grandmother, mezzo-soprano.

EXCERPT 1c Esch sp, f pp. 22/2/1–29/1/6 5 min.

A scene for Salud, supported by the voice of a tenor and a men's chorus. The chorus could be eliminated as in excerpt 1a. The beauty of Salud's music is like that of a folk song, and indeed it is founded on the Andalusian style.

EXCERPT 1d Esch sp, f pp. 29/2/1–44/1/1 7 min.

Salud, Paco, Grandmother, and Uncle Sarvaor (see excerpt 1 for descriptions) are heard in this excerpt. If the cuts recommended in excerpt 1a are used, the men's chorus is not needed.

EXCERPT 1e Esch sp, f pp. 31–37 3 1/2 min.

The love scene between Salud and Paco from excerpt 1.

EXCERPT 2 Esch sp, f pp. 73–89/1/3 8 min.

Salud, her Grandmother, and her Uncle Sarvaor are involved in this scene as they watch Paco and Carmela and Carmela's brother, who have a limited amount of singing. There also is a short amount of chorus singing, and dancing would be appropriate.

At the wedding celebration of Paco and Carmela, Salud observes Paco laughing and talking with the girl who is separating him from her forever. She sings a lament and longs for death. Her Grandmother and Uncle arrive, and the latter tries to relieve the situation by cursing Paco. Salud hears Paco's voice and makes up her mind to speak to him once again.

EXCERPT 3 Esch sp, f pp. 111/2/1–121 4 1/2 min.

This last scene of the opera includes Carmela, Paco, Manuel, Salud, Grandmother, and Uncle Sarvaor (all described in previous excerpts). The mixed chorus is not necessary in this scene.

Paco is nervous because he has heard Salud's voice. Manuel makes a speech to congratulate Carmela and Paco, but Paco becomes even more uncomfortable when Uncle Sarvaor, followed by Salud, comes into the patio. Salud denounces Paco's treachery toward her in a calm tone concealing deep feeling. She falls dead of shock at Paco's feet, and Grandmother and Uncle Sarvaor curse Paco as the opera ends.

Le Villi (The Willis)

Giacomo Puccini (1858–1924)

The Black Forest, late nineteenth century

EXCERPT 1 Ric i pp. 22–38/3/2 9 1/2 min.

An excerpt for Roberto, tenor (D2–A3) who needs strength throughout his range, and his village sweetheart, Anna, soprano (C3–A4). Anna has an aria in this scene, and she and Roberto have a duet.

Roberto is preparing to leave on a long journey. Anna picks a bouquet of forget-me-nots and is just about to put them in the bag he has packed, when he arrives. She is sad that he is leaving, but he reassures her that he loves her and will return to her.

The Voyage of Edgar Allan Poe

Dominick Argento (1927–)

Baltimore and a fictional area, 1849

EXCERPT 1 B&H e pp. 72–97/1/4 10 min.

Poe, tenor (C♯2–A♯4); Griswold, baritone (D2–F♯3); Aunt Nancy, mezzo-soprano (C3–G♯4); Mrs. Allan, mezzo-soprano (C3–E♭4); the Doctor, tenor (E2–A3); and Virginia, Poe's wife, soprano (C♯3–B♭4), sing in excerpt 1. An offstage chorus could be used or the few chorus lines could be omitted. There is one mute woman in the scene.

A small troupe of actors is presenting a melodrama. Poe becomes aware that it is a reenactment of his own mother's death when he was a small child. He is drawn into the scene, which becomes "real" to him. Griswold, dressed as Mr. Allan, pops up from beneath the sheet covering the corpse of Poe's mother, and the two men grapple amid the bedclothes. In the confusion, Poe finds himself wrestling with a large rag doll in the form of Virginia. Griswold has disappeared. A small boat with Virginia, Poe's wife, slowly drifts across the water. Poe steps into it, and they relive the happy memories of their love. A second boat appears with Griswold and another Woman, her face hidden. When she turns, Poe sees it's his mother and shrinks back.

EXCERPT 1a B&H e pp. 87/2/1–97/1/4 6 1/2 min.

This is the second portion of excerpt 1 and includes Poe and his wife, Virginia, and Griswold with a mute woman.

EXCERPT 2 B&H e pp. 220–39/2/1 9 min.

This scene opens the second act of the opera with the Ballad Singer, who is Mrs. Poe, soprano (D♭3–A♭4), and others watching Edgar Allan Poe, tenor (D♭2–B♭3) who has a long, difficult aria in this excerpt. Also included but with little singing are Mrs. Clemm and Mrs. Allan, mezzo-sopranos, with Mrs. Clemm singing the higher line in the ensembles; the Doctor, tenor (A♭2–G3); Griswold, baritone (D♭2–E♭3); and the Theater Director, bass (C2–B♭2). Other characters could be present if desired; and two instruments, viola and cello can be used onstage.

Poe is lying on the floor and struggles to consciousness. After some ensemble singing, Poe sings of preceding events, and the passengers conclude that he is insane.

EXCERPT 3 B&H e pp. 351–70/2/1 9 1/2 min.

A scene with Poe, tenor (F2–B3); Griswold, baritone (C2–A♭3); with most of the singing by Virginia, lyric soprano (D♭3–A♭4, with opt. C♯4). A silent Priest could be included in this scene.

Poe is kneeling at his wife Virginia's bier, with Griswold and a Priest in the background. A heartbeat is heard and Virginia's body comes to life in Poe's embrace. Despite a warning not to ask about life beyond the grave, Poe cannot refrain and as he persists, her voice rises in ecstasy and then abruptly ceases as she falls lifeless back into Poe's arms.

EXCERPT 4 B&H e pp. 370/2/2–391/1/2 8 1/2 min.

The Theater Director, bass, begins this excerpt and is joined by Griswold, baritone; Mrs. Clemm and Mrs. Allan, mezzo-sopranos; the Doctor, tenor; and Poe, tenor (see above excerpts for descriptions); and two lesser characters—Rosy, soprano, and Willie, bass. All need to be able to sing fortissimo in this scene, and Griswold has a sustained G♯3 at the climax of his accusation. If desired, more singers may be used to supplement the principals when they sing as a chorus.

The Theater Director plays Auguste Dupin, Poe's fictional detective, and Griswold plays the judge as they try Poe for the death of his wife in a very dramatic scene. Poe, trying to defend himself, sees Griswold, now without his judge's robes, standing behind the mirror frame and cries, "Who dares judge me?"

"Myself," replies Griswold, "Your soul. Your secret self."

La Wally

Alfredo Catalani (1854–1893)

Tyrol, about 1800

EXCERPT 1 Ric i pp. 7/3/2–18 5 1/2 min.

This is a scene for Walter, trouser role for light soprano (D3–B4); Stromminger, bass; Gellner, baritone; and a women's chorus, which sings only briefly.

As part of Stromminger's seventieth-birthday celebration, Walter, a minstrel and friend of Stromminger's daughter, Wally, sings a Tyrolese song.

EXCERPT 2 Ric i pp. 42/5/2–59/4/1 11 1/2 min.
(or 59/2/2 with an E-minor tremolo)

A scene for Wally, spinto soprano (D3–B4); Gellner, baritone (D2–G3); and Stromminger, bass (A1–E3).

Gellner is in love with Wally and has been promised by her father, Stromminger, her hand in marriage. When Stromminger finds out that Wally loves Hagenbach, a young man whom he dislikes, owing to an old family feud, he demands that Wally marry Gellner within a month. She refuses, saying that she will leave the village and wander by herself (this is the well-known aria "Eben ne andrò lontana").

EXCERPT 3 Ric i pp. 76/3/2–86 3 min.

This excerpt is for Walter (see excerpt 1); Afra, mezzo-soprano (A2–F♯4); Hagenbach, tenor (F2–B3); and the Wanderer of Schnals, bass (B♭1–E♭3).

In Solden, where Wally now lives, Hagenbach is now betrothed to Afra, the innkeeper. This quartet is part of a holiday celebration that is taking place.

EXCERPT 4 Ric i pp. 97–2/1–110/2/3 6 1/2 min.

Wally and Gellner, both previously described, are in this scene.

Gellner arrives in Solden for the celebration, again pursues the affections of Wally, who continues to resist him because she is in love with Hagenbach.

EXCERPT 5 Ric i pp. 138/4/5–160 11 min.

Wally, Walter, Gellner, and Wanderer sing in this excerpt in which Hagenbach appears briefly.

Wally has been the victim of a cruel joke; thinking Hagenbach really loved her, she allowed him to kiss her while dancing and then found out he was only making a bet with his friends that the reserved, unapproachable girl would yield to him. She is now so furious that she will marry Gellner and wants him to kill Hagenbach. In this scene, however, she regrets her anger too late; when Gellner pushes Hagenbach from a bridge, Wally decides to try to save him.

EXCERPT 6 Ric i pp. 183–221 20 min.

The complete act 4 calls for Wally, Walter, and Hagenbach, with an offstage chorus for storm effects. The technical effects at the end of the scene are difficult to achieve.

Walter has followed Wally into the mountains, begging her to return to the safety of the valley. She refuses, and Walter goes home alone. Hagenbach comes in search of Wally, whom he still loves. All is forgiven and they dream of a future together, but a blizzard surrounds them and they are buried in the avalanche.

EXCERPT 6a Ric i pp. 183–98/3/1 8 1/2 min.

The portion of excerpt 6 with only Wally and Walter.

EXCERPT 6b Ric i pp. 196/2/3–221 11 1/2 min.

Wally, Hagenbach, and the offstage chorus are in this portion of Excerpt 6.

The Wings of the Dove

Douglas Moore (1893–1969)

London and Venice, 1900

EXCERPT 1 GS e pp. 1–35 16 min.

Kate Croy, strong mezzo-soprano (C3–A4); Homer Croy, her father, baritone (C♯2–E3); Miles Dunster, young jounalist, baritone (E2–F3);

and Aunt Maud Lowder, contralto (A♯2–E4), are in this excerpt. The servant Steffens, baritone, only announces the guests when they arrive. The music, though through-composed, is melodic with conventional harmonies.

This scene takes place in the ornate parlor of Aunt Maud Lowder at Lancaster Gate in London. Kate Croy, whose father has gambled away all of the family money, desperately loves Miles Dunster and wants to marry him, but not without money.

EXCERPT 1a GS e pp. 1–24/2/3 10 min.

The opening of excerpt 1 to the end of the love duet with Kate and Miles, which includes Homer Croy, the father, and Steffens, the servant.

EXCERPT 2 GS e pp. 65–98 16 1/2 min.

This scene opens with the Lecturer at the National Gallery, tenor (E1–F2), talking to the tourists who are going through. Milly Theale, soprano (F3–A4, opt. C♯5), and Susan Stringham, soprano (D♯3–G♯4), are among them. Kate and Miles, described in Excerpt 1, are included in the excerpt.

In the National Gallery in London, a Lecturer is showing tourists through and telling them about the paintings. Milly Theale, a beautiful, frail American heiress, and her middle-aged companion, Susan Stringham, are in the Gallery. They have met Kate and Dunster earlier; in fact, Miles Dunster and Milly met in America, and Milly has fallen in love with him. It is not difficult for Kate to arrange a marriage between the two, believing that Milly will die soon and Miles will inherit her wealth and marry Kate.

EXCERPT 2a GS e pp. 70/1/2–98 14 1/2 min.

Excerpt 2 beginning after the Lecturer, Susan, and the tourists have exited. It remains a scene for Milly, Miles, and Kate, and Susan, who reenters.

EXCERPT 2b GS e pp. 70/1/2–80/2/2 5 min.

The portion of excerpt 2 for Milly and Kate only.

EXCERPT 2c GS e pp. 84/3/1–98 7 min.

The duet between Kate and Miles Dunster only.

EXCERPT 3 GS e pp. 99–121/1/2 12 1/2 min.

In Venice, Milly, Miles, and Susan (all described earlier) are watching a masque. Included in the excerpt are Guiliano, baritone (B♭1–E3), and a Minstrel, tenor (F2–A♭3), who sings the masque while it is pantomimed by a young man and a young woman. Mute servants may be used.

Guiliano, the Majordomo at the Palazzo Leporelli, announces that a masque is to be performed. When it is over, Susan tips the performers and leaves Milly and Miles alone.

EXCERPT 4 GS e pp. 131–52 13 min.

Milly, Susan, Miles, and Giuliano, all previously described, are in this scene. There is also a silent Sister of Mercy, who is arranging flowers when the excerpt begins.

Lord Mark, an evil, bitter man, has told Milly about Kate's plot of having Miles marry Milly for her money. He has claimed that Kate is Miles' mistress as well, and this gossip has weakened the frail Milly. She has not let Miles visit her for some time, but now she has called for him to come so she may learn the truth.

EXCERPT 5 GS e pp. 154/3/2–183 16 1/2 min.

The final scene of the opera with Kate, Steffens, Mr. Croy, Maud, and Miles (see excerpts above).

Kate is reading a letter from Susan when the excerpt begins. When her father enters, she hears that Milly has died and left her money to Miles as Kate had hoped. Miles, however, has grown to care for Milly, and though he promises to marry Kate if she will renounce the money Milly has left him, they reach an impasse and Miles leaves her.

Wozzeck

Alban Berg (1885–1935)

Germany, 1836

EXCERPT 1 UE g pp. 9–26 8 min.

A scene for the Captain, tenor (B1–C4), and Wozzeck, dramatic baritone (F♯1–G♭3). This twelve-tone score should be attempted only by singers who are solid musicians with mature voices; however, some higher and lower options are offered by the composer in passages that go to the extremes of the vocal range.

In the Captain's room, Wozzeck is shaving the Captain, who criticizes the morals of Wozzeck for having an illegitimate child. Wozzeck answers that he is too poor to be virtuous; the Captain tells him to think less.

EXCERPT 2 UE g pp. 30–40/3/3 6 1/2 min.

Andres is a lyric tenor (C♯2–B3) who, with Wozzeck, baritone, has many sprechstimme passages in this scene.

Wozzeck and his friend, Andres, are cutting sticks for firewood in a field. Wozzeck feels that the place is cursed and frightens Andres with his description of fire ascending to heaven.

EXCERPT 3 UE g pp. 40/3/4–55/2/1 9 min.

The major characters are Marie, soprano (G2–B4, with lower spoken pitches and less extreme options in sung passages), and Wozzeck, baritone, described earlier. Margret, mezzo-soprano, speaks briefly, and the Drum Major, tenor, appears, but neither sings in this excerpt. The scene requires a small boy (silent).

Marie, Wozzeck's mistress, stands at her window with her child, watching the regiment and admiring the Drum Major. Her neighbor, Margret, accuses her of flirting with the Drum Major, and they hurl names at each other. Marie closes the window and sings her child to sleep; Wozzeck arrives but cannot stay because he must report to his barracks. Marie worries that Wozzeck will lose his mind.

EXCERPT 4 UE g pp. 55/2/1–72 8 min.

This is a scene for Wozzeck (see excerpt 1) and the Doctor, bass (D1–F♯3, with less extreme options).

In the Doctor's office, the Doctor upbraids Wozzeck for misbehaving; he is using Wozzeck in scientific experiments and orders a diet of beans to which Wozzeck submits in order to earn money for Marie and their child. The Doctor is delighted to hear about Wozzeck's hallucinations; Wozzeck may make the Doctor famous.

EXCERPT 5 UE g pp. 73–81 4 min.

This excerpt is for Marie (see excerpt 3) and the Drum Major, dramatic tenor (C2–A3).

In the street in front of her house, Marie talks with the Drum major whom she admires. At first she resists his advances but eventually gives in as they enter the house together.

EXCERPT 6 UE g pp. 82–94/2/2 5 1/2 min.

Marie, Wozzeck, and their child are in this excerpt.

Marie is admiring herself in the mirror, her child in her lap. The child falls asleep before Wozzeck enters and notices Marie's earrings, a present from the Drum Major. He apparently believes her when she tells him she found the earrings; as he gives her some money and leaves, she feels remorseful for her behavior.

EXCERPT 7 UE g pp. 96/3/1–124/2/3 9 min.

Captain, Doctor, and Wozzeck, all previously described, are in this excerpt.

The Doctor is in a hurry, but the Captain insists on stopping him. Almost in revenge, the Doctor diagnoses the Captain offhand and scares him with tales of death. Wozzeck passes by, and the two make fun of him and torment him, the Doctor beating time with his cane like a drum major.

EXCERPT 8 UE g pp. 124/4/2–134/2/2 3 1/2 min.

This is a short scene for Marie and Wozzeck, both previously described.

On the street outside Marie's house, Wozzeck accuses her of deceiving him. She warns him not to touch her—better a knife in her heart. Her words haunt him.

EXCERPT 9 UE g pp. 181–97 8 min.

Marie, Wozzeck, and the child are again in this scene.

Marie reads to her son from the Bible and prays God that Wozzeck will return to her. Later, she and Wozzeck are walking near a pond. He recalls their first meeting and comments ironically on her fidelity. When she wishes to escape, he stabs her in the throat and rushes off.

Index of Operas
Index of Composers
Index of Arias and Ensembles

Index of Operas

Index of Composers

Index of Arias and Ensembles

MARY ELAINE WALLACE was, for twenty-five years, professor of voice and director of opera at Louisiana Tech University, the State University of New York at Fredonia, and Southern Illinois University at Carbondale. In addition, she directed the opera workshop for the Chautauqua (NY) summer school of music. Many of her former students are now singing in opera both in the United States and abroad, and others are opera directors themselves. Now living in Texas with her husband, Dr. Robert House, she is serving as executive secretary for the National Opera Association and editor of the NOA Newsletter.

ROBERT WALLACE is currently adjunct professor at New York University, where he serves as music director for the Kurt P. Reimann Opera Theatre. As an operatic coach and conductor, he has also worked with the New York City Opera, Minnesota Opera, New Orleans Opera, Mississippi Opera, and Opera Metropolitana of Caracas, Venezuela. A graduate of the Manhattan School of Music, he is cofounder of Singers Theatre of New York, under whose auspices he has conducted a series of workshops in which opera scenes are studied and performed.